Keeping Up
Appearances

WHEN WE LONG FOR AN EARTHQUAKE!

"I know nothing more awful than turning up at a function in fancy dress when it isn't a fancy dress function after all

—except, of course, turning up in the wrong kit"

Throughout the 1920s and 1930s ignorance of dress codes could be a social disaster.
(Tatler, *25 December 1929, Illustrated London News Picture Library*)

Keeping Up Appearances

FASHION AND CLASS BETWEEN THE WARS

CATHERINE HORWOOD

SUTTON PUBLISHING

For Dominique, Katy and Emily

First published in the United Kingdom in 2005 by
Sutton Publishing Limited · Phoenix Mill
Thrupp · Stroud · Gloucestershire · GL5 2BU

Paperback edition first published in 2006

British Library Cataloguing in Publication Data
A catalogue record for this book is available from the British Library.

ISBN 0 7509 3958 3

Typeset in 11/15 Ehrhardt.
Typesetting and origination by
Sutton Publishing Limited.
Printed and bound in England by
J.H. Haynes & Co. Ltd, Sparkford.

Contents

Acknowledgements

This book is about people and their choices and tastes in dress. Photographs alone cannot tell you why someone has chosen to wear a certain outfit or why they disapproved of it on someone else. Nevertheless, they are a vital tool in piecing together reality as opposed to fantasy. So I would like to start by thanking the Baxendale, Hendrick, Styles and Sharp families among others for scouring their family photograph albums and allowing me to reproduce their family memories, as well as friends, family and the oral history interviewees who also gave me access to their albums.

I would like particularly to thank those anonymous men and women who talked to me as part of my oral history research. Over endless cups of tea, we pored over old magazines and picture books together to retrieve memories that had not been thought about in many cases for over sixty years. Their testimony, together with the hundreds of records left by the respondents of the Mass-Observation Archive, added enormously to the richness of this work. I am so grateful for the unfailing helpfulness of Joy Eldridge and the team at the Mass-Observation Archive at the University of Sussex led by Dorothy Sheridan. I am also indebted to Monty Moss of Moss Bros, staff at T.M. Lewin of Jermyn Street, and Robert Fearn, Secretary of the Stourbridge Rotary Club for the information they shared with me.

The staff of the British Library, the British Newspaper Library at Colindale, the London Library, the Punch Library, the National Portrait Gallery, and the Bedford Centre for the History of Women at Royal Holloway College, have all been unstintingly helpful. I would also like to thank the staff at the John Lewis Partnership Archive; the Documentary Photography Archive at the Greater Manchester County Record Office; the Hat Works Stockport Museum of Hatting; Luton Museum Services; the Museum of Costume, Bath; Simpson's Archive; the History of Advertising Trust in Norfolk; and the Oxfordshire County Record Office. My thanks go to Honor Godfrey at the Wimbledon Lawn Tennis Museum for her continuing support. I am, of course, greatly indebted to the Arts and Humanities Research Board for their generous funding of the research that has culminated in this book.

Over the years I have received hugely helpful feedback and support from a large number of friends and colleagues, in particular Barbara Burman, Carol Dyhouse, Edwina Ehrman, Martin Francis, Hannah Greig, Clare Langhamer, Clare Lomas, Sharon Messenger, Niki Pullin, John Styles, Pat Thane, John Tosh, Judy Tregidden, Alex Windscheffel, and everyone else who listened to and read my work over the years. An enormous thank you goes to Amanda Vickery, my outstanding Ph.D. supervisor, whose energy and enthusiasm have been an inspiration.

As the mother of three fashion-conscious daughters, I have no shortage of advice on how to 'keep up appearances' these days but I owe a deep debt of gratitude to my late mother who passed on to me her love of dress and dressmaking. As a young woman in the 1930s she always managed to be stylish at a time when quality did not come cheap, a talent that remained with her throughout her life. Finally, though he is often bemused by my fascination with *schmutter*, my love and thanks go to Paddy for listening, commenting and just being there.

Introduction

When Daisy was bidden to some entertainment for which she was tersely requested on her invitation card to don Morning Dress, she discovered, on considering her wardrobe, that she possessed no Morning Dress. . . . She did not think that she even had an afternoon dress . . . she certainly had not a rest gown (apart from her nightgown) or a tea gown . . . Life must be, to those who lived sartorially, a complex and many-changing business; they must be at it from morning until night, in order not to risk being caught in the wrong clothes. Daisy knew that she would never be any good at this game.[1]

R. Macaulay, *Keeping Up Appearances* (1928)

By the time Rose Macaulay's heroine describes this 'game' in the 1928 novel *Keeping Up Appearances*, it had already been played for some time by the British middle classes. Clothes have always been a key component in that most British of rituals, maintaining class distinctions. Nevertheless, by the interwar years the rules were pettier and more challenging than ever before.

Broadcaster René Cutforth pointed out the pitfalls of getting it wrong:

the universal game was class assessment and judgement . . . what made the game more complicated was that different middle-class sections played it by different rules. In the matter of what was done and what was not done, every white-collared Englishman daily walked a tightrope over a deadly chasm.[2]

The middle classes had to be adept at this game, whether at work, socialising with neighbours, or holidaying at the seaside. But who were Cutforth's 'white-collared Englishmen'? And why were they so anxious about what they wore?

The complexities of interwar class are encapsulated in the comment of a 43-year-old office worker from London, who described himself in 1939 as 'upper class by education (P[ublic] S[chool], Balliol), middle class by profession (sort of clerk) [and] lower class by residence (small house)'.[3] In spite of his private education and Oxford degree, this man believed that neither his job nor his home matched up to the standard of his background and, because he felt he had slipped down the class ladder his position in society was ambiguous.[4]

Analysts during the 1920s and 1930s struggled to make their own class definitions. A survey conducted in 1927, in the days before accurate consumer targeting, looked at reading habits but found it hard to pinpoint clear differences within the middle classes. It defined the middle classes vaguely as 'well-to-do and comfortably off' while the lower-middle classes were significantly defined as having limited money but the same buying habits and social outlook.[5]

A review of the middle classes by Roy Lewis and Angus Maude shortly after the Second World War categorised them in terms of material culture. The middle classes were those 'who used napkin rings (on the grounds that the working class did not use table napkins at all, while members of the upper class used a clean napkin at each meal) and that the dividing line between the upper-middle and lower-middle classes [was] the point at which a napkin became a serviette'.[6] This deliciously captures the complexities of a stratum of society bounded at one end by top professionals mixing with 'high society' and at the other by a struggling group 'newly emerged from the working class'. The latter were people who 'had to dress to the public' and were mocked as 'all fur coat but no breakfast'.[7] The middle classes were minutely stratified, 'less a class than a society of orders each with its own exclusion rituals and status ideology . . . exquisitely graded according to a hierarchy of rank'.[8]

Yet rather than a strict hierarchy, the middle classes comprised segments more like an orange than a layer cake.[9] Even people of seemingly similar status often chose not to socialise with each other. 'The clergyman's widow, in reduced circumstances, would not make friends with the elementary school teacher, though she might have her round for tea . . . The academic in cap and gown would not mix with the chain-smoking, shirt-sleeved journalist, nor the goggle-eyed motorist with the poet.'[10]

Class analysts Lewis and Maude estimated that 40 per cent of England's population could be categorised as middle class by the early 1950s, using five 'income brackets': 'A', head of household earning more than £1000 per annum; 'B', earning £650 to £1000; 'C', earning £400 to £650; 'D', earning £225 to £400, and 'E', earning less than £225. The problem with this system, as Lewis and Maude found, was that some men in traditionally working-class jobs such as steel manufacturing, could earn in excess of £1000 per annum. Similarly, a young man just starting out in a profession might well earn less than £225. Just as in the

Any item of clothing could become unacceptable once it was seen being worn by the lower classes. *Punch* charts the route spats took as they slipped down the social ladder. (Punch, *19 April 1922*, © *Punch Ltd*)

case of the confused public school-educated office worker with a degree from Balliol, economic recession could alter a family's income bracket while they retained their middle-class status.[11]

What bound all portions of the middle classes together were the ropes of respectability knotted against fears of unemployment and social disgrace. Yet they were the section of society least affected by the economic 'depression' of the interwar years. In real terms, although consumers across the middle classes may have felt they were becoming the 'new poor', in reality they were increasingly able to get more for their money. There was patchy unemployment all over the country but by the late 1920s average earnings had regained the losses of the early 1920s, only to drop again slightly in the early 1930s. In contrast, the Cost of Living Index did not rise again until the mid-1930s, having fallen steadily after 1920.[12] The net result was that many people – particularly among the middle classes – were better off than they perceived themselves to be.

After the First World War there were new economical and political pressures on society which meant everyday life had to change. Many of these changes have been captured in travelogues such as J.B. Priestley's *English Journey* and in histories such as Robert Graves and Alan Hodge's *The Long Weekend*.[13] Both recreate a vivid picture of a Britain divided economically and geographically by the depressed economy in the north and the burgeoning new domestic industries in the south. Priestley saw that the 'new industries ha[d] moved south . . . potato crisps, scent, tooth pastes, bathing costumes, fire extinguishers', and was intrigued that a living could be made from them.[14]

Yet there was a living to be made. In 1931, 400,000 of the one million men employed as managers throughout England and Wales were based in the south-east, in addition to all the thousands of small businesses and retailing operations that would have been considered middle class.[15] Most men saw job security as vital, especially as they were under pressure to provide a 'family wage'. A wife who did not have to work was a key marker of middle-class respectability.

Because of this, most middle-class women expected to give up paid work on marriage and did not need to worry about keeping a job for life. It is not surprising then, that contrary to opinions held by some well-known women of the time such as Winifred Holtby and Ray Strachey, there were few career opportunities for middle-class women. Teaching and clerical work was available and there were opportunities within retailing particularly for lower middle-class women. But the pattern of many middle-class women's lives in interwar Britain was traditionally school, briefly a job, then marriage, children and the usual trappings of domesticity.

For young middle-class women there were also new excitements to enjoy. Formal chaperonage at public events for girls was now outdated. Dancing and the cinema became an important part of their social lives. Smoking and make-up gradually became socially acceptable among all classes, encouraged by the popularity of the cinema and American films. All this meant that women ostensibly had far greater freedom of choice in how they looked and dressed. In reality, however, the constraints placed upon them by the society they moved in were still a controlling factor.

There was a surge in popularity of all sports and leisure activities which became more widely available across the classes and to both sexes. Women in particular gained once again in terms of becoming more physically emancipated through sport and travel. The practicalities of everyday living encouraged change. Many women now had access to a motor car as either a passenger or a driver. Contemporary dress historian James Laver recalled that 'the daughters of the middle classes were whisked away in two-seaters; the daughters of the lower classes on the pillions of motor-cycles'.[16]

All these improvements had their influence on dress codes. In the 1930s, for example, increased holiday opportunities encouraged daring women to wear trousers on the beach or for sport and even as evening wear. By the outbreak of the Second World War freedom of movement was replacing modesty as the key fashion issue in leisurewear.

The revolution in dress in turn necessitated the rewriting of the codes by which men and women negotiated the formality and informality of their lives. Therefore it is hard to find a period in the history of dress, for women in particular, that witnessed a greater change than that between 1900 and 1939. By the 1920s and 1930s women's clothes were seen as being healthier and less restrictive than men's, a complete *volte-face* in dress terms.

However, although menswear design in particular appeared to be reactionary and thoroughly traditional, it was also being influenced by developments in sportswear particularly from America.[17] Many changes in menswear were extremely subtle. However, such subtlety contributed to the male obsession with small details in matters of appearance, 'the width of a lapel, the angle at which a hat was worn, the colour of handkerchiefs and hosiery'.[18]

Judgement by one's peers was of primary importance. The overriding factor in matters of dress was social status rather than any attempt at individuality or sexuality. 'Correctness in dress extended to the minutest particulars . . . Men were forever fidgeting with their tie to see that it was level and that the top button of the shirt did not show; women were forever feeling for the slipping petticoat and falling hairslide.'[19] In contrast to their parents' generation, interwar children, were relatively immune to the vagaries of changing fashions and class pressure. Opportunities for buying clothes were changing steadily during the interwar years. The arrival of the department store as a shopping forum by the end of the nineteenth century heralded a more forceful marketing approach by suppliers. The private dressmaker, the local draper's shop and the Savile Row tailor all faced new rivals. Vast department stores provided a showcase for 'correct attire', demonstrating to a much wider public what they were expected to wear.[20] Stores were able to stock their shelves with an increasing array of goods available through new technological processes of manufacturing.

The widening of markets for goods heralded the start of a democratisation of sorts. Cheap mass production of garments challenged the old class demarcations that Savile Row and *haute couture* stood for. These were indeed the first attempts to bring high fashion within the reach of all. These events were encouraged by the increasing availability of synthetic fabrics, which, although of basic quality, allowed for the manufacture of scaled-down Parisian designs. In contrast to the pre–First World War period, by the 1930s there was a strong ready-to-wear trade.[21] The success of ready-to-wear in turn encouraged the development of mass-produced clothes, although the full effects of this were not truly felt until after the Second World War.[22]

Many of the items of clothing associated with the 1920s and 1930s are so familiar – the winged collar, the pair of gloves, the pinstriped suit, the floral frock – that the significance of choice, why people chose to wear what they did, when they did, is lost. There is no shortage of excellent empirical works which chart the changes in both men's and women's fashions during this period. However, taken out of context it is hard to pass on the wearer's motives for either purchase or display, or to demonstrate the tensions between modesty and modernity.

Everyone, consciously or unconsciously, sends out a message with what they wear. Rebels are easy enough to spot, but those seeking the safe haven of respectability also send out visual signals through their clothes to display this message. The British desire to look respectable – in contrast, that is, to 'looking a tart' – has 'at different times this century, kept ankles from view, cleavages hidden, colour sombre and figures rigidly controlled by inhibiting underwear'.[23]

The pursuit of respectability in the mid-twentieth century led to a definite feeling of 'anti-fashion' among the middle classes. The irony is that respectability

"THAT'S BETTY GRANT'S NEW MAID."   "SHE'S MUCH SMARTER THAN HER MISTRESS."
"WELL, THEY CAN'T *BOTH* AFFORD TO DRESS LIKE THAT."

Much to the dismay of the middle classes, higher wages for staff – prompted by the interwar servant shortage – allowed them to take advantage of the ready-made clothing appearing in department and chain stores across the country. (Punch, *16 March 1921* © *Punch Ltd*)

forced the middle classes to change their appearance so that they could dissociate themselves from anything that might be considered 'too cheap, too expensive, too formal, too slovenly, too old-fashioned or too trendy'.[24] There is also a conceit in clothing that can deceive not just the viewer but also the wearer into believing the message of the garments.[25] Which man or woman does not move differently when in full evening dress than when dressed for gardening? In a less obvious way quality clothes gave the wearer a feeling of confidence in their class status.

Yet by the 1930s advertisements and the media were suggesting that one could no longer judge class distinctions by what someone wore. When Jaeger relaunched their clothing in this period, they claimed that 'thanks to [us] you can no longer tell a shop girl from a Duchess'. The *Daily Mail* ran stories such as the difficulty that traffic staff had in 1936 of distinguishing 'working girls' eligible for cheaper travel tickets since 'these days girls dress so ingeniously that it would be almost impossible for any omnibus conductor to detect whether a girl is of the working or middle class'.[26] Just before the outbreak of the Second World War the author Antonia White praised this social levelling effect of fashion in the 1930s in *Picture Post*: 'It was so easy to look smart when everyone from duchess to mill girl wore exactly the same type of clothes.'[27]

These all suggest that mass-production techniques were helping to level class barriers in Britain. Yet there is another side to the story that shows that this certainly was not readily accepted as happening among the middle classes. Here clothes mattered a great deal and were still important class signifiers. As the mythical mill girl gained access to better quality clothing, so the middle-class shopper had to find other ways to distinguish him- or herself visually.

Of course, this is nothing new. Clothes have been used as a way of demarcation for centuries. Feudal class recognition by dress was signposted by legislation, and clothing was used as a method of social control. Even after specific sumptuary laws had died out, the economics of society as much as its social mores dictated that it was always relatively simple to judge a person's class through the newness, cleanliness and quality of their clothes. What makes the interwar period different and its dress codes important is the social unrest and struggle with modernity that they reflect. Unravelling the messages behind dress codes of this time helps us to understand the social and economic upheaval that was taking place in Britain between the two world wars. This in turn was to shape the postwar society for the rest of the twentieth century.

In an attempt to dissect the complexities of the interwar middle classes and their dress codes, this book has made extensive use of the Mass-Observation Archive now held at the University of Sussex. Mass-Observation was started in 1937 with the aim of doing 'sociological research of the first importance, and which has hitherto never been attempted'.[28] The object of its founders, Tom Harrisson, Humphrey Jennings and Charles Madge, was to create a 'people's anthology' of British life, for the people, by the people.[29]

In the early months of 1939 Mass-Observation began to send out monthly questionnaires or 'directives' to their 'respondents'. Respondents had volunteered from a variety of backgrounds, though they were predominantly middle-class, and were identified only by a number. However, the archivists kept basic biographical details of each person for their own research purposes. By combining all these details it has been possible to work out the age of a particular respondent, where he/she lived, and what their occupation was, thus we are able to place them geographically as well as socially within the class structure of the time. It was even possible to establish precisely which part of the middle classes they came from, sometimes through their occupation but more often through their own replies to the directive on class.[30]

Founder Harrisson recognised that the real value of the replies to the directives was that they recorded 'what people *thought* they were doing'. Whereas this might make the evidence unreliable for other forms of research, it was exactly the sort of information needed to find out people's motives for wearing the clothes they did. Directives on dance, clothes, personal appearance, class and age differences, together with reports compiled by contemporary Mass-Observation researchers, all combine to paint a revealing picture of the fragmented interwar middle-class society. In addition, a wealth of material from magazines to shop and store records, from didactic literature to personal testimony, contributed to this book's exploration of the relationship between dress and decorum between the wars.

In 1903 George Bernard Shaw commented that 'acquired notions of propriety are stronger than natural instincts. It is easier to recruit for monasteries and convents than to induce . . . a British officer to walk through Bond Street in a golfing cap on an afternoon in May'.[31] By 1939, in spite of all the social and cultural upheavals of the First World War and the economic progress made in terms of retailing and manufacture, the British middle classes remained steadfastly conservative, reluctant to step outside the cloistered and socially secure world of tennis clubs and bridge parties. Sporting the uniform of respectability, they were clinging to a class system whose days were numbered as the social upheaval of another traumatic world war approached.

ONE

Shopping for Status

Shun the cheap and shoddy as you would a contagious disease and . . . sink your all in a few perfect clothes. Well-made shoes, well-cut clothes of classic, lasting style, good hats, however few in number – these form the foundation of our lady's wardrobe.[1]

Vogue, 1931

Where people shop has always been a good indicator not just of their taste but of their social aspirations. *Vogue*'s advice from 1931 encapsulates the aims of the female middle-class shopper. Achieving them was another matter. First, there was the question of how to pay for these quality goods. Salaries and housekeeping rarely matched expectations. Secondly, people's loyalties to their traditional style of shop were being challenged as new types of shops and stores started appearing across the country.

During the interwar period large-scale manufacturers and retailers gradually changed the face of the British high street forever. Lawrence Neal, head of Daniel Neal's, famous until the 1960s for their range of 'sensible' children's shoes, wrote a review of British retailing in 1933.[2] He divided it into six categories: department stores; multiple shops, such as Burton's or Freeman, Hardy & Willis; speciality shops such as Austin Reed's; the Co-operative Movement; 'fixed-price' chain stores such as Woolworth's, Marks & Spencer or British Home Stores; and finally, small independent shops. In addition he looked at 'clothing clubs' and mail order, but makes no mention of the 'hire' and second-hand markets even though they clearly existed. Nevertheless, he accurately assessed that there was a wide and growing variety of retailing outlets across the country to suit all tastes and classes.

Most of England's department stores had been established in the early twentieth century. By the 1920s major cities had at least one department store while mid-sized towns had large specialist clothing stores. Department stores sold 10 per cent of all clothing and footwear in 1920, increasing to just over 15 per cent by 1939.[3] Sales were buoyed by the development of mass production. In 1920 there were also nearly 6,000 branches of smaller multiple clothing retailers, such as Burton's and Freeman, Hardy & Willis, which grew to nearly 10,000 by 1939.[4] Their market share rose from 8.5 per cent in 1920 to just over 20 per cent in 1939. These figures, when combined with figures from the Co-operative Societies, which went from 5 per cent in 1920 to 7.5 per cent in 1939, show how shopping habits changed within twenty years.[5] In 1920 75 per cent of clothing and footwear was bought from small independent retailers but by 1939 this figure had dropped to 50 per cent as larger chain stores increasingly dominated the market.[6]

From the turn of the twentieth century department stores had aimed at the middle-class market.[7] During the 1920s and 1930s, for example, within the Debenhams network stores were graded 'A', 'B' and 'C', being 'high class', 'popular to medium class' and 'just popular' respectively.[8] This was reflected in the standard of goods they sold. Management advised 'C' class stores to be 'second in fashion, whilst the first burnt their fingers'.[9]

Stores increasingly used inducements to entice customers through their doors. Publicity stunts included celebrity visits and roof-garden fashion shows such as those held at Selfridges throughout this period.[10] Simpson's had three aeroplanes on the top floor of its store in Piccadilly in 1936,[11] while Kennards of Croydon, a 'C' group store aiming at the 'just popular' market, borrowed two elephants from a visiting circus in the 1930s to promote a 'jumbo' sales event.[12]

Large retailers also encouraged consumers to linger by installing hairdressing and beauty salons and coffee shops. City businessman's daughter Eileen Whiteing remembers taking tea with her mother at Kennards of Croydon 'all to the strains of light music from the inevitable trio or quartette [sic], often of ladies only, hidden behind a bank of palms and plants'.[13] Selfridges was also among the first stores to use not only celebrity appearances but also marketing of particular lines of clothing to capture sales. In the 1930s they devoted a section of the women's wear department to promoting a range of clothes inspired by the popular female flying 'ace', Amelia Earhart.[14] Earhart was one of many sports stars in the interwar years who endorsed clothing lines.

Stores which wanted to attract a higher class of customer concentrated on offering good service. Harrods Man's Shop, for example, aimed to give a standard

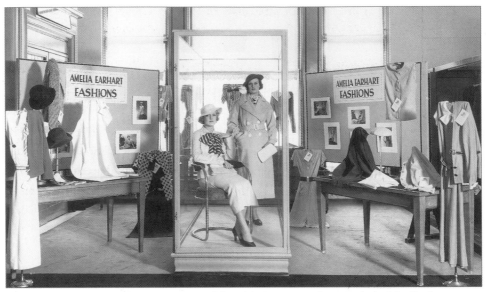

Stores tried to attract new customers with celebrity promotions such as this display put on by Selfridges in Oxford Street of a range of clothes inspired by American female flying ace Amelia Earhart and featuring the top model of the time, 'Gloria'. (*From the Selfridges collection at the History of Advertising Trust Archive*)

of personal service similar to that of a smaller specialist quality shop such as Austin Reed.[15] Most major department stores offered to send goods 'on approval'. Ordering an item 'on appro' was a form of mail order and a way of offering customers extended credit since they did not need to pay for the goods until they had been received and accepted. Eileen Whiteing's mother, wife of a City managing director, regularly ordered a selection of hats 'on approval' from Aldis & Hutchings in Croydon.[16] Harrods chairman Sir Woodman Burbidge claimed in 1933 that the approval system worked because advertisements had improved so much that 'a woman would know that the article she was ordering would suit her requirements'.[17] Figures for items returned are not available to confirm or deny his claim but it was undoubtedly a popular marketing ploy aided by a cheap and reliable postal system.

Department stores such as John Lewis and Harrods carefully fostered and maintained their middle-class status. In 1932 Harrods regularly sent out brochures to their account customers to encourage sales. The John Lewis Partnership followed suit with 'Customers' Gazettes' and 'Monthly Special Notices'. There was great concern that the newsletters should avoid 'such vulgarities' as the use of words such as 'kiddies'.[18] Similarly, the chairman of the

John Lewis Partnership was horrified by the 'nastily cheap' reproductions of women's clothing:

> I am writing this in ignorance of the opinion of the Deputy Chairman. I am waiting with real interest to hear whether she considers that for our real public, that is to say the cultivated people, who are thrifty but not 'impossibly' hard up, the kind of cheap-and-nastiness, that we seem to me to be failing at present to avoid, is of serious importance . . . I am not suggesting for a moment that the opinion of any one lady, however typical a customer she should seem to us to be, should be accepted at all uncritically. I have a strong suspicion that Sir Algernon has been misled quite seriously by the extent to which he has relied upon the guidance of his own wife whom I should certainly consider to be typical of the public at which I have sought to aim the steering of his company.[19]

Unfortunately, the reply of the deputy chairman is not recorded but clearly 'cheap-and-nastiness' is something to be avoided.

Department stores catering for the lower middle classes were challenged by the newer concept of chain stores selling only own-label clothes.[20] One such clothing chain, C&A, openly targeted the lower end of the market. Retailer Lawrence Neal, writing in 1933, felt its new style of selling was 'particularly interesting . . . in that it illustrates the combination of mass-production methods with a multiple distributive organization'.[21] When C&A opened its first major store in London in 1922, it was among the first to offer only its own-label clothing, 'the Height of Fashion at the Lowest Cost'. They made a point of saying that they did not offer a mail-order service.[22] This was presumably in an effort to keep down costs.

C&A's second major British store was in Liverpool. Advertisements for the opening played on the London/Paris fashion connection promising 'the wonderful shopping atmosphere associated with Paris and the West End of London'.[23] In contrast, advertising for the London opening had stressed the economic value of their clothes without mentioning Paris. Subsequently, no distinction was made between advertisements for its various stores, which soon included Birmingham, Glasgow and Southampton.[24] C&A, aiming at the lower middle classes, rarely suggested emulation as a motive for buying their clothes. Apart from the initial mention of Paris and 'the height of fashion', thriftiness became their *leitmotif*.[25]

The small shops could not compete with department and chain stores in terms of advertising expenditure. Even C&A, among the top ten retail advertisers of women's clothes, was regularly surpassed by store giants like Barkers and Selfridges.[26] Barkers dominated West London, offering in its namesake store 'high-class lines' while its junior partners, Pontings and Derry & Toms, carried their middle-class counterparts.[27] Nevertheless, there is little doubt that Barkers had to move with the times and introduce facilities such as tearooms and toilets as inducements to female customers to lure them away from the West End.[28]

In contrast, a local store could provide the personal touch that many middle-class consumers liked.[29] Residents would be aware of the status of both the large and the small shops in their area. Mrs B. noted as a teenager that in Croydon where she grew up there was a 'very nice shop . . . called Grant's, and a not at all nice [one] called Kennedy's'. She envied her best friend Susan who 'used to have very expensive clothes from Grant's'.[30] Similarly, Cape & Co., a department store in Oxford, with a working- and lower-middle-class clientele, found it hard to compete with Elliston & Cavell, the 'grander and larger business'.[31]

The upper-middle-class man or women would try to buy clothes in the leisurely manner of someone who had time and money to spare. Families were loyal to stores that treated them with the appropriate deference.[32] Ella Bland remembers women talking of 'my milliner', 'my furrier' and 'our tailor'.[33] Shop-keepers would open the door for regular customers and 'shop-walkers', senior store staff, would cater for the needs of favoured customers. The walker in Brighton drapers Chipperfield & Butler was 'always flawlessly dressed in frock-coat and tails', recollects Leonard Goldman who worked there as a junior salesman in the 1920s.[34] In Croydon Eileen Whiteing recalls her and her mother being given chairs to sit on in local drapers Aldis & Hutchings 'while we made a leisurely selection'.[35]

The ties of loyalty could be strong. When Mrs A. moved from Wantage in Berkshire to Croydon in south London she continued to buy clothes from her favourite local drapers, Arbery & Son.[36] Mrs R., an MP's daughter from Gloucestershire, remembers her mother getting her clothes from a shop in Cheltenham called 'Madam Wright': 'Practically once a week I think she managed to go there. She was pretty extravagant about clothes. They weren't terribly fashionable, but they weren't frumpish either, not at all. They were just like the sort of clothes you would expect from a shop that called itself Madam Wright.'[37]

Most towns offered a selection of clothing retailers to suit different price ranges. Worthing had 'a considerable number of shops specialising in clothing as well as private dressmakers catering for the wealthy clientele of west and north Worthing, and the affluent areas nearby'.[38] Lewes in Sussex had five shops that sold menswear. Although they may have had to pay a little bit more than in larger towns, locals felt no need to leave the town to buy clothing.[39]

Most towns in southern England had a selection of small dress shops called 'Madam' shops in the trade.[40] One such was Joan Laurie's of Worthing and Brighton, owned by a Mrs Fletcher, confusingly known as Madam Barnett.[41] Records of such shops are rare since they were usually owned by individuals and documentation was often destroyed when they closed. Although there were fewer shops of this type in the North, they did exist. Leonard Goldman's aunt Esther ran such a shop in the Gorbals district of Glasgow. He describes his aunt as having been 'somewhat flamboyant', saying 'she knew what suited her and within the limitations of her background, she had, if not exactly good taste, then at least a flair, which certainly drew attention to her even in a fashionable [southern] resort like Brighton'.[42]

Esther Goldman's shop would have been similar to the one set up by Blackburn-born Dorothy Whipple's heroine in *High Wages*.[43] Having worked for little money for a draper's in her unnamed northern town, the heroine Jane decided to open her own shop. Whipple's description of the window display on its opening day captures its trim modesty and daintiness.

> In the window . . . was an elegant white embroidered frock with a yellow necklace laid on it. Three equally elegant white embroidered blouses were disposed on the other side of the window; and just where it should be was a bowl of yellow globe flowers to point the colour of the necklace. Jane thought it discreet, fresh and delicious.[44]

'Madam' shops such as these tried to offer a personalised service, knowing each customer's requirements intimately. Eric Newby's experience as a wholesale representative for his family's London-based firm shows that little had changed even in the 1950s.[45] A Scottish shop owner with a business in the Borders told him, 'it seems to us that you are not *au fait* with the requirements of our ladies. They do not want *mass-produced* garments . . . our ladies would not wear such a garment, Mr Newby!'[46]

In the late 1930s there were also around 30,000 retail drapers and gentlemen's outfitters, selling socks, shirts, haberdashery and underwear to a clientele they would have known well.[47] As a young sales assistant in a Brighton drapery store in the 1930s, Leonard Goldman learned quickly that there was more than taste in clothes to master.

Several of the staff were from a middle-class background and as, in those days, accent mattered, it wouldn't do to be heard using an 'inferior' one. One had to keep up with the Jones's. But perhaps this was even more true when it came to the customers. If they spoke that way you had to match them. If they didn't, your assumed upper-class accent somehow gave you the edge.[48]

BALANCING BUYING AND BUDGETS

For women with a comfortable income shopping was often a treat. For those on a lower income it was sometimes a struggle but nevertheless pleasure could be taken in the planning of a purchase and the shopping trip itself.[49] Mass-Observation surveyed their respondents on shopping habits in April 1939, asking them to describe the steps leading to the purchase of a main article of dress. By far the most popular activity was window-shopping. Two-thirds of the women looked in shop windows for ideas while just under half used magazines and advertisements for inspiration. *Vogue* was the fashion mentor of the time with women across the middle classes referring to it as a fashion guide and mentioning it more than any other magazine.[50]

Not surprisingly, young working women under thirty showed the greatest interest in shopping for clothes. Few respondents took sales assistants' advice, preferring to discuss what they might buy with female friends instead.[51] Mrs B., a housewife from Dorking in Surrey, bemoaned the problems of dealing with assistants working on commission, which was common practice in many smaller shops and stores until the 1970s, showing that 'service' can itself be a problem: .

The biggest pitfall to be avoided is falling into the clutches of the Jewish type of saleswoman, who will over-persuade you with glib patter. Then you will find yourself with a garment which usually spends the rest of its life hanging in your wardrobe and which reproaches you each time you see it. I am very easily persuaded by people like this, so the only thing to do is to avoid all such shops (they are a very definite type) and only go to big shops or shops where you know the salesgirls are reliable.[52]

This unmistakably anti-Semitic tone was not uncommon in references to sales assistants.[53] Shopping for 'costumes' to go up to Oxford for the first time, Jenifer Wayne recalls her mother, with 'Anglo-Saxon determination' delighting in visiting little 'gown shops' in Soho, each with 'its full-blown Jewess beaming in the doorway between the small plate-glass windows'.[54] Yet, as Leonard Goldman confirms, a young sales assistant like him could get into trouble if a customer 'swapped', meaning walking out without buying.[55]

Outside the big cities those on a lower income also used the media and shop windows for inspiration, as Mrs E., a housewife from Burnley, showed:

I always study fashion articles, advertisements, women's magazines to keep my ideas up to date. I never discuss with friends, but I take note of what well-to-do people wear, and notice photographs of the Queen or Duchess of Kent as naturally the fashion houses who dress these people should know what is coming in. I take every chance of studying the displays in the best shops though I could not afford to patronize them. Fashion in this locality lags behind the fashion in a large city like Manchester so I like to see the shops there.[56]

Professional working women were not above window-shopping either. The memoirs of Marion Pike, both a student and later staff member of Royal Holloway College, reveal that staff members frequently browsed the London shops for an hour before late afternoon meetings, enabling them to 'get one's eye in for really earnest shopping, which was done in vacations'.[57]

The pitfall of mass production was that a wider class spectrum could now buy cheaper variations of smart clothes. Therefore women who wished to be fashionably turned out not only had to keep abreast of current trends but they also had to be aware of what, as one Mass-Observation respondent, Miss D., a female secretary in London, put it, was 'going to be "run to death" and therefore . . . quickly disappear from the better shops'.[58]

Whether for work or for leisure, the selection of clothes for the middle-class woman's wardrobe was governed by a longing for quality. As Mrs E.E. from Pwllheli notes, 'We were all taught "one good thing was better than two cheap ones".'[59] A middle-class housewife from south London, who considered herself impoverished, admitted she felt superior to those who had the money to dress well but not, in her opinion, the taste. She did feel embarrassed when staying with her husband's 'people' who were 'very county'. There she would be attended by her aunt-in-law's maid and felt that her wardrobe was 'lacking'. 'I spend less and have practically no clothes as compared with the other women around here,' she noted, 'but I do not think I look too badly dressed.' Since she lists the places she shopped at as Debenhams, Harrods, and Reville & Bradley's, all high-class stores and shops, she was obviously looking for quality rather than quantity, the mark of the aspiring middle-class woman.[60]

The necessity to buy quality was a burden for many middle-class women. From the early 1920s women's magazines such as *The Lady* increasingly acknowledged that there was a financial pressure being felt by what were termed the 'new poor'.[61] At the same time Browns of Chester, 'the Harrods of the North', brought in a 'new lower price level policy [knowing] the purchasing power of the great majority of people has been drastically curtailed'.[62] Whether this was a perceived pressure or a real one is hard to judge since in real terms the pound in the pocket was steadily buying more for consumers during the 1920s and 1930s.[63]

Figures for middle-class expenditure in 1938–9 show that both men and particularly women in the lower income groups spent significantly more proportionately on clothing than those better off.[64] It is not surprising either that the lower income groups' repair bills were higher as well, a consequence of their efforts to economise and maintain standards. With new domestic consumer goods, particularly electrical items, becoming available, budgets had to be stretched that much further. In all middle-income households, from those earning more than £250 a year to those earning over £700 a year, 20 per cent more is spent on clothing than on household items including furniture and domestic equipment, confirming the importance of appearance to the middle-class family.[65]

A rare set of accounts left by a wealthy Yorkshire housewife in the early 1920s gives a tantalisingly limited glimpse of the spending patterns of a woman with a healthy personal allowance of about £300 a year. 'Mrs Pennyman' of Stokesley, North Yorkshire, spent between one-third and one-sixth of her income on clothes, travelling regularly to London to shop at Harrods, Selfridges and Fortnum & Mason as well as patronising local department stores such as Binns of Middlesbrough and Fenwick of Newcastle.[66]

For those less fortunate there were various ways in which a middle-income woman could make her salary or dress allowance go further. This often involved financial juggling since it was the norm for women to settle accounts with stores and shops on an irregular basis rather than when the items were bought. Hire purchase was looked down upon so it was important to be able to meet one's obligations to tradesmen when they became due. This financial balancing act is a constant theme in E.M. Delafield's fictional classic, *The Diary of a Provincial Lady*.

Should like new pair of evening stockings, but depressing communication from Bank, still maintaining that I am overdrawn, prevents this, also rather unpleasantly worded letter from Messrs. Frippy and Coleman requesting payment of overdue account by return of post . . . write civilly to Messrs. F. and C. to the effect that cheque follows in a few days.[67]

Some middle-class women on limited incomes managed this juggling act of maintaining a higher-class front by buying good-quality second-hand clothes. Middle-class families would never have bought second-hand clothes from market stalls because of anxieties about cleanliness but even more of a concern would have been the stigma attached if one was seen.[68] Yet, although none of the interviewees or Mass-Observation respondents admitted to it, there plainly was a thriving second-hand clothes trade among upper- and middle-class women.

There were two ways of going about shopping for second-hand clothes. First, one could buy and sell anonymously through classified advertisements in upper-middle-class magazines, in particular *The Lady*. Secondly, one could use the services of a dress agency. The reasons why women used the columns of *The Lady* were all too obvious. Middle-class women advertised wanting, typically, a parcel of clothes for a large family 'trying to keep up appearances'.[69] One explained that 'having expensive taste, but greatly reduced income', she would 'be grateful if another would sell her exclusive wardrobe regularly and cheaply; only really good things; privately'.[70] A 30-year-old widow, 'income reduced', writes plaintively 'accustomed buy from best houses, would take entire wardrobe, day and evening, undies, from lady same age . . . must be moderate in price'.[71]

Phrases that crop up regularly, such as 'originally expensive' and 'high class' for example, show the keenness to keep up standards.[72] Both sellers and buyers often proclaimed their status – 'barrister's wife', 'London lady', 'Titled lady' – but more generally these advertisements were phrased using anonymous language. One can assume that the majority were from individuals although it is clear that professional clothes buyers also used the columns to find stock since occasionally the phrase 'no dealers' appears.

The Lady had started its classified columns from its first issues in 1885, offering free advertising for selling or buying 'personal items'. It quickly became a money-making section of the magazine, often carrying nearly a thousand individual advertisements. While the majority were from sellers, there were those appealing to a middle-class clientele anxious to purchase from, as one advertisement put it, 'a society lady only or maid to same, fashionable wardrobe'.[73]

By 1920, in addition to the lengthy columns of classified personal advertisements, small display advertisements were appearing in *The Lady* from the likes of Mr and Mrs Blandford of Gray's Inn Road, offering to buy cast-off clothes. Since they claimed to have been in business since 1857, it was evidently an established trade.[74] While middle-class women rarely used mail-order catalogues, the personal touch of a dress agency appears to have made it more acceptable.

It is difficult to estimate the extent of the dress agency business since discretion was an important aspect of this trade. Patricia Carr advertised her 'Exclusive Dress Salon' in Buckingham Palace Road, SW1, 'now showing new and little worn Models bought from Society ladies [a] speciality'. It was discreetly pointed out that the 'salon' was on the first floor, thus eliminating any possible embarrassment for clients being seen through a ground–floor shop window.[75]

During the 1930s there were additional advertisements in *The Lady* for agencies such as 'Titled Ladies Gowns' at the 'Regents Dress Agency', which was 'stocked with Right Clothes'.[76] Cora Bee's 'Different Dress Agency' offered 'everything inexpensive but good'.[77] One particular advertisement from the Regent proclaimed it had just purchased stock 'from a well-known Marchioness . . . wonderful recent Model EVENING and DAY GOWNS, 2 and 3–PIECE SUITS, etc. Created by Vionnet, Chanel, Worn only once. Our price 2 to 8 *gns*. Orig. cost approx 40*gns* each.'[78] Discretion was paramount – 'Mrs Selway' of Portobello Road claimed 'courtesy, privacy and exclusiveness' were her 'dominating features'.[79]

Robina Wallis ran a postal dress agency, taking over her mother's business in Tiverton, Devon, in 1929. The few records that survive throw a little light on this shadowy service. Extant correspondence shows that 'Mrs' Wallis, as she was known, advertised anonymously throughout the 1930s in *The Lady* magazine. She purchased clothes which she then sold through the post to customers. The address book listing the clients whom Mrs Wallis bought from reads like a copy of Debretts, an alphabet of aristocracy including the Countess of Arran, the Marchioness of Dufferin & Ava, Mrs Dudley Ward and Lady Victoria Wemyss.[80] One customer claimed she had been given Mrs Wallis's name by Buckingham Palace 'with whom you have previously done business with'![81] The customer's poor standard of writing suggests that the recommendation probably came from below stairs rather than above.

It is clear that the clothes Mrs Wallis bought from her aristocratic customers were generally months rather than years old since, on occasion, outfits coming from the Duchess of Roxburghe at Flores Castle were asked to be returned if unsold so that they could be worn again.[82] These women evidently did not suffer as E.M. Delafield's *Provincial Lady* had done when using a dress agency.

March 12th. – Collect major portion of my wardrobe and dispatch to address mentioned in advertisement pages of *Time and Tide* as prepared to pay Highest Prices for Outworn Garments, cheque by return . . . March 14th. – Rather inadequate Postal Order arrives, together with white tennis coat trimmed with rabbit, which – says accompanying letter – is returned as being unsaleable. Should like to know *why*.[83]

Letters to Mrs Wallis from women who bought her clothes confirm that the business covered a vast area of Britain, from Scotland in the north to London and the Home Counties in the south. It is evident from the financial details in the letters to Mrs Wallis that her purchasers were of a lower social status than her aristocratic sellers but they were invariably from the middle classes. Pleas for extended credit owing to dress allowances being needed to tide over bereaved relatives or extravagant sons are legion.[84] 'I don't wonder you are angry and truly I would have sent you the money at once if I'd had it,' wrote a customer from Cricklade who was regularly in arrears between 1932 and 1936.[85]

Businesses such as Mrs Wallis's and the classified column inches in *The Lady* plainly thrived during the interwar period. The anonymous nature of the contact between buyer and seller was a perfect way of dealing with what otherwise could have been a socially awkward situation. The fact that evidence relating to dress agencies is so scant confirms that secrecy was paramount. These shops were never to be found on a high street displaying their wares in the window but were always discreetly up a flight of shadowy stairs. There was a sector of middle-class women who would rather 'keep up appearances' by buying second-hand quality clothes than consider the growing quantity of mass-produced styles that were coming on to the market.

The growth of mass production did mean that many women no longer expected to make most of their wardrobes themselves or, depending on their income, to have them made. In spite of the enduring popularity of fabrics from specialist stores such as Liberty's, the sale of 'piece goods' – that is, fabric bought to be made up at home or by a dressmaker – had plummeted since before the First World War and departments selling ready-made items replaced those selling rolls of material.[86] For example, after the First World War, Lewis's department stores 'placed far less emphasis on "yardage" and far more on "taste"'.[87]

Children's wear was still mostly handmade. When Mrs E.E. was a young girl 'a little woman' came in twice a week for 'half a crown a day and all her food' to make her clothes.[88] Mrs S.R.'s mother made all her and her sisters' frocks but she remembers the thrill of buying her first ready-made outfit: 'I thought I was really dressed because I had a bought dress on.'[89] When she needed a tailored suit, she saved up from her wages of 15 shillings a week as a trainee hairdresser, and paid 12 guineas to have it tailor-made.[90]

Nevertheless, home dressmaking was extremely popular and was another way middle-class women improved the quality and stylishness of their wardrobe. Paper patterns were widely available and often given away with women's magazines. Records from Arbery & Sons Ltd of Wantage, Berkshire, 'drapers, outfitters and dressmakers', contain lists of haberdashery items such as Sylko thread and petersham ordered regularly by in-house dressmakers and customers.[91] *Vogue* ran articles suggesting ways in which 'a girl with nothing a year' could improve her wardrobe. These articles were visibly aimed at a readership from the middle classes struggling to maintain social standards. 'At this time of year, when the rich woman is buying new items to refresh her winter wardrobe, the girl with nothing a year is dyeing, turning, or altering hers, and having just as good a time at it, especially when she appears in a camouflaged creation that fools everybody.'[92] The success of homemade creations in fooling people that they were shop-bought is obviously hard to ascertain. It is significant that Mrs E.E. did not feel properly dressed until she was wearing a bought frock and would not have attempted any tailoring at home.

TAILORING TRENDS: CHANGING CHOICES FOR MEN

For middle-class men shopping for clothes was a quite different experience to that of women. Yet for them also, this was a period of change ushered in by mass production and the rise of a new breed of shops. There was still less flexibility in the buying of men's clothes than women's. Men did not have the option of going to 'a little woman round the corner' to have things made up. The male equivalent of the dress agency appears to be almost non-existent. Bespoke tailoring dominated at the top of the market.

Advice for men on what to wear still came from a tailor. There was no male equivalent of *Vogue* to be consulted and it was rare for newspapers to carry features on menswear. The 'man on the street' had little access to printed advice in the form of men's fashion magazines. The short-lived *Men Only*, first published in 1935, was a lone exception in including a small section on men's clothing called 'The Well-Dressed Man'. The trade itself was well supplied with journals full of suggestions ostensibly on correct dress codes but obviously

Pont's cartoon was a particularly accurate parody of the 'club-like' atmosphere of the tailor's fitting room where women were rarely welcomed. (Punch, *15 December 1937* © *Punch Ltd*)

designed to boost business. Titles such as *Man and his Clothes*, *Men's Wear* and *Sartorial Gazette* regularly carried articles with titles such as 'The Influence of Clothes', 'Clothes and the Job' and 'For Better Business'.[93]

For men of the lower-middle classes information increasingly came from tailoring assistants employed by chains such as Montague Burton's and Hepworth's. Burton's published a highly confidential 'Managers Guide' (sic) full of advice on sales tactics. 'Make your customer feel he is welcome and that you are anxious to please him,' Burton's encouraged their sales staff. 'Avoid the severe style of the income tax collector, and the smooth tongue of the fortune teller. Cultivate the dignified style of the "Quaker tea blender" which is the happy medium.'[94]

Traditionally the world of the bespoke tailor was indisputably exclusively male. Little had changed since the pre-war Edwardian period when small tailoring establishments and gentlemen's outfitters predominated. In the old-established businesses tailors encouraged their customers to rely solely on their advice. Not that the tailor's advice was always sycophantic. One young man was warned that a double-breasted suit made him look as though he 'was on board a yacht, i.e. dressing above his station' while turned-up trousers would have made him look as though he 'was ploughing a field'.[95] Just as the customer desired the correct clothes, the assistant thought it part of his role as salesman to help maintain the status quo.

By the mid-1930s the traditional tailoring industries felt threatened by outside influences, specifically the burgeoning ready-made industry. In an article in 1935 subtitled 'The frightful results of the intervention of Outsiders', the anonymous writer damns 'speculators . . . selling inferior goods' and spurious advertising campaigns by multi-national retailers. Even the aristocrat's valet is warned to leave the advice-giving to the bespoke tailor. The rallying cry from the industry was that there should be 'definitely agreed codes and fixed standards, so that tailors could adhere to them and thus avoid conflicts of opinions offered and clashes of advices tendered'.[96] This is obviously not an unexpected reply when trade might be threatened. Most upper-middle-class men were resigned to this system of control. One Mass-Observation respondent, ex-colonial Mr A., is typical of many who took their tailor's advice. 'He knows more about it than I do . . . manage to look reasonably presentable, so suppose it's all right.'[97]

Tailors themselves had long been provided with style charts by trade magazines. In 1929 Austin Reed's started publishing a publicity pamphlet for its customers called *Modern Man*, 'a masculine magazine'.[98] It was aimed at reassuring their customers on how shopping at their stores would confirm their superior class status with articles such as choosing the upper-middle-class necessities of 'flying-clothes' and 'tropical kit'. By 1937 Simpson's had published a chart for their customers in one of their publicity booklets detailing how an annual budget of £50 or £115 should be spent, down to the last set of studs. The two luxuries the higher-income man is allowed are a 'bath gown' and '6 silk handkerchiefs at 7/6'. Otherwise the difference is in quantity, and, to judge by the difference in price, in the quality of the goods listed.[99]

While advertising campaigns and shop displays became increasingly influential, the trade press suggested that 'any customer who desires to see clothes as they look when worn has only to be observant of the well-dressed man that he meets in the course of a short walk down the street'.[100] A few men did look to shop windows. Window displays had vastly improved, grouping items from various menswear departments to demonstrate a look rather than a single unit.[101] One Mass-Observation respondent enjoyed 'the more amusing advertisements, e.g. Austin Reed, Hector Powel'.[102] A few made considered choices. Mr M., an engineer from London, wrote that he studied 'tailors' windows and other men's styles and eventually decide on the kind of suit I want. I then go to the shop where I think I should get the best bargain and buy or am sold a suit similar to one I have chosen.'[103]

Some men left the choice of their clothes to their wives. A middle-aged man from Swindon admitted that his 'choice of a suit [was] guided very largely by [his] wife's strong prejudices in favour of respectability'.[104] Nevertheless, the female influence was tacitly ignored by the tailoring industry that controlled menswear trends. Women were discouraged from entering the inner sanctum of the tailor's fitting room and were only reluctantly welcomed into the male department store.

In contrast, general department stores were less successful at luring in men than women.[105] Their percentage of total sales nearly doubled during the interwar period but was still only 6.6 per cent of the total market by 1939. Men, it was believed, did not enjoy such a frivolous occupation as shopping and even today one invariably finds the menswear departments of larger stores on the ground floor safely surrounded by exits for a quick getaway. In contrast, menswear sales by multiple shop retailers leapt from 9 per cent to over 30 per cent in less than twenty years.[106] This included sales of other menswear garments such as shirts and ties.

Nevertheless, with the growth in numbers of department stores and multiples such as Burton's, accessories such as ties and socks and items such as underwear were increasingly being bought by women. It was also a challenge to the men's outfitters in much the same way that the stores stole business from the 'Madam' shops. This was particularly true in the north where Burton's in Bolton found that 'at least half the customers in the men's department are women. This is in contrast to the practice in the South "and adds to our difficulties"'.[107]

Old-established tailoring businesses continued to service the upper-middle classes. However, the division of quality that had previously marked out the lower-middle-class man's suit was lessening. There was far more choice on the high streets across the country. From 1920 to 1939 the number of multiple tailoring shops with fewer than twenty-five branches remained relatively stable, while these old companies had doubled the number of branches they had countrywide by 1939. Similarly, the number of larger firms competing for business increased slightly and tripled the number of outlets they had.[108] During the 1920s new menswear multiples opened at a rate of two to three a week across Britain.

As with women's clothing, new cutting techniques enabled the development of chains such as Henry Price's 'Fifty Shilling Tailor' and Burton's, which catered predominantly for a mass market, patronised by the lower-middle and working classes. Burton, who used as his slogan 'a Man of Taste', aimed just a little above his long-time competitor Price, with suits starting at 55 shillings. Since 50 shillings was estimated to be an average weekly wage, this was a relative bargain: residents of Lewes in Sussex, who did not have a nearby Burton's, reportedly had to spend three weeks' wages on a suit.[109] In 1919 Burton's had forty shops, of which half were in London and the non-industrial regions. By 1939 they had 565 shops, over 90 per cent of them outside the south-east.[110]

While the term 'bespoke' indicated a hand-stitched suit made by a 'Savile Row'-style tailor, the term 'tailor-made' was most often used to indicate a machine-made semi-tailored suit bought from a chain such as Burton's. The newest innovations were 'ready-mades', a term only just a little more acceptable than the earlier 'reach-me-downs'.[111] There was a stigma attached to buying these until well after the Second World War. A retailer recalled 'one of our regular customers for years [was] the managing director of So-and-so's across the street . . . a year ago he came in here to buy a suit and found himself standing beside one of his junior clerks . . . we haven't seen him since.'[112]

Further up the social scale there was a relatively new marketing phenomenon – the specialist store aimed at middle- and upper-middle-class men, which sold a full range of menswear from suits to socks, combining the roles of tailor and outfitter. Stores such as Austin Reed, with what they termed 'New Tailoring', and later Simpson's, bridged the gap between the two extremes of the expensive and exclusive Savile Row tailor and mass-production chains such as Burton's.[113] Whereas Burton's modelled their stores on a style reminiscent of a gentlemen's club, encouraging the illusion that their customers were entering a true tailor's,[114] Austin Reed and particularly Simpson's were more forward-looking and introduced male customers to a style of shopping more familiar to their wives. This was not just a London phenomenon. Countrywide sales of the Simpson's and Daks brands were 'making Lancashire people more dress-conscious, more ready to follow the leaders,' claimed a Bolton tailor.[115]

Research carried out by *The Statistical Review of Press Advertising* during the 1930s shows that Austin Reed regularly spent four times as much as their competitors such as Horne Bros in promoting their essentially upper-middle-class brand. Over 50 per cent of this advertising went into the national newspapers with another 25 per cent going into magazines. Aiming at men in the upper middle classes, Simpson's of Piccadilly played on the success that would await those who dressed correctly. In 1938 they ran a series of advertisements, one of which read, 'A rising architect yes, but what a pity he doesn't get his clothes at Simpson's', the implication being that this man would be more successful if smartly dressed by the menswear store. Similarly they targeted the 'member of the board', the doctor with 'a good bedside manner' and the 'Captain of the club'.[116] All these jobs were high-status positions within the middle classes and so the clothing worn by men who held these jobs was a form of 'uniform' proclaiming their standing and disassociating them from the lower ranks within the same career structure. By contrast, Burton's preferred direct marketing, sending out booklets to every man in a town's local directory four times a year.[117] The place of Austin Reed and Burton's as brand leaders in their fields suggests that both these campaigns were successful.

There were noticeable regional differences in menswear sales patterns. Easter and August were the busiest times for the tailoring industry across Britain. In the north-west business peaked around June, a traditional holiday period.[118] Menswear retailers from the Midlands northwards emphasised lower prices as opposed to variety.[119] Austin Reed opened branches in Liverpool, Manchester and Preston during the early 1920s; the Liverpool and Manchester stores flourished but Preston floundered. Their first-ever market research campaign revealed that in Preston's business area collarless coloured shirts outnumbered the formal white shirt by eight to one. This was in contrast to the figures in Liverpool and Manchester, where the ratio was virtually 50:50. Austin Reed duly closed the Preston store, accepting that the social mix in the town was not enough to sustain their middle-class business.[120]

A lower income did not necessarily mean a lower spend on clothing but this largely depended on where one lived. In 1926 Londoners needed to spend less on their clothes than those living in large towns, probably because more choice made prices slightly more competitive. In the lower-middle-class wage range those living in small towns with limited access to large department stores necessarily had to spend more on their clothes. In mathematical terms the provincial shopper felt the need to spend 1.5 per cent more of their income on clothes than Londoners did.[121]

To take one example from a man's wardrobe, an evening suit was, for most men, likely to be their biggest clothing purchase. In 1929 Austin Reed advertised evening wear that would not 'depart by a hair's breadth from those standards which are implied by the very words "dress clothes"'. Such correctness came at a price. Jackets cost 4½ and 6 guineas, waistcoats, 30 shillings and trousers, 45 shillings. The longevity of such a purchase was emphasised by the fact that all the items could be bought separately and replaced 'at any future time'.[122] Although 80 per cent of clerks working within government, banking and insurance earned over £150 a year, salaries dropped slightly during the late 1920s and early 1930s and 6 guineas for one jacket would have been a major investment.[123]

It is not surprising that the expense but also the necessity of correct evening dress led to the growth of one of Britain's most famous outfitting chains, Moss Bros. The company started by specialising in the hire of ceremonial dress from the turn of the twentieth century, and one general, Sir Ian Hamilton, found himself hiring a campaign uniform he had sold to Moss Bros thirty-six years before.[124] This is a rare indication that there may have been a hidden second-hand menswear market as well though it was most likely confined to dress clothes. For example, clients of Moss Bros have always been able to purchase outfits that they have hired.[125]

The firm capitalised on the middle classes' need for a correct but economically priced evening wear hire facility in the 1920s and 1930s. As store buyer Ethyle Campbell noted in 1939, Moss Bros served 'those who have all the impulses towards gentility, but lack the necessary money to equip themselves in accordance with their real or imaginary status in life'.[126] There had been a reluctance to use the facilities of a hire shop in the early 1920s. While the aristocracy had no such compunction, Moss Bros found the trade among the middle classes slow to start with.[127] Ethyle Campbell explained:

> This hush-hush attitude about the hiring of ceremonial garb is a peculiarly English one. The Englishman doesn't really mind admitting that he is hard up. He doesn't mind driving a shabby old car, wearing practically worn-out flannel bags, travelling third class by train, eating at cheap restaurants and risking wet feet to save a taxi fare . . . but – the ordinary, decent, reasonably truthful young man will shift, prevaricate, shuffle and lie sooner than admit that he has hired any garment.[128]

The social necessity for such outfits soon left many men with no choice but to hire rather than buy if they wanted to be seen in anything other than a poor quality suit. Men's attitude to hiring their dress clothes is just one example of the angst that clothes-buying in the interwar years induced. Whatever the situation, at home, at work, on the golf course, even on holiday, dress mattered during this heyday of sartorial correctness.

TWO

Black Coats and White Collars

It is reasonably easy to give an almost exact guess as to what class of person is engaged on from his or her personal appearance. Also a person takes a pride in this is nearly always found to have a keenness and pride their work. If they are neat and smartly dressed then they are also usually neat and smart at their work and in their habits. [1]

Mr J.L., a buyer from Birmingham

For the last one hundred years phrases such as 'black-coated', 'white collar', and 'white blouse' have labelled middle-class occupations. The above comment from a 32-year-old buyer from Birmingham in 1939 shows how important it was to 'dress the part' for one's working environment. Similarly, his use of the phrase 'class of job' suggests that employment had social as well as economic implications. Whether a man was a lowly clerk or a High Court judge, wearing the 'correct' clothing was vital to maintaining his social standing in the employment market-place.

During the early 1920s the tailoring industry felt that the First World War had engendered a relaxation of dress standards. Judging by anxious editorials in journals like the *Sartorial Gazette*, it seems tailors feared that informality might become the norm.[2] However, this did not happen. One of the reasons for this is that the perception of increased job insecurity led to the re-embracing of formality. Although many of the middle classes thought they were suffering from the effects of the economic slump in Britain in the early 1930s, the reality was that in material terms salaries and employment remained steady across the middle classes.[3]

Whatever the job, long-term security was always seen as desirable in employment. While many middle-class careers offered such security, promotion could be slow and domestic budgets tight.[4] Individuals were reluctant to step out of line for fear of losing their jobs or holding themselves back within their sector. This also involved adhering to the many codes of dress decorum of office life. Thus a man's choice of wardrobe had to reflect his working environment and aspirations.

By 1938 one in seven working adults was employed in a salaried occupation.[5] In *The New Survey of London Life and Labour*, published in 1932, class was defined by the occupation of the head of the household, occasionally using the benchmark of the £250 minimum annual income as well. Therefore, a self-employed man would not be counted as middle class unless his income was over this level. Similarly, while shopkeepers were ranked as middle-class, shop assistants had to have both a managerial or supervisory position and the higher income to qualify as middle class. In the police force, only those holding the rank of inspector or above counted as middle class.[6]

To help establish who was who in the middle-class pecking order, it is useful to look at contemporary business societies at a local level. For many middle-class men across Britain in the 1920s and 1930s social aspirations took the form of membership of local business organisations such as Chambers of Commerce and Rotary Clubs. The latter, many of which were established in the 1920s and 1930s, were important both socially and in allowing networking among other local businessmen, particularly since a man could not apply to join but had to wait to be asked.[7] In addition, each club maintained a list of acceptable occupations or 'classifications' and was supposed to have only one representative from each trade or profession, although this was frequently flouted. 'If they want you in Rotary, they'll find a class for you,' claimed one member.[8]

Significantly, membership was also supposed to be confined to men in 'executive' positions but this could, and did, include men running their own small business or a shop. Indeed, the membership list of most Rotary Clubs paints a picture of middle-class society in the 1930s. Two-thirds of the twenty-two founder members of the Rotary Club in Poole, Dorset, were based in the High Street though not all were retailers; the other third included a bank manager, an architect, an inspector of taxes and a mineral water manufacturer.[9]

The classifications show what were considered to be acceptable middle-class occupations. The organisation aimed to recruit 'men whose occupational interests would inform them of the trends and activities of "big business" without offering

In the 1930s there was little difference in the way most middle-class businessmen across the country dressed as they enjoyed the networking opportunities afforded by organisations such as the Newcastle Rotary Club. (*Hulton Getty*)

the means of controlling events'.[10] The wide range of jobs is significant. Birmingham had nearly two hundred classifications in the early 1930s. Of the initial thirty-eight members of the Rotary Club of Stourbridge in the West Midlands when it was started in 1922 the occupations of twenty-nine are known and are typical of middle-class occupations: there was a group of professionals including an accountant, two architects, a bank manager, a doctor and three solicitors; there was a group representing local retailing, including six shop owners and two estate agents; and finally there were various other disparate local worthies such as a newspaper proprietor and the town clerk.[11]

There is little evidence that in the 1920s men in business felt the need to compete in terms of appearance. However, as job security became more important in the 1930s the maintenance of standards also strengthened in importance. Men working at managerial level felt duty-bound to present an image of a 'gentleman'. This was an image that was a 'clearly identifiable icon of masculinity . . . it was taken as given that the gentleman always appeared correctly dressed, for clothes were a public sign of social honour'.[12]

In surveys of the middle classes between the wars family incomes were set between £250 per annum to in excess of £700.[13] Many men within this salary

Even in what might have been expected to be the more relaxed atmosphere of a national newspaper press room, journalists at the *Daily Express* stuck to the traditional suit, collar and tie with not a shirtsleeve in sight. (*Hulton Getty*)

range felt they had a great deal of financial pressure on their wardrobe requirements, in contrast, for example, to the clerks who worked beneath them.

> Those whose wage is . . . £100–130 often do not require to keep up appearances to the same extent [as us] and can therefore manage with one very good suit and wear for everyday a selection of reach-me-downs or odd garments, whereas the necessity to attend important meetings and the feeling that one must not 'let the side down' means that such as I must have at least 1 good suit for special occasions, one 'decent' suit for every-day business wear, 1 good looking heavy overcoat and a rain-coat.[14]

An insurance agent vented his frustration on what he saw as the main pressure on his clothing budget. 'BUSINESS demands that I dress well. That is why I do . . . My profession makes it necessary for me to be always well-dressed.'[15] Even a

While 'shabbiness' was unacceptable, overly new clothes also drew suspicion that the wearer might be too concerned about his appearance, prompting accusations of dandyism and effeminacy. (*Estate of H.M. Bateman*)

The New Suit

Mass-Observation respondent who was a journalist, a less traditional profession, noted that he was expected to wear 'a darkish respectable suit at the office', a version of the by now ubiquitous lounge suit.[16]

The lounge suit, that is matching jacket and trousers, was thought by the tailoring trade to be the instigator of slovenly dressing, and was initially associated with a derogatory vocabulary of, 'lounge 'abits, lounge lizards and dole drawers'.[17] Because it was seen as a suit for 'everyman', magazines such as the *Sartorial Gazette*, the self-appointed purveyors of 'good taste', suggested that the lounge suit was contributing to the lowering of class barriers which in turn would damage the mystique surrounding the bespoke tailoring business.

Correct dressing did not end with the purchase of the correct suit. Ostentatious newness could draw mockery. Razor-sharp creases in the trousers might come with a new suit but might also convey the message that the wearer was trying too hard. Subjective comments by the Mass-Observation team show the ease with which a man might be misjudged. In the hand-written notes made on the survey of clothing, one analyst has written 'dandy?' next to the entry for one respondent, Mr A., who owned six suits. Mr A. was, in fact, a chemist who felt he was 'conservative in matters of male fashions and only modest changes made in what I consider "good taste" find favour with me'.[18] The selection of clothes for work by the man in the middle range of the middle classes is exemplified by the sentiments of a 28-year-old office worker from Manchester, who chose 'quiet clothes, chosen to be in keeping with the position in life of the wearer, and not with the purpose of trying to appear what one is not'.[19]

By the end of the 1930s, among middle-class men working in business, with the exception of the professions, the difference was in quality rather than styling. Occasionally, a small degree of freedom was allowed depending on the occupation. Note the relative flexibility enjoyed by an analytical chemist:

> The middle-class man must be a 'black coated' worker, he must be able to maintain a 'respectable' appearance, I mean that the type of work must be such as to allow him to do so even if he does not always present such an appearance. For example, I often go to work in the summer in an open-necked shirt, flannels, no socks and sandals (hardly 'black coated') but even so, I present a different appearance to the ordinary workman – my clothes are newer, I am not so dirty and so on.[20]

Similarly, the self-employed businessman or shopkeeper was answerable only to himself (or his wife) and could therefore show a degree of individualism not available to the company man. Writer Eric Newby recalls his father, the owner of a large ladies' clothes manufacturing company in London, always being immaculately dressed. 'None of the clothes made by his tailor ever wore out. They belong to a period before the First World War when a button once put on was on for ever.'[21]

Similarly, novelist Elizabeth Jane Howard's father, who worked for the family timber-merchants business in the City, owned 'many and varied' suits, 'beautifully-cut – with an enormous silk handkerchief in the breast pocket'.[22] Historian Richard Cobb remembers Mr Edwards who ran a prestigious sports shop in his home town of Tunbridge Wells, 'not *quite* a shopkeeper, certainly not *just* a shopkeeper'. He wore a blazer in his shop 'as if he were just looking in between two games, so that one felt rather apologetic about catching him on the wing and keeping him from playing for Kent or Sussex, or both'.[23]

By the late 1920s men working in the City or central London expected to wear a version of 'London clothes . . . a very dark suit and overcoat worn with bowler hat, black or very dark brown shoes, crook-handled umbrella and light gloves'.[24] Morning suits were not commonly worn outside the professions or the City however high a man's status. The clothes of politician and 'man of the people' Stanley Baldwin epitomised the complexities of middle-class masculinity. In public his appearance, always correct with no hint of flamboyance, supported Baldwin's 'national persona of imperturbable trustworthiness', a persona many middle-class men were striving to achieve in their own business and professional worlds.[25] Yet he did not dress to impress and the American press felt that 'in baggy clothes, smoking his inevitable pipe and wearing that look of detachment' it could have been interpreted that Baldwin, a Midlands industrialist's son, would have preferred 'being a drowsy country squire in Worcester, tending to pigs'.[26]

The middle-class look of another Prime Minister, Neville Chamberlain, grandson of a shopkeeper and son of politician 'Radical Joe' Chamberlain (noted for always wearing an orchid in his buttonhole), was also part of his popularity.[27]

> The ordinary Englishman sees in him an ordinary Englishman like himself; one who has been in business in a small way and has made a little – but not much – money; one who has been happily married and brought up a family of which the world knows little; one who wears the same business-suit every day, the black coat and vest, the striped trousers, the laced boots, and carries the same umbrella whether he is walking on a cloudless morning in the Park with Mrs Chamberlain (which he does every day at the same hour) or whether he is flying across Europe to meet the dictator to settle the affairs of nations.[28]

Even in these pre-television days politicians' appearance was important and commented on.

Large towns and cities in the north were not so strict in following the rules of 'London' clothing conventions, to the despair of the tailoring industry. Interviewed in the *Manchester Evening News* in 1933, an optimistic tailor predicted a revival of the 'black-jacket-and-striped-trousers rule', seeing this as the optimum choice. 'Sooner or later . . . business chiefs will realise that clothes are an advertisement, and will issue an edict that all their employees must wear black coats and striped trousers . . . if women can go to so much trouble over their clothes why don't men?'[29]

However, photographs that appeared in the *Manchester Evening News* indicate that few businessmen in the north-west actually wore morning suits. Standard wear appears to be the classic three-piece pinstripe suit as worn by Major J. Becke, Chief Constable of Cheshire, when he was photographed for the *Manchester Evening News*.[30] Indeed, across the north it appears that businessmen other than professionals such as doctors, solicitors and bank managers rarely wore morning suits. However, they differed from the city gentlemen of the south-east in sartorial touches such as the patterned tie and tiepin worn by Mr William Sucksmith, senior partner of the Valley Scouring Company, wool scourers and carbonisers, of Shipley, in a photograph in the *Bradford Times & Argus*.[31] Wealthy northern businessmen and entrepreneurs appeared to prefer the flamboyance of the flowery buttonhole, the silk handkerchief or the gold watch-chain, echoing the Edwardian period and T.S. Eliot's 'silk hat of the Bradford millionaire', to the sombre suiting of the professional.[32] They clearly did not feel the need to adopt 'London' clothes among northern society.

MARKING OUT THE PROFESSIONAL

It was left to the professionals – doctors, lawyers and the like – to develop a recognisable dress code that set them apart from other middle-class men. Professional men have long been central to the identity of the British middle classes despite being only a relatively small section of it. It has always been difficult to dissect the various sectors of the professions. The dictionary definition of a 'professional' as a person 'engaged in a profession, especially one requiring advanced knowledge or training' is of little help in distinguishing the multitude of occupations that the label could cover.

In 1851 twenty-two different professional occupations could be identified ranging from civil servants (the largest number) to scientists (the smallest).[33] By 1931 twenty-seven occupations were listed as 'professions', including new categories such as librarians, laboratory assistants and industrial and trade association officials.[34] Teaching and medicine were the largest professions closely followed by engineering and other sciences, law and architecture. Significantly, classifications were not made through 'amount of income or possession of wealth'.[35] Men in business often earned more than doctors, for instance.

Professionals have been seen as a 'maverick fourth class' who 'rightly, or wrongly, see themselves as above the main economic battle'.[36] All professional men and their families would have been acutely aware of the differences within their social networks and outlook. It is hardly an exaggeration to say that 'barristers and solicitors inhabited separate universes, the one a refuge for impecunious gentlemen, the other a summit of ambition for the tradesman's brightest son'.[37] These disparities were increasingly used by mid-ranking professionals to distinguish themselves from differing segments within their own class group.[38]

The tailoring trade put pressure particularly on the professions who dealt directly with the public, such as doctors, solicitors and bank managers, to use

FOR BETTER BUSINESS

THERE is, of course, a kind of junior-clerk version of the black-jacket ensemble, but there is no fear of confusing it with this, which can be seen at a glance to belong in the large room with the pile carpet, often distinguished by a neat card on the door, marked "In Conference." It blends just as well with a Harley St. address as with Throgmorton St., or, for that matter, the Inns of Court. Or your own needs. The choice of trousering gives the chief touch of distinction ; a grey Cheviot is recommended, with well covered ground, either in stripe effect or in miniature check. The collar is white, and in most cases the shirt also, though a neat stripe is quite in order. Similarly, a slight touch of colour is excusable in the black of the sock. A coloured boutonniere finishes the ensemble rather better than white.

In 1935 *Style Guide*, a menswear trade magazine, featured a highly stylised version of the look they felt professional men such as doctors, lawyers and solicitors should aim for. Note the rolled umbrella and Homburg hat neatly placed on the desk. (Style Guide, *1935*) dress to distinguish their status from those in 'trade' – or indeed in other professions, which were seen as less highly skilled. Increasingly during the late 1920s many complied and wore the distinctive morning suit and bowler hat associated with the City of London until well into the 1960s.

The wearing of morning suits by non-professionals or City businessmen was seen as presumptuous although it did happen. Mr and Mrs Tom Hendrick of Ealing remember their fathers, a commercial traveller and a shop manager respectively, always wearing spats, pinstriped trousers with a black jacket and 'the mandatory brolly' for work in the 1930s.[39] 'Morning suits', noted a 29-year-old clerk from Newcastle, 'are suitable for business men, solicitors, and others who hold *responsible* positions [original italics] but appear unnecessary and rather snobbish when worn by clerks generally.'[40] His comment shows that 'business-men' at top managerial level, such as company directors, used the morning suit as a dress code to reinforce their positions of responsibility. It also suggests that men in these groups felt threatened by men of lesser status attempting to emulate their style of dress. Some 'junior clerks' did attempt to emulate senior figures in the way they dressed but may have been let down by the quality of their outfits.

The tailoring industry insisted that the key to suitable dressing was quality. The editorial in *Style Guide* shows a highly idealised version of the look they felt professional men should aim for. 'There is, of course,' runs the caption,

> a kind of junior-clerk version of the black-jacket ensemble, but there is no fear of confusing it with this, which can be seen at a glance to belong in the large room with the pile carpet, often distinguished by a neat card on the door marked 'In Conference'. It blends just as well with a Harley St. address as with Throgmorton St., or, for that matter, the Inns of Court.[41]

Tailors actively encouraged a wider embrace of this formal style of clothing confirming the morning suit, that is black jacket without tails and 'sponge-bag' striped trousers, as a visual uniform for professionals and businessmen. The *Style Guide* makes it clear that there ought to be no comparison between this outfit and the cheaper version of the black jacket ensemble:

> Doctors, dentists, opticians, bankers, company directors and heads of firms in general should all dress severely and with care. In the first place, because serious matters and weighty responsibilities call for a serious demeanour. Secondly, to set an example to their employees and the public in general.

The clothes worn by the harassed doctor in Pont's cartoon are clearly a cut above those of his waiting patients. They are typical of those worn by fee-earning GPs at this time. (Punch, *27 July 1938 © Punch Ltd*)

Thirdly, as a continual reminder to themselves should their thoughts tend to wander from their ordained paths.[42]

The tailoring industry implied that if a doctor wore a lounge suit instead of a morning coat, he would be bringing himself 'down to the level of "the man in the street"'. Similarly, the trade warned the solicitor that paying clients would be less likely to part with their money to a lawyer in a jacket than to one who dressed the part.[43]

The implication that professional men needed to dress well rippled out from the traditional professions. In 1939, a 40-year-old osteopath from Birmingham felt that 6 guineas was 'the cheapest figure at which I can get a suit that will pass muster in a first-class hotel or in the company of well-to-do people'. He stressed that he was 'careful' with his appearance because his job demanded that he wore 'decent' clothes, 'the general inference being', he continued, 'that a man cannot give a really skilled osteopathic treatment if he cannot afford to wear the "right" clothes'.[44]

A popular formal alternative to the black jacket and 'sponge-bag' trousers was the chalk pinstripe suit. Balfour Barwise, a dentist with a practice in central Oxford during the 1930s, wore a dark blue three-piece pinstriped suit every day until the 1950s. It was made for him by Shepherd & Woodward, Oxford's leading tailors, and Mr Barwise would wear it without the jacket for work, the waistcoat and watch-chain covered by his short white dentist's robe. 'He was always dapper, a neat and smart man with neat and tidy clothes.'[45]

ACADEMIC ALTERNATIVES

Not all professionals dressed in such a conventional manner. The formality of morning dress was in clear contrast to the relatively relaxed attitude to clothes taken by most male academics for example. R.H. Tawney, Professor of Economic History at the London School of Economics, was known in the 1930s for carelessly emptying his pipe into the cuff of his tweed trousers.[46] Sir Frederick Hopkins, a scientist and President of the Royal Society from 1935 to 1940, chose to wear for his portrait by Meredith Frampton in 1938 a pale cream jacket, blue shirt and green tie and waistcoat without robes standing at a laboratory workbench.[47] This is in marked contrast to a portrait of Reginald McKenna, Chairman of the Midland Bank from 1918 to 1943.[48] He is wearing a morning suit of black jacket and waistcoat together with dark pinstripe trousers and a barely visible discreet watch-chain. These clothes are clearly part of the banker's 'uniform' and can be seen as representing respectability and status in contrast to the academic's degree of individuality. The clothes chosen for portraits often reveal the persona the sitter wants to present. It is no surprise that most board-room portraits followed a predictably familiar format.

Teachers also had a degree of flexibility depending on their level of income and their interest in clothes. Wilfred Blunt describes an eccentric maths teacher at Haileybury public school in the 1930s (where Blunt was himself a teacher), who wore 'clod-hopper boots, trousers too short, a four-inch collar and a five-buttoned coat. Every four or five years a postcard inscribed "same again please" brought another identical ill-fitting suit from his tailor.'[49]

In contrast, Mr R.B., a 45-year-old teacher from Liverpool, spent the considerable sum of 14 guineas on his new suits, which he had made in London. His wardrobe always included one morning suit with black and white 'shepherd's plaid' or 'sponge-bag' striped trousers. However, since Mr R.B. describes his suits as being kept for interviews and social occasions, the assumption must be that he wore one of several pairs of grey flannel trousers and a sports jacket for work under the usual black academic gown worn by teachers, since he lists these as being 'everyday wear'.[50]

Similarly, a 25-year-old chemistry teacher from Leicester owned three suits, the newest being kept for 'best', the second, a two-year-old suit, 'used weekdays' for work, and the third 'is not used, although it is by no means thread-bare, but merely shabby'.[51] At the lower end of the scale academic Bryan Magee remembers that his teachers in Hoxton, in London's East End, 'always wore suits, because it was expected of them, but with most of them it was the same very cheap suit every day, bagging and shiny at the joint'.[52]

Whether teacher or salesman, 'shabbiness' was something to be avoided at all costs without the security of academic tenure. 'Lack of money does not necessarily mean that a man should dress shabbily,' pontificated a respondent, while another felt that 'having out of necessity to wear shabby clothes has a demoralising effect'.[53] Several Mass-Observation respondents, including the young teacher from Leicester, admitted that they were more concerned about having a clean collar and shirt together with a 'tidy' tie and handkerchief than whether their trousers were creased.[54] Thus the standard cliché of cleanliness equalling respectability was still in evidence and more important than sartorial detail. Cleanliness also firmly distinguished the blue-collar worker from the higher status white-collar worker.[55]

CLERKS: THE WHITE-COLLAR PROLETARIAT

Many young men from the lower middle classes started their careers as clerks in a variety of business environments. These were the young men who, prior to the First World War, formed 'part of [a] large, shifting, single-male population . . . fac[ing] the material consequences of keeping up appearances on a minimal income'.[56]

After 1918 clerks were still comparatively poorly paid in jobs such as local government and insurance, but about 90 per cent were earning more than £150 a year in 1924.[57] With a great deal of overlap between clerks from the traditionally white-collar lower middle class and the aspiring working class, it is clear that many young men felt that by donning a suit and tie they were elevating themselves socially. So it is not surprising that they frequently held strong 'middle-class' attitudes since 'they stood in the front line of the class war'.[58]

In 1935, when reviewing the employment conditions of clerks, Klingender pointed out it was a mistake to assume, because clerks appeared to be higher up the social scale than skilled workers, that they were better off. Not only were they likely to be earning less than skilled workers, they also had to pay more for their 'outward signs of respectability' such as clothing.[59] One young man confided in his Mass-Observation reply that 'my job as a clerk necessitates that I look tidy so that I am unable to economise below a certain limit in the matter of clothes'.[60] A 26-year-old clerk from central London who spent the large amount of 7 guineas on his suits confirms this. 'Wanting to get on in my job I cannot afford to be ill-dressed.'[61] Even a respondent who spent only 3 guineas on his suits thought, 'there is no possible excuse for economising on clothes; a man should spend all he can afford on his wardrobe. Appearances are everything – a man with money will naturally dress well, being able to afford it; lack of money does not necessarily mean that a man should dress shabbily.'[62]

Tailors played on their young customers' social insecurities. A pamphlet on salesmanship included advertisements from a small London tailoring business: 'It is no use going to a New Job with poor clothes/You get the job and leave the clothes to me.'[63] The *Sartorial Gazette* offered advertising aphorisms to encourage sales such as 'As people cannot *see* our characters or abilities, they judge us by our clothes', 'Dressing correctly and well commands respect' and 'You too can win your chief's approval and secure that better job if you dress with good taste as well as prove a good worker'.[64]

In spite of the need to look tidy and respectable for work and the increased availability of cheaper suits through tailoring chains such as Burton's, young men were surprisingly reluctant to wear their new suits for work. Many respondents call their newest suit their 'best', worn for social occasions, while the second best becomes the office suit. One youth quantifies this: 'Usually a suit is best for 6 months, then work for 9 months.'[65] One man who had four suits all bought for under £4 thought two were 'as good as new' while two were 'only suitable for office'.[66] As one Mass-Observation respondent commented, 'I have to choose a cloth & style [of suit] that will not date quickly & that will be suitable for office wear later in its life.'[67]

From the end of the nineteenth century clerical work had increasingly been seen as 'unmanly'. By the end of the First World War more women were going into office jobs and the threat of women's presence in the office was a recurring theme in the trade press:[68]

Never forget that the modern girl, who is your competitor in business nowadays, takes [her appearance] most seriously. She realises that she has to if she wants to get on, and you'd better realise you have to if you want to get on. It costs you rather more for one rig-out than it does her, because all your clothes are tailor-mades; but she needs more variety in dress than you do, so you and she start more or less even.[69]

The male respondents for Mass-Observation did not mention this as a strong concern yet spoke of other influences in their choice of clothes. A 19-year-old planning assistant from York voiced the feelings of many when he said he regarded 'personal appearance as a definite social and business help, in addition to which it gives me a clean and respectable feeling to be smartly (tho' not ostentatiously) dressed'.[70] A 22-year-old clerk from north London noted that although he was 'a long long way from being rich', he failed to see that 'that was a reason why the appearance [he presented] to the community should not be one of pleasantness and general correctness'.[71]

In 1930 psychologist J.C. Flugel published his significant work pronouncing that 'The Great Masculine Renunciation', the move of men's clothes from ideals of beauty to the purely practical, had started at the end of the eighteenth century. Flugel may have been wrong about when the 'Great Renunciation' began but he was writing quite accurately about his own time when he said in 1930, 'So far as clothes remained of importance to [man], his utmost endeavours could only lie in the direction of being "correctly" attired, not of being elegantly or elaborately attired.'[72] He reiterated this in 1934, adding 'modern clothing . . . allows few outlets for personal vanity among men; to be dressed "correctly or in good taste is the utmost that a modern man can hope for"'.[73] While there were no doubt exceptions among the young, on the whole, whatever style of suit was worn, at work 'correctness' reigned supreme for all interwar middle-class men.

THREE

Business Girls and Office Dresses

It has been said so many, many times – I hate to rub it in – don't drape yourself for office hours like a haberdashery counter. Resist brooches, bows, necklaces. There is only one frivolity I won't deny you – feminine and unnecessary though it be – a buttonhole. A bunch of cowslips under one's nose somehow brings spring into the most unromantic office.[1]

Daily Mirror (February 1935)

This advice on what a working girl should and should not wear in the mid-1930s focuses on the dilemma women faced between fashionability and correctness and also between femininity and the traditionally masculine arena of work. Whereas for most of a man's adult life, his world was clearly shaped between the areas of work and home, a typical middle-class woman's life followed a different pattern and the pressures on her wardrobe reflected this.

During the interwar years, despite the Sex Disqualification (Removal) Act of 1919, young middle-class women often found paid work but generally their working life finished on marriage. In 1931 only 16 per cent of the female work-force was married.[2] It appeared that for most young women work was 'a dreary routine, an interval . . . en route to a trousseau, marriage and a home of her own'.[3] But many young women enjoyed this time in their lives which gave them brief economic independence before marriage.[4]

Middle-class women were actively discouraged from working after marriage. This was less to do with taking jobs away from men, as was the feeling immediately

The 'office' costume worn by the female members of the National Provincial Bank, Manchester, in 1933 was chosen with function not fashion in mind. The women would have been clerical staff and they dressed with a modest formality not officially regulated by the bank since they were not in the public eye. (*National Portrait Gallery*)

after the First World War, but rather to do with the implication that a man should be earning enough to keep his wife and family – the family wage. To endorse this, the civil service and schools operated a marriage bar. During the interwar period women made up 25 per cent of the Civil Service but a marriage bar obliged them to give up their jobs on marriage.[5] Women were still outnumbered four to one within the Service's General Clerical grades.[6] In contrast, the numbers of women working in offices increased dramatically after the First World War. Figures leapt from just under 200,000 in 1911 to nearly 600,000 by 1931.[7]

Within the professions, while there were nearly twice as many female teachers as male, at nearly 130,000, the numbers of female solicitors, architects and accountants could only just struggle into the low hundreds by 1931, a small improvement on the figures from 1927.[8] From 1921 to 1931 the percentage of working women teachers in Britain among professionals actually dropped from 42 per cent to 38 per cent because of the bar.[9]

Business dress for women altered little during the 1920s and 1930s. In 1922 the *Girls' Favourite* recommended either a coat-frock or 'a coat and skirt with neat blouse beneath'.[10] For those who did go out to work, there was a hierarchy of dress for women within the office environment. The shorthand typist wore a flannel or serge suit, the typist more generally a dark frock or skirt and white blouse. The shorthand typist or secretary could distinguish herself from the lowly typist by the formality of her costume or suit. The 'office' costume was still functional enough for it never to be mistaken for that of the 'society' lady. Women working as clerical staff in institutions such as banks dressed with a modest formality which did not have to be officially regulated since they were not in the public eye.[11]

Didactic lists of correct female clothing for the office, but more often lists of what was incorrect, abound in this period:

> Remember that appearances reveal more than they hide – and that a lost button may mean a lost job . . . Wear a costume that fits you, and look trim and spruce. . . . Choose the hat that suits you best, letting it frame your face, not smother it. You may be asked to take it off so be prepared for this. It is better to uncover a well-dressed head than explain why your hair wants doing. Above all, avoid that Christmas-tree look. Noisy blobs of ornaments are not only distracting; they suggest you have the wrong sort of mind for business life. Match your stockings with an eye to your hat, your blouse, your gloves. There is still an almost superstitious faith in shoes and gloves as marking a woman's standard of refinement. Neat gloves should cover hands as neat, and a business girl's hands are as important as those of an actress.[12]

Gloves, hands and stockings were expected to be scrupulously clean with handbags 'emptied of all but necessities'.[13] Some offices had rules about what could not be worn, such as short sleeves (whatever the weather) or brightly-coloured frocks. Jewellery was considered unsuitable for the office, making the wearer look 'over-dressed and common'.[14] To 'over-dress' was seen as a sign of lack of breeding, noted a clerk from Newcastle-upon-Tyne. 'Fortunately, very few girls overdress for business, and this minority are too obvious. A girl can look smart and efficient without over-emphasis. Those who do overdress, both male and female, generally give the impression of being social climbers – from the bottom rung.'[15]

While it would be a mistake to read too much into such advice, the plethora of such articles in magazines shows women's concerns. There was a balance to be achieved between the indulgences of femininity and fashion and the constraints of modesty. Therefore, in contrast to the men's lists, rather than indicating what *was* correct, more often than not they listed what was *not* correct. 'Never adopt fluffy frocks for the office, or your employer may think your mind is on a par with your dress, and you may never secure a responsible position' is just such an example.[16] It was pointed out that 'a man's physical appearance does not affect his mental reactions as it does a woman's . . . she is terribly conscious the whole time of how she looks and of what she is wearing . . . [men] work better because of [women's] beauty just as they work better because of their own beauty'.[17] There were clear concerns about women's sexuality that were never voiced in men's tailoring literature.

BUYING FOR THE OFFICE

Dressing well for work did not come cheap. In 1924 over two-thirds of male clerks earned over £150 whereas less than one-third of female clerical workers did.[18] In 1927 the *Daily Mail* stated that women in business 'kept their position partly, if not chiefly, by their appearance'. Among the most poorly paid of the lower-middle-class female workers were shop assistants. The *Daily Mail* quoted a Miss Gladys Burlton, who trained shop assistants and recommended to her girls that if they earned £3 a week they needed to spend £1 of it on dress. The proportion could be less if they earned more. 'A business girl', she commented, 'cannot dress as a private character.'[19]

In 1938 just over half of all female shop assistants were earning between £90 and £125 a year. Rates had remained steady throughout the 1920s, fallen slightly in real terms during the early 1930s, but increased by nearly 4 per cent by 1939.[20] In 1934 Ruth Bowlby studied the spending patterns of middle-class girls between the ages of 20 and 30 working in London. The girls all came from families where the parents' income was over £225. Although the sample size was limited, it covered a variety of occupations from office workers and saleswomen to librarians, teachers and journalists. Bowlby herself eliminated the budgets of girls with dress allowances from their parents, and for the purposes of this work girls who lived at home have also been excluded.[21] She found that the reality was that young working girls were spending far less than a third of their income on clothes.

In general shop work was not considered suitable for a middle-class girl – 'unthinkable in our circle to serve in a shop,' commented Eileen Whiteing, a City businessman's daughter from Wallington in Surrey.[22] Lower-middle-class girls in retailing were assumed to be in a better financial position than skilled working-class girls. However, an example of the extremes gone to by some of these girls was given by Miss O. of Glasgow:

Clerks and shop assistants, many of whom in order to find money for smart clothes, cut down their allowance on food, light, [heating] . . . a sales girl at

Magazines such as *Weldon's Ladies' Journal* acknowledged the rise in the number of young women who worked, targeting the young 'business girl' who could improve her working wardrobe if she had good dressmaking skills. (Weldon's Ladies' Journal, *September 1930*)

> Copland & Lye's, a tip-top drapers . . . after paying for her room, clothes and travelling . . . is left with five pence a day for food, and recently collapsed from what the doctor termed 'malnutrition'. Yet her wardrobe is full of lovely clothes. This could not happen in less 'snooty' circles.[23]

Women outnumbered men three to one in retailing but only a sixth of them were married.[24] There was no official marriage bar in the drapery trade although women were always known as 'Miss'.[25]

Women in a position of more responsibility in retailing, such as the top female managers of Fenwick's department store in Newcastle-upon-Tyne, adopted the costume of matching skirt and jacket or dark dress rather than the secretarial white blouse and skirt of the more lowly clerks. While a few might add a masculine-style tie, most of the women chose individual feminine touches such as a string of pearls or beads.

Cleanliness was always an issue. Work clothes, although they might not be in the height of fashion, were valued and cared for assiduously. To preserve the freshness of their clothes, office workers usually changed when they got home.[26] This was doubly necessary to give an airing to outfits worn day in, day out. Frances Donaldson, in charge of a London typing pool in the 1930s, remembers being asked to speak to the girls about perspiration smells. Her reply to her boss was that not to smell involved expense. If he had doubled their wages, they could have afforded more than one dress to wear to the office.[27]

Miss Modern, a magazine aimed at women at the lower end of the salary scale, such as typists and shorthand typists, recognised the financial burden on young women to provide special clothing for work. In 1936 it was assumed by the magazine that its readers would be buying just 'one good suit a year':[28]

> I wonder if [employers] ever pause to consider that most girls wear last year's best frock to the office *this* year, and that salaries seldom run to two complete outfits: one for the office and one for the home. Therefore, Miss Modern should be allowed the privilege of wearing what she likes in the office provided she is neat and tidy, unless her employers are prepared to pay for the regulation long sleeved, navy blue dress which seems to them so suitable for the business girl (poor dear).[29]

In early 1935, when the *Daily Mirror* publicised a new 'Best Office Dress', they also took the opportunity to advise their female readers on the finer points of office etiquette:

> Here is an advance photograph of 'Miss 100 per Cent', one of the best office dresses to be displayed . . . Detachable collar and cuffs . . . When you go to the White City you might take a leaf out of the mannequins' book. You will notice the girls who display work-a-day dresses give us good tips on what to avoid in office hours. Notice their hands. No brilliant lacquers. Although bright nails are the thing, they are out of place in business hours, and however modern the 'Chief' and the office furniture no businessman likes his girls flashing carmine over typewriters.[30]

There is no doubt also that in many offices a girl's looks were just as important as her typing skills:

> A pretty, charmingly turned-out secretary is a great asset to a busy man. Being pretty she has confidence in herself, and so is more self-reliant than a plain girl.

She can be trusted to soothe irritable callers and people who want to quarrel over the telephone. Also she adds brightness to an office and helps to give it a cheerful atmosphere.[31]

Girls were aware of ways to use these visible assets even in the most constricting of office environments. A 23-year-old shorthand typist in Liverpool considered herself to be upper middle class as she thought 'middle class to be something better than working black-coated workers in routine jobs', and puts the prefix 'upper' to 'distinguish the more educated persons in better positions from the ordinary workers'.

It's always a source of amusement to me to watch the reactions of the men in the office if I wear an old dress coupled with a white collar. They don't notice the dress – the collar does the trick! Give me a white collar! The same thing applies to a transparent blouse – although perhaps in this case it's easier to analyse the reaction! A transparent blouse will keep you busy all morning, dealing with the visitors to your desk.[32]

Magazines disapproved of georgette blouses that displayed a 'vast amount of cami . . . they are not only out of place, but get grubby quickly, and grubbiness is an unforgivable sin for the office worker'.[33]

Transparent blouses were not an option for the older women at work. Sombre colours such as navy and black were seen as 'suitable' and 'becoming according to . . . age'.[34] As single 36-year-old journalist Miss B. explained, 'in answer to "are you well-dressed?" no, I am not well dressed, I am respectably dressed but not fashionable'.[35] Women such as Miss B., who were from the upper middle classes and held positions of responsibility, were under just as much pressure as the lowly typist to present a dignified front. Among the Civil Service's predominantly middle-class grammar school-educated girls 'all took great care with [their] appearances . . . all dressed nicely', according to a young civil servant clerk in the 1930s.[36]

DRESSING AT THE TOP

Women in senior management positions in business were a rarity. In 1938 only 4 per cent of salaried women were earning more than £250 a year as opposed to over 50 per cent of men.[37] The most visible women were those involved in politics, still a tiny number, dropping from fifteen in 1931 to nine in 1935. Nancy

Astor, for example, dressed to avoid undue attention being paid to her clothes. As the first woman to take a seat in Parliament, she was aware that she would be judged as much by her appearance as by her policies.

On the day Astor took her seat dozens of milliners sent hats to her at the House of Commons in the hope of future business.[38] She appeared wearing 'a beautifully cut, simple black coat and skirt with a white blouse open at the collar, and neat brimless black hat,'[39] and she would continue to wear a variation of this costume, which she designed herself, throughout her twenty-five years in Parliament.[40] Nevertheless, manufacturers recognised the influence that the small but significant batch of female MPs might have on women of a similar standing and produced costumes with names like 'Westminster'.[41]

For many middle-class women the only way they could become involved with the non-domestic world remained the traditional route of charity work, which many women pursued to a high level of proficiency.[42] Well before this period, all over the country single and married women who were not in paid employment had made use of their spare time by doing voluntary work with charities and other philanthropic organisations. Although the 1920s and particularly the 1930s are seen as a time when most women saw their role as going 'back to home and duty', in fact, just as in the nineteenth century, the idea of separate spheres takes little account of just how much women who did not work for money achieved in the community.[43]

Similarly, there were many married women involved in voluntary work who, by virtue of their husband's standing in local or national society, were in the public eye. *Success in Dress*, published in 1925 by the Hon. Mrs C.W. Forester, pointed out the pitfalls for all such women:

> What I have said of the business woman applies also to the woman who takes a big part in public life – the Town or County Councillor, the official for societies, the public speaker, and so on . . . many a cause has been numbered among the lost because its champions were ill dressed, and therefore unconvincing . . Audiences – political, social, or otherwise – are very quick to notice the wrong note in dress, whether it suggests undue ostentation, garish colours, or exaggeration in cut and style, or that accentuation of masculinity that irritates and repels.[44]

The era of the Prime Minister's wife as 'First Lady' or fashion icon was yet to arrive and Mrs Stanley Baldwin, for example, was more concerned with her

charitable works than with her media image. Indeed, she was notoriously
unconcerned about fashion. At a major event to launch her favourite cause, the
National Birthday Fund (a children's charity), newspapers reported that the
society ladies present all wore the currently fashionable black but that
Mrs Baldwin wore brown.[45] Just as her husband embodied the solid respectability
of the country squire, so Lucy Baldwin as his consort personified the sort of
respectability emulated by a tranche of middle-class wives of a certain age,
anxious for acceptability rather than fashionability.

Attitudes had not softened much by 1939, as shown by a Mass-Observation
respondent who was a Member of Parliament:

> My profession influences my clothes and appearance to a considerable extent.
> As my income is limited I cannot have too many clothes and they must be of a
> kind that I can wear on the platform or the office and to meet every class of
> person. Hence they must look 'right'; be of fairly good quality and cut so that
> when I am with well and expensively dressed women I feel sufficiently smart to
> maintain my poise and self confidence, yet should I be with working class
> women who cannot afford to dress well I shall not make them feel
> uncomfortable by my appearance. . . . to dress 'down' to a person or audience
> creates a bad impression and in many cases is looked upon as an insult. My
> clothes must not be 'flighty' or many of the older women would consider me
> lacking a sense of responsibility and be suspicious of my capabilities. As a
> general rule when moving to a new constituency I wear tailored coats and skirts
> with rather severe ['plain' crossed out] hats. Once my Committees have gained
> confidence in me and know me I then begin to wear rather more daring
> millinery without serious effect to my position.[46]

As an MP's wife commented, 'I like wearing new clothes . . . I want my husband
to like them, and hope that his constituency will not find them too highbrow!'[47]
Ethyle Campbell, a fashion buyer and perceptive observer of dress codes,
summed up the pressures on women in the public eye in 1938:

> The attitude of men towards the adornment of their women becomes largely a
> question of class. The Cabinet Minister requires that his wife be clothed in
> accordance with his station . . . The wives of doctors, parsons, borough
> surveyors and aldermen, in less degree than those of Cabinet Ministers, must
> combine a certain standard in dress with their other qualities.[48]

THE PROFESSIONAL WOMAN

At the top of the employment tree there were still few women in the professions. Given the working and domestic restrictions women were under it is not surprising that, while just over half of all teachers were women, less than 1 per cent of doctors were female.[49] There was certainly no female equivalent of the morning suit and striped trousers for these few professional females.

One might have expected the almost exclusively female environment of interwar women's schools and colleges not to be greatly concerned with fashionable clothes. With 130,000 women teachers, they were the largest group of professionals throughout the interwar period. Women in the teaching profession have traditionally had a reputation for presenting a masculine appearance.[50] The Merchant Taylors' School for Girls in Crosby, Lancashire, was a typical staunchly middle-class school where all the staff were single and some were 'noticeably mannish' – sporting short hair and wearing 'severely tailored suits' made from 'masculine worsted material, complete with shirts and ties'.[51] Girls lived in dread of curly hair becoming unruly when they might be told that they were 'no better than a "street-girl"' without having a clue what that actually meant.[52]

Many head teachers insisted on their staff being dressed as 'correctly' as the pupils. W.E. Wightman's illustration for one of Angela Brazil's enormously popular boarding-school novels, *Joan's Best Chum*, published in 1926, shows a young teacher wearing a plain dress and white collar almost indistinguishable from her pupils' uniform.[53] Miss Fordham, headmistress of the Merchant Taylors' School for Girls throughout the 1920s and 1930s, held to such a regime. Her staff were allowed to wear only sober navy or grey costumes with long-sleeved blouses, short-sleeved blouses never being allowed whatever the weather. A member of staff who turned up once wearing beige stockings was sent home so she could change into the regulation black ones, which 'constituted correct wear for both staff and pupils alike'.[54] Occasional rebellion was quickly dealt with. Miss Allan and Miss Powell, both of Merchant Taylors', liked to be different, 'sometimes wearing bright orange and yellow blouses'. Miss Powell was thought particularly daring for not wearing a dress under her chemistry overall during hot weather. Unsurprisingly, both teachers left for other jobs not long after Miss Fordham took over.[55]

Other teachers found ways round the dress regulations of their particular school. Miss H., a 37-year-old teacher, bought

Although a degree of individuality was acceptable among female teachers, the ladies of the National Union of Women Teachers Board of Management in 1935 show that sensible shoes and tied-back hair remained unmovable fixtures. (*Archives of the Institute of Education, University of London*)

plain, basic clothes for everyday and work wear, usually especially made for the purpose. I usually try to have on hand frocks which can quickly be made more frivolous on leaving work, by the addition of a flower, scarf, belt, necklace or ear-rings, if I am not going to change before going out to supper, cinema or meeting. This addition has an immense psychological effect upon one's enjoyment of the evening, I think.[56]

Photographs of women teachers in the 1930s show a slightly more relaxed attitude to dress with small touches of individuality under the traditional black academic gown where it was worn. Costumes buttoned to the neck were increasingly replaced with suits and blouses with a single row of pearls or a similar single-strand necklace. Sensible shoes, however, remained an immutable fixture as did the tied-back hair and hats and gloves in public.

Higher up the academic ladder there were fewer women and a slightly more relaxed atmosphere. At teacher training colleges female students were encouraged to dress in a 'neat and simple' way . . . a serge or tweed coat and skirt with a shirt of washing material are most suitable for everyday wear'.[57] Photographs of three female heads of teacher training colleges during the interwar period, Florence Johnson,

Staff and students of Bedford College pose in the grounds of their London campus in 1932 and demonstrate a clear interest in clothes through the variety of styles. Skirt lengths remain defiantly of an acceptable 'academic' length rather than reflecting any of the vagaries of fashion at that time. (*Archives, Bedford Centre for the History of Women, Royal Holloway, University of London*)

Principal of Bishop Otter College from 1919 to 1930, Elsie Bazeley, who followed her from 1930 to 1935, and Freda Hawtrey, of Avery Hill College from 1922 to 1938, show their own tastes as being conventional but artistic rather than masculine.[58]

Personal albums from Bedford College in the 1930s illustrate that female undergraduates and staff wore a variety of styles of outfit but most generally skirts with either a blouse or jumper indicating that there were no obvious dress regulations other than uniforms for sport.[59] While a minority of female staff adopted a masculine-style tailored jacket, stiff collar and tie, on the whole the staff dress was perhaps surprisingly individual and idiosyncratic. Similarly, photographs of college students and staff in London's Regents Park during both the 1920s and 1930s show by their variety a clear interest in clothes.[60] The only dress rule at the Bedford Froebel College, attended by Mrs J.B. in the late 1930s, was the wearing of a hat with 'a plain brim and piece of band'. She and two other college seniors 'revolted' and managed to abolish the wearing of these hats.[61]

In spite of the absence of men, a wardrobe of unexpected range was needed for college life. Marion Pike, a student and later staff member, longed to give Royal Holloway 'a fashion show from a first-class house, of clothes for all College occasions – lectures, sports, elegant afternoons, town and country travelling, summer days, dinners, dances and dazzling evening gala nights – all to be shown with the necessary hats, gloves, handbags, shoes and stockings'.[62] Not surprisingly, she wistfully yearned for a 'beautiful complete minimum new outfit of clothes suitable for all occasions, light-weight, uncrushable, easily packed in an equally superior minimum set of travelling cases'.[63] One of the reasons for this may well have been the judgement of women by their peers when it came to dressing for reunions. Marion Pike's memoirs describe the trials of selecting outfits for 'Old Students' Days' at Royal Holloway:

> A certain amount of planning was needed. Three toilettes had to be carefully chosen – an elegant plain suit or nice cotton dress for Saturday afternoon, a best evening dress for Saturday dinner and something approaching garden party style for Sunday. Staring was quite *comme il faut*; one almost expected it.[64]

The 'certain amount of planning' gives confirmation, if ever it has been needed, that women dress just as much to win the approval of other women as for the admiration of men. There were female academics in the humanities departments of other universities who showed a clear interest in clothes. At the London School of Economics Lilian Knowles was 'known for her flamboyant hats'.[65] Friends said of Eileen Power, Professor of Medieval History at the London School of Economics, that 'every time she got an article published she would go to Croydon, and take a flight on Imperial Airways to Paris, to buy herself a new dress'.[66]

The insight given above into a female academic's attitude to clothes is a rare one. Autobiographies by several professional women, particularly those involved in the sciences, such as Louisa Martindale, an eminent surgeon in the interwar period, make absolutely no mention of dress at all.[67] Similarly, when Louisa's sister Hilda Martindale wrote a review of female civil servants during a seventy-year period up to 1938, she also ignored both the clothing tastes and requirements of her subjects.[68] Whether this is simply a familial lack of interest in dress is hard to know yet it is surely significant that two such tough and ambitious women did not feel their wardrobes were worthy of comment. Similarly, when Dorothy Hodgkin, the eminent scientist, was photographed by portraitists Ramsey & Muspratt in 1937, there is no hint of vanity or interest in clothes in the resulting photograph.[69] Clearly, whatever job or profession a woman might have been in, her wardrobe needed to reflect a sensitivity to her surroundings at the same time as remaining resolutely correct and respectable at all times.

FOUR

In Home and Garden

No matter what your circumstances may be, you cannot afford to neglect your appearance, nor must you ever forget that to look your best *at all times* is your duty – towards yourself and towards the man you married.[1]

Woman's Own, October 1932

Woman's Own did not mince its words in telling its female readers where their duty lay in 1930s Britain. It highlights the importance of the home in interwar society and the pressures to maintain correct standards even behind closed doors. For the majority of middle-class men the routine of their lives followed an established pattern. Their activities were neatly divided between work, domestic and social activities with clearly defined wardrobes to match. Their home was somewhere to come back to and relax in after a hard day's work, an opportunity to escape the formality of the office – albeit one many were slow to take up. In contrast, most women within the middle classes stopped work on marriage and the home became their central domain.

In 1931 only 16 per cent of married women went out to work.[2] Raising a family, running a house and neighbourhood society occupied their time and required flexible wardrobes to cope with changing demands throughout the day. The daily routine for a married woman depended on her family situation, the age of her children, her class status and where she lived. The 1920s and 1930s saw a spectacular house-building boom with housing developments spreading like tentacles along Britain's newly-built arterial roads. Between 1919 and 1939 just under four million new homes were built, almost three-quarters of them for private buyers.[3] This enabled almost 60 per cent of middle-class families to own or buy their own homes.[4] By 1938 two-thirds of civil servants and teachers on salaries of £250–£500 a year had a mortgage.[5] House-builders advertised for 'families of good breeding', aiming to keep each road to 'a definite class', and even asking for high deposits to keep 'estate[s] select'.[6] Since families were usually trying to 'better themselves' by buying one of these homes, the pressures on maintaining the correct social etiquette were considerable. Even codes of speech, such as saying 'my husband' instead of 'my Bill', had to be remembered.[7]

These suburban homes, usually built outside the major cities across the country but predominantly in the Midlands and south-east, brought with them a pre-occupation with the home environment. Events such as the annual *Daily Mail* 'Ideal Home Exhibition' recognised a new obsession with all things domestic. It was not surprising that the imagery of women at the Exhibition was 'overwhelmingly middle-class – well-dressed, affluent and glamorous – and, almost certainly, married'.[8]

THE SERVANT PROBLEM

Organisations such as the Women's Institute that focused on encouraging the domestic skills of their predominantly middle-class married members, thrived. This was in part because middle-class women were finding it increasingly difficult to get domestic help. Although servant numbers increased slightly overall during the interwar period, the number of individual family homes also grew, effectively creating staffing shortages.[9] By the end of the 1920s the term 'daily' had come into common usage to describe the older, local woman who would come in and help with domestic work replacing the traditional live-in servant.[10]

Domestic staff were also becoming more demanding about pay, hours and social restrictions. Their new financial status showed in the clothes they wore, something noticed by *Punch* particularly in the early 1920s.[11] It was also noted in the *New Survey of London Life & Labour* published in 1931:

> With the better pay that she now commands the domestic servant is quite as well dressed as any others in her class . . . Well-cut ready-made garments of all kinds, artificial silk stockings and under-clothing, and fur-trimmed coats came within the reach of young ammunition workers during the war, and domestic servants now generally look on them as a necessary part of their equipment.[12]

Women from the lower middle class spent a great deal of time doing their own domestic chores. The designs of many newly built homes took this into consideration by ensuring that the cooking area of the home was not open to view, so that guests could not see the housewife working in her kitchen. In addition, advertisements in magazines such as *Good Housekeeping* and *Ideal Home* increasingly offered women new domestic appliances.[13] Take-up of this type of equipment was slow but the middle classes were the first to buy them. Equipment with no direct relation to housework such as electric lights and radios quickly arrived in most households.[14] But middle-class women benefited most from supposedly 'time-saving' appliances such as cookers and vacuum cleaners both in their usage and in their appeal to servants.[15]

Married women felt under pressure to maintain not only certain standards of 'housewifery' in their homes but also high standards of respectable dress within the home and neighbourhood. As Mrs P., a 36-year-old housewife from Surrey, explained,

> I have no best or second best in the generally accepted sense. I have various frocks of which I have become very fond and as I choose patterns that don't date I wear my frocks for three years on an average. I have no old clothes for wearing about the house liking to keep up to the same standard all the time. An overall protects them from dirty works. I don't believe in -old-thing for the home.[16]

The preoccupation with high standards of dress started before women got married. A telling quote comes from *Miss Modern* in 1   When a man looks for a wife,' it said, 'she must have a nice taste in dress .   s are so important to a *man's* success.'[17] [My italics] *Woman's Own* rem   ied women that they must not let their standards slip after the wer   tain loveliness . . . is born of a healthy mind and a healthy body, plus   about one's toilet. This is the only beauty a man understands.'[18]

Mrs P., a 36-year-old housewife and M   ontributor from Surrey, thought that 'one should look as r   and children as for anyone' and coyly comments that she does   much effect on strangers – that can be inconvenient at times!   bserving that:

> one of the biggest differences in the matt   -days between my generation and those immediately before   omen continue to take a pride in their appearance after dome   My grandmother assumed cap, shawl and apron when she bec   settled down to be middle-aged. My mother never could both   lothes, because she

hadn't the time with the children – and I take more interest in clothes and make-up now, after twelve years of married life, than I ever did when I was in my 'teens.[20]

The need to 'keep up appearances' in a variety of situations meant that most middle-class women felt they required a selection of clothes to suit varying occasions. Suitability was the critical dress criteria for Miss D., a 43-year-old unmarried organising secretary from London:

I am actually embarrassed if I find myself *unsuitably* dressed for an occasion but it does not worry me if other women have more fashionable or more expensive frocks. Having once satisfied myself that a garment is suitable, and having got 'the feel' of it, I do not consciously worry myself about its effect on others.[21]

Most middle-class women would change at least once in the day. For many this was a habit that did not change until after the Second World War. Mrs D.R.'s mother, from Lanarkshire, would wear 'old things in the morning . . . with an apron on' and change into a better dress in the afternoon.[22] While fashionability was an important criterion in a dress, anything conspicuous or daring was considered 'in very bad taste' and 'the mark of vulgarity'.[23] The dictum of the time was: 'Be not the first by whom the new is tried, Nor yet the last to cast the old aside.'[24]

Women at home regarded the clothes they wore in the morning as 'work' clothes. New electrical equipment such as irons and vacuum cleaners helped make housework a marginally less dirty job than it had been when carpets had to be brushed on hands and knees and irons heated up on a coal-fired stove. Not surprisingly, the iron and the vacuum cleaner were the most popular domestic items purchased during the 1930s. In the early 1930s less than 20 per cent of homes had an electric vacuum cleaner but by 1938 nearly 40 per cent owned one. Figures for take-up of irons were even greater and by 1936 70 per cent of homes had an electric iron.[25]

Advertisements no longer featured a maid using domestic machinery but the housewife herself, reflecting the increased involvement in the home of the middle-class woman. However, magazines such as *Good Housekeeping* rarely depicted women in anything other than a small dainty apron.[26] Therefore there was little confusion between the maid's apron – plain with an equally simple

Advertisements for new electrical equipment for the home demonstrated their labour-saving properties for both mistress and maid. However, there was little confusion between the apron of the maid (left), plain with an equally simple uniform dress, and the apron worn by the middle-class woman (right) doing her own cleaning. Hers was often decorated with flowers or trimmed with a coloured frill and was ready to be whipped off as soon as the doorbell rang. (*Hulton Getty*)

uniform dress – and that worn by the middle-class woman doing her own cleaning; hers was often decorated with flowers or trimmed with a coloured frill.

Attitudes to aprons and overalls were changing as more women had to take on their own domestic chores. Throughout the 1920s and 1930s the wrap-round overall was associated with working-class 'char' women. Miss M., a 28-year-old pianist from Croydon, had a different attitude from her parents in such matters: 'They hate to be caught by visitors if they are wearing old or working clothes, especially an apron. Myself I think a clean white overall is as pleasant as a frock and I do not mind who sees me. Most of my friends agree.'[27] Many women chose to wear an apron that could be taken off as soon as the front door bell rang. As Miss M. shows, there was a need and a desire for respectability even within one's own home. Worse would be to forget to take the apron off when 'crossing the road to see a friend'.[28] Even in the 1950s it was still considered the 'height of bad manners and bad taste, very rude' to answer the door with an apron on.

In the mid-1920s Mrs Gertrude Naylor (centre) poses with daughters Rita, Rose and at their feet Kay, elegant and confident of their middle-class status as the family of a Bradford industrialist. (*Prof J. Styles*)

OUT AND ABOUT

The housework done, a married woman's day might continue with shopping trips, library visits, a trip to the cinema or appointments for tea. All required a degree of correctness greater than in the home. When Mrs P., a 36-year-old housewife from Surrey, went up to London once a week she wore her 'smartest clothes'.[29] Miss D., the 43-year-old secretary from London, found the need to change regularly put pressure on her wardrobe:

> Except for three weeks holiday, there are few occasions when I can wear 'any old thing'; hence my clothes are divided into formal, all-day, or country wear, rather than best and second best. Formal clothes are needed for 'functions', afternoon or evening, and social occasions; all-day clothes are those which do not look out of place in the office but can be also worn for informal evenings; country tweeds and a softer style of dressing is needed for week-ends in the country. Dress for formal occasions can seldom be more than two seasons old, after which it will probably be adapted for one of the other categories. In general coats and suits last three years, also dresses.[30]

What to wear for what occasion was a regular topic of female conversation. Female Mass-Observation respondents showed an acute awareness of the seemingly minor details of their appearance that sometimes exposed regional differences. Mrs T., a 30-year-old housewife from Otley, explained that in Yorkshire

> it was considered fast to wear your best clothes for every day. Provincial middle-class people didn't 'dress up' in their own homes. Even now my mother doesn't 'dress up' to the same extent for a party in her own home as she does when she visits other people. She regards 'dressing up' as a compliment to her hostess but it would be showing off if she dressed to the same extent when she was receiving guests.[31]

This attitude reflects the general view among the middle classes that to be *too* fashionable was to border on the ostentatious or vulgar. The ideal middle-class woman should be, according to London dress buyer Ethyle Campbell, 'just a little behind the current fashion – weeks, not years – rather than quite abreast. She would then be well turned out in every sense of the word without being conspicuous.'[32]

In *John Bull at Home*, written in 1933, the author Karl Silex suggests that the reason why Englishwomen were 'smart' while Frenchwomen were 'chic' is that Englishwomen viewed their clothes as a form of uniform.[33] A traditional rather than ultra-fashionable style of costume or frock brought a certain reassurance with it. Established styles offered a social safety net. Even in maternity wear, women were encouraged to 'conform' as much as possible 'so the wearer doesn't look different to other women'.[34] Specialist maternity wear was hard to find and pregnant women usually had to make their own outfits or use a dressmaker or tailor.

The key to this British style of correctness was 'good taste'. As medical researcher's daughter Eileen Elias pointed out, '"taste" was something I was very careful about . . . I had no clear idea of what it was, but I knew it was terribly important.'[35] Harold Nicolson wrote in 1930 that 'the people who are the most lavish in maintaining the ideal of good taste and in decrying its opposite are in most cases people who are not very certain of their own sense of values'.[36] During this period the wearing of correct and 'tasteful' clothing alleviated a woman's social anxieties. Mrs K., a housewife from Yorkshire, echoes the sentiments of Miss D., a secretary from London, admitting, 'If I'm not well-dressed – suitably for the occasion – I feel self-conscious. When I know I look "right" I can forget myself.'[37]

The desire for anonymity lead to a definite feeling of 'anti-fashion' among the middle classes, the irony being that it forced them to change their appearance so

"WELL, DEAR, YOU DON'T WANT TO OVERDO IT, AND YOU DON'T WANT TO LOOK DOWDY. SEEING IT'S IN A CHURCH HALL, I SHOULD WEAR A SEMI-FULL AFTERNOON DRESS WITH A CHIFFON SCARF, AND CHANCE IT."

The agonies women went through in deciding what to wear for what occasion were rarely more complicated than in the interwar years. While styles appeared to be less rigid than before the First World War, there was still a complicated code of dressing that had to be adhered to. (Punch, *13 January 1937 © Punch Ltd*)

that they could disassociate themselves from anything that might be considered 'too cheap, too expensive, too formal, too slovenly, too old-fashioned or too trendy'.[38] Older women, for example, often took to wearing black indefinitely after the death of their husbands. Mrs E.E. of Pwllheli remembers her mother dyeing all her clothes after she was widowed.[39]

The younger the person the less concern they showed for 'keeping up appearances' though this did not exempt them from social awareness. Miss M., a young girl from Romford who describes herself as middle class, would not be seen locally with 'a shiny nose or laddered stockings or shabby coat' but was far less worried about her appearance away from Romford or at home. Sagely she explains that 'this points to my taking care over myself only to impress the people I know . . . "No-one knows me around here" exempts me from taking pains.' Within the home, the divide between the generations on matters of fashion was becoming more noticeable. Miss M. mocked her parents for thinking that short skirts were not 'nice'. 'The not-nice attitude is typical,' she wrote, quoting other aphorisms of her parents such as 'nice girls don't wear slacks in the street' and 'nice men' don't wear 'brightly-coloured suits'.[40]

CLEANLINESS AND CLOTHES CARE

There was no debate over matters of cleanliness. It was not just a vital part of daily living but had to be seen to be so as well. Because of the atmosphere of 'niceness', titled ladies such as Lady Troubridge warned in magazines that the dangers of poor dress care could be far-reaching: 'Many a "marriage will not take place" notice has been traced back to a dusty black velvet frock.'[41]

E.M. Forster cruelly said that the middle classes of this period smelled, but personal hygiene was a constant battle at a time when even many upper-middle-class homes had only the most basic of washing facilities.[42] The 'stink of unwashed humanity' was so great in one cinema, according to a chemist in Lancashire, that he was forced to buy more expensive tickets in order to avoid it.[43] Attitudes to hygiene varied between the sexes. For most men, it was accepted that 'a man should not seem to have tried consciously to do anything about his appearance other than the minimum demands of hygiene'.[44] Yet the standards of a civil servant from Yorkshire who prided himself on his tidiness are typical:

I like to keep suits on coat-hangers while not in use – I always fasten the top waistcoat button and the middle jacket button when on a coat-hanger. Press occasionally, I brush weekly. Other clothes – I rotate on 3 shirts, wearing one

Established styles offered a social safety net, as shown by the Davies family from Crosby in Lancashire, gathered for a family christening; all the women look relaxed and 'suitably' dressed. (*Mrs A. Sharp*)

for week; clean collar every other day, clean handkerchief every day in winter; clean socks every other day. Vest I changed weekly, I don't wear pants; pyjamas I change fortnightly.[45]

Women were increasingly becoming aware of body odour through magazines. Removable dress shields were sewn into clothes to protect them from underarm staining. Basic deodorants such as 'Odorono' could be bought but were frowned upon by the older generation. Amazingly, a book published in 1936 called *The Modern Woman. Beauty, physical culture and hygiene*, with subjects ranging from corsets to constipation, managed not to mention perspiration once.[46] 'Ladies', believed the elder relations of Miss H., a 37-year-old housewife from Blackheath, 'do not perspire so deodorants are not a necessary adjunct to the bathroom and it's perfectly horrible to wear protectors in one's dresses'.[47] Instead, toilette water or 'scent' – the word 'perfume' was thought common – were used to mask body smells to some extent.

Clothes care was important to both sexes and every middle-class home had a clothes brush on the hallstand ready to brush down a suit or costume and a darning 'mushroom' in its mending box.[48] An indication of this perceived respectability was intimated by the requirement suggested by Ethyle Campbell that a woman should 'have a fresh, wholesome appearance, turned out in such a way that it subtly conveyed, without investigation, that her underclothing was spotless'.[49]

Achieving spotless underclothes required careful cleaning. In 1938 only 4 per cent of UK households owned a washing machine.[50] Laundry services were still relatively cheap but clothes cleaning and repairs were still one of the largest chores for the middle-class woman either to cope with herself or oversee. For many middle-class women evening leisure involved some element of darning, mending or knitting for the family while listening to the radio.[51]

With few homes having any form of central heating, families wore clothes in the home for warmth as much as for comfort or elegance. Knitting was therefore a practical and valuable craft for women to master. More than a hobby, it was a way of economically expanding the family wardrobe. Great skill was often required to create the complicated patterns that were so fashionable. With so much knitwear made at home, broadcaster René Cutforth claimed it was 'a notable stroke of the universal one-upmanship to own a genuine Fair Isle sweater'.[52]

POWDER AND PAINT

Another area which caused sparks to fly between the generations was that of make-up. The use of cosmetics by middle-class women slowly developed during the 1920s. The older generation and the more staid middle classes still considered lipstick taboo until much later. They considered vulgar not just the use of it, but its application in public. In 1925 Mrs Forester wrote in *Success Through Dress*, 'Well-bred women do not so often offend in this prospect, but it is a pity our ultra-modern girls seem unable to grasp the fact that the use of the lip-stick in public is not all a question of morals, simply of taste.'[53] Make-up was problematical for the young female, as this verse from 1927 shows:

> A powder-puff or a shiny nose – a shiny nose or a powder puff?
> A problem this, it seems to me, on which some girls cannot agree.
> From good taste it is very far, to make up like a cinema star.
> But you *can't* look pretty with a nose like sun,
> So *my* puff will always be my good, staunch chum![54]

By the 1930s, when a shiny nose was deemed 'unpardonable', a matt-powdered face was the only acceptable face for a woman. Miss M., a student from Romford, recorded her friends' comments: 'Yes, my dear, she's quite nice looking, I suppose, but her nose! Hasn't she ever heard of powder?'[55]

By the late 1920s the increase in the use of cosmetics was inexorable. Within the middle classes, while public use was still associated with low morals, in 1930 magazines were cautiously acknowledging that some use of cosmetics was inevitable even for job interviews. 'You may need a little powder, but if so, choose it with care and apply it with discretion. As for lipstick, if you use it at all, remember that art lies in concealing art.'[56] In 1932 Godfrey Winn, writing in *Miss Modern*, was outraged when the Bank of England banned its female employees from wearing make-up. 'The majority of business men, from chief down to office boy, delight in the pretty, varied clothes and the lovely (though artificial) complexions of the women members of staff. . . . they introduce glamour and romance into our humdrum routine.'[57]

For many girls a dance or theatre trip was the first opportunity they had to wear any form of make-up though cosmetics were still frowned upon by the older man. 'Ladies now do not hesitate to powder their noses and rouge their lips and even comb their shingled locks not only in public places but at one's private dining table,' complained a correspondent in *The Times*. 'Surely the proper place is in the dressing-room and not where it causes offence to others?'[58]

Similarly, some young men were suspicious of cosmetics. 'I am always over-awed by splendid coiffures and elaborate make-up,' confessed a 24-year-old local government clerk from Sutton in Surrey, '[and] aim at a girl who I can safely lay hands on without anything coming to pieces or smearing.'[59] The too obvious wearing of lipstick and rouge was seen as vulgar. This sort of snobbery was confirmed even by a young middle-class girl who was interviewed for Mass-Observation outside the Streatham Locarno in South London; she said, 'I don't like the girl[s] in there . . . [they are] too heavily made-up.'[60]

Early 1930s advertisements aimed at married women show that many men also disapproved of their wives wearing make-up since it might make them look cheap. Cosmetic advertisements tactically acknowledged this male reticence. 'There's one thing even a loving husband won't forgive . . . a cheap, painted look!'[61] The dilemma was that fashionable women were increasingly using make–up and therefore not to use it could be seen as being distinctly behind the times.

Make-up was a particular cause of disagreement between the younger and older generations. Miss H., a 21-year-old hospital almoner's clerk from Bromley in Kent, had problems getting her parents to accept her wearing of make-up:

> My people are reluctant but willing to accept any fashion, but lipstick is a veritable red flag to a bull in my home! It is, I am told, muck, horrible and never used when they were young and definitely not necessary. I use lipstick and make-up in moderation, if applied carefully looks well, and certainly gives me added self-confidence.[62]

But given the popularity of the glamorous film stars seen every week at the cinema, it is not surprising that the popularity of cosmetics was unstoppable. Manufacturers were quick to respond and there was a giant leap in advertising expenditure on face powders in the early 1930s. Within two years spending had leapt by 50 per cent from £18,315 a quarter to £27,606. The top company, Tokalon, spent over £3,500 in the national press in September 1934 alone.[63] This was an enormous amount considering that it was more than the total spent by eighteen competing firms advertising perfumes in one quarter in 1933.[64]

Advertising on face powder continued to grow, increasing by nearly 40 per cent in one year.[65] In late 1936 magazines carried 60 per cent more advertisements for lipstick than in the same six months of the previous year.[66] While the consequences of impending war during the first half of 1939 must be taken into account, it is clear that advertisers were reacting to increased demand for their products.

By the end of the 1930s only the older generation still considered make-up vulgar. The complication remained that a shiny nose and laddered stockings were also thought of as 'inferior'.[67] Mrs H., a 37-year-old housewife from Blackheath, came from a family who disapproved of cosmetics. Her aunt used books of *Papier Poudré*, pocket-sized leaves of powder-impregnated papers for blotting, 'so thinks she has evaded the daily sin of powdering her face'.[68] In 1939 many older women regarded 'unusual hats and lipstick as an outward sign of complete lack of morals and sense and no capabilities for business'.[69] However, figures detailing advertising spending on lipstick and rouge between 1935 and 1939 show they were fighting a losing battle.[70]

Magazines for the middle classes such as *Good Housekeeping* were important influences in middle-class women's lives. When it came to writing about cosmetics, they concentrated their editorials on the less frivolous aspects of beauty care such as weight control and anti-ageing exercises. In 1931 *Good Housekeeping* ran a light-hearted article called, 'Do Women Dress to Please Men?', berating the 'habits of modern woman, her paint and powder, her reddened nails . . . and plucked eyebrows . . . [do] many women realise how deeply men are revolted by some of their habits?'.[71] This reaffirms the pressures women within the middle classes were under to remain feminine without incurring the dreaded vulgarity that too much make-up might bring them.

A survey published in *Good Housekeeping* in 1930 had revealed that the use of obvious make-up was still frowned upon and 'very much [in] a minority among women of the middle classes'. Only 20 per cent of their readers used lipstick, 7 per cent rouge and 5 per cent scent. Yet few used no make-up at all, only 7½ per cent.[72] In 1935 a feature called 'What Price Beauty?' revealed that whereas a provincial typist might be expected to spend just over £3 a year on her cosmetics budget, *Good Housekeeping*'s average reader would spend £8–9 a year to cover rouge, lipstick and face powder plus visits to the hairdresser and beauty salon.[73] This appears to confirm Robert Graves's much-quoted observation that the course for the acceptance of cosmetics went 'from brothel to stage, then on to Bohemia, to Society, to Society's maids, to the mill-girl, and lastly to the suburban woman'.[74] Rather than trickling down the social ladder, make-up bounced through the various different groupings before finally coming to rest among the staid middle classes.

MENSWEAR AT HOME

Unlike housewives, whose weekend wardrobes were on the whole the same as their weekday wear, most middle-class men did have separate clothes that were worn only at weekends. Many men felt constrained by the clothes they had to wear for work and young men in particular were relieved to be able to wear more relaxed clothing when they were not working. Mr H., a 17-year-old articled clerk from Sunderland, expressed how many felt: 'Apart from office occasions, I usually dress in plus fours or something which leaves the office behind, something which I feel free in.'[75]

Yet whereas women usually changed during the day into a smarter 'afternoon dress' for socialising, a man's wardrobe would only change completely when the working week ended. Leisure did not necessarily start immediately when they returned home from the office. A man might take off his jacket and put on a cardigan or jumper, but in general he would keep other items for weekend wear.

Men were therefore not free from social dress codes in or around their own homes. For example, although there was a tongue-in-cheek call for more colourful braces through the columns of *The Times* in 1932, braces, along with sock suspenders, were expected to be invisible in polite society.[76] The necessity for men to have three-piece suits was in part to use the waistcoat to cover up braces which were still required to hold up suit trousers. But to display them even in their own home was 'low' and 'common'.[77]

The tale of a man being berated by his wife for sitting in his garden in his braces, reported in *The New Statesman and Nation* in 1938, is revealing. Her use of words such as 'uncivilised', 'country bumpkin', 'indecent' and 'bad example' show the strength of feeling that such an action induced. This woman was not concerned with the styling of her husband's outfit but with what the neighbours would think if they saw him. The author acknowledged that there was what he called 'a social vendetta against braces' publicised in the *Sunday Express* and led, he claimed, by women.[78]

Since it was considered extremely 'bad form' for a respectable man to take his coat off and reveal his braces, it is not surprising that men from the middle classes were reluctant to take their jackets off in public, whether through pressure from their wives or from their own social conscience, however informal the surroundings might be. The relaxed attitudes of the 'rough' working-class man in his shirt-sleeves were anathema to the 'Pooterish' respectability of the lower middle classes. The less socially confident could easily slip up by misjudging their 'off-duty' clothes. When a Scotland Yard detective joined the well-to-do Newby family on their boat on the Thames, he was damned for taking off his black suit jacket and revealing 'a thick flannel shirt and rather grubby braces', and was forever known as 'that fellow who wore braces'.[79]

Many middle-aged men in particular did not feel relaxed without a jacket even in their own homes. Playwright John Osborne's grandfather was 'always dressed . . . as if ready to go out at any moment'.[80] Even on retirement, men did not necessarily discard formal outfits completely. I cannot remember my own grandfather, a retired economist, wearing anything other than a three-piece suit daily until his death in 1957.

Mr A., a 31-year-old married retail chemist from Colne in Lancashire, owned one business suit and five suits all 'worn in leisure time': a one-year-old grey lounge suit, a four-year-old navy blue suit, a three-year-old tweed suit, and a six-year-old plus-four suit and a sports suit, both worn mostly for holidays. 'I like the right thing for the right occasions,' Mr A. commented. 'I do not wear sport suits for business or formal occasions, or indoors generally.'[81] And as Mr A., a 23-year-old journalist from Chelmsford, said, 'There is a considerable difference between my dull workaday appearance and my appearance at weekends and other times when I do not have to be about our office.'[82]

Mr R. of Tamworth was unusual in changing immediately he got home into what he termed 'free-and-easy garb':

I like as much freedom as possible in the matter of clothes, and wear sports attire with open-neck shirt whenever possible, even in winter. In summer I wear shorts and sleeveless shirt at home, in the garden and when hiking and cycling (my favorite [sic] recreations). On returning home each evening I always change into this free-and-easy garb, and I never wear anything else at weekends. I hate 'best clothes' for Sundays and am usually more unconventionally dressed on that day than any other.[83]

Plus-fours and patterned socks for weekend wear were popular during the 1930s even for those who never played golf. Mick Borgars and his friend, both from Wiltshire, look relaxed with their contrasting styles of leisurewear. (*Mrs E. Baxendale*)

Many men felt uncomfortable without the armour of a formal suit jacket around them, even in their own homes. According to his daughter, this is a rare photograph of her father, Richard Williams, an accountant with the Liverpool Gas Company, wearing a jumper rather than a jacket in 1935. (*Mrs A. Sharp*)

In the 1930s most men would have had knitted for them a sleeveless 'vest' worn instead of the formal waistcoat, the third part of the three-piece suit. The adaptability of patterns was part of their popularity, as can be seen from a knitting pattern for the 'David' pullover, possibly named after the family name that Edward VIII was known by. It was described as a

> serviceable pullover, knitted in a neat vandyked design, [and] is suitable for the older man no less than for the younger. Made up in a fawn or grey shade of wool, it would be right for wearing during working hours; or, knitted in one of the lighter colourings, it would be useful for wearing at tennis or on other sports occasions.[84]

The idea of the 'Sunday Best' was rapidly dying out within the middle classes.[85] At home at weekends, particularly on Sundays, since many men still worked on Saturday mornings, there was an opportunity to escape the formal suit. The attitude of Mr B., a 26-year-old clerk from central London, is typical. 'At weekends I wear plus-fours or an old suit or grey flannel trousers and sports coat if there are visitors at home. If not, old trousers and khaki shirt for gardening, etc.'[86]

With many families owning their own home for the first time, gardening became a popular hobby for many men in the 1920s and 1930s. Old lounge suits were often kept for pottering around in but popular fashions such as plus-fours and patterned knitwear were regular weekend wear as well. The winged collar is a satirical dig at the Englishman's seeming inability to reject formality completely. (Punch, *29 April 1925 © Punch Ltd*)

Old suits were frequently kept for wearing while gardening.[87] Cartoons allude to the fashion for middle-class suburban man even to wear golfing clothes while gardening. Gardening was a popular hobby encouraged by the design of the new suburban house which gave every householder a back garden and often a front garden to care for. The man of the house did most of the work and most male respondents mention keeping old clothes for gardening.

Mass-Observation respondents knew what was thought correct for men to wear at weekends. Miss H., a hospital library assistant from Liverpool, was quite clear that it was not acceptable to her for a man to wear an open-necked shirt in the street. 'This can be obviated by filling in the space with a scarf . . . Also it is not "done" to wear a lounge jacket with flannels – a blazer is the correct thing. Then there is the fact of not doing up the bottom button of your waistcoat.'[88]

In spite of the fact that the term 'sports' clothes was used for informal clothes not necessarily worn for a particular sport, much of men's leisure clothing did reveal the influence of participatory sports. Virtually all the men questioned by Mass-Observation mentioned 'sports' jackets and flannels in their wardrobe listings. Mr A., the young journalist from Chelmsford, wore what he called the 'usual week-end wear, unless hiking or biking is to take place'. His weekend wear comprised grey flannels, 'Kantabs' (a brand of flannel trousers) and a dark blue blazer with his school crest on the pocket, the typical middle-class system of branding. Mr A. also owned a plus-four suit, which was 'rather dirty' and had been 're-seated with material from similar previous plus-4 suit'. This he wore 'only if hiking and biking, usually with a blue-grey roll-neck pullover'.[89]

The origins of plus-fours are obscure. Clearly related to breeches, the 'four' is most likely to indicate the number of inches below the knee these garments should correctly be worn at, a practical and, as it turned out, fashionable altern-ative to tucking one's trousers into one's socks to prevent them getting wet or muddy when following country pursuits such as shooting and, of course, golf. They were looser and longer than knickerbockers, which had traditionally been worn with the Norfolk jacket since the mid-nineteenth century.[90] The high point of the plus-four suit was around 1927, prompted by the Prince of Wales's passion for them together with checked socks and Argyle jumpers.[91] Although *The Drapers' Record* mentions record sales of plus-four suits in 1930, they gradually fell out of fashion for golf after that to be replaced by the traditional trouser style.[92] By the mid-1930s the figure of the 'knickerbocker glory' was a regular object of ridicule in the satirical press.[93]

Much as the tracksuit and trainer wearer of today may never have set foot inside a gym, plus-four trousers were often worn by men who had rarely, if ever, swung a club. Yet it was a popular item of menswear particularly in the 1920s. Many Mass-Observation respondents still owned a pair for 'weekend wear' in 1939, clearly reluctant to part with a garment that was comfortable if outdated.[94] Mr M., a 30-year-old married man from Ayrshire who worked in the steel industry, owned a plus-four suit he had bought seven years previously for golf. 'Now that I've stopped golfing I use the trousers for cycling along with a leather jacket that I had for golf.'[95]

British middle-class men seem to have remained untouched by the new breed of American male film star who successfully wore a smart but casual look. Women's magazines bewailed the fact that few men looked to the cinema for dress guidance while acknowledging that 'too much obvious interest in his clothes on the part of any man is not a trait which is regularly admired among men'.[96] Much as women may have wanted their sweethearts or husbands to emulate a certain film star's style, the truth was that in Britain, as in America, women's opinions appeared to have little impact on manliness or men's dress, especially with regard to what they wore at home. As many think is still the case, during the interwar years, British men did not take easily to 'casual' dressing.

FIVE

From Seaside to
Sports Club

[He wore] an impeccable fawn pin-stripe suit, with a brown silk handkerchief
in the breast pocket, a cream-coloured shirt and cream and down spotted
bow tie . . . [while her rich young cousins] were both wearing khaki shorts,
old tennis shoes, and faded, coloured shirts . . . Pierre did not look right in
the country.[1]

Monica Dickens, *Mariana* (1940)

In Monica Dickens's *Mariana*, the heroine Mary realises she cannot marry her
suave Frenchman when she sees that he has completely misread the nuances of
English leisure clothes in 1930s Britain. It is little wonder that he was confused. If
many middle-class men were reluctant to take their jackets off in their own
gardens, it is not surprising that clothes for holidays and sporting activities were
another sartorial challenge.

By the 1920s and 1930s the routine of the British seaside summer holiday was
established. In 1935 *The New Survey of London Life and Labour* stated that
'practically all persons following "middle-class" occupations, including
professional and commercial employees, shop assistants and clerks . . . [had] long
been entitled to a week or fortnight's holiday on full pay'.[2] The late Victorian
period had seen the start of the major development of select resorts preferred by a
wide range of the middle classes, 'from the plutocratic (bankers, industrialists)
through the opulent professionals and substantial employers to the still-growing
army of administrators, subordinate professionals, tradespeople and "black-coated

workers"'.[3] By the interwar period they would have shied away from working-class resorts such as Blackpool and Southend which by then achieved visitor numbers of 7 million and 5½ million respectively.[4]

Time & Tide and *The Lady* magazines ran travel correspondence columns advising their readers on suitable – and select – accommodation predominantly in the United Kingdom but also in Europe. Middle-class families headed for the smaller resorts such as St Anne's in Lancashire, Bexhill in Sussex, Brancaster in Norfolk and Southwold in Suffolk.[5] *The Lady* carried nine or ten pages on average of property either for sale or to let for middle-class families for the summer months. One advertisement in July 1937 offers a coastguard's cottage to rent facing the sea in Southwold, 'available for £50 for 4 weeks in August'.[6] In comparison to the 6 guineas on average charged for a whole family by boarding houses, this sort of holiday was definitely in the upper-middle-class league.[7]

Author V.S. Pritchett remembers with great envy his neighbours preparing to decamp to Wales, 'where they always went . . . for years they had gone, every year, and their mother and father before them. They always went to the same house, they always had the same rooms. They had a photograph album with snapshots of years of Welsh holidays.'[8] This was a pattern repeated across thousands of middle-class homes.

One would expect that on family holidays the dress codes might have been more relaxed. Yet when Pritchett himself went away, to stay with relatives just inland of the Yorkshire coast, a visit to the seaside was fraught with social and sartorial anxieties:

> [This] place was so dominated in our minds by the terrifying social eminence of certain relatives by marriage who owned property in the town . . . that we dared not dig in the sand, eat ices in the street or take off our shoes and stockings, in case the great respectability of the family should become creased or spotted.[9]

However, for some the holiday was seen as an opportunity to relax their dress codes. A 21-year-old planning assistant from York saw holidays as a break from social judgements: 'As distinct from work and social duties, when on holiday, my one thought is for comfort, and then I rake out all old or worn clothes, and don't care at all for the comments of my friends.'[10] Seventeen-year-old Mr H., an articled clerk from Sunderland, also relished the opportunity for dressing 'down' on holiday: 'On holiday, I wear shorts and an open-necked shirt simply because a

Three generations of the Naylor family on a beach at Scarborough in the early 1920s. Around them, all the men maintain strict standards of respectability by keeping their jackets and their ties on even in this holiday environment. (*Prof J. Styles*)

holiday is made to be free from everything else one has one's mind on and I dress in clothes which I think will suitably do that to me.'[11]

Photographs from family albums of the 1930s consistently show that older men in particular were reluctant to wear distinctively different clothes for the beach. Mrs D.R. from Lanarkshire in Scotland remembers photographs of herself and her mother 'walking on the prom' at St Anne's, 'complete with hat, gloves, umbrella'.[12]

The fact that most municipal beaches charged visitors for the use of changing facilities might have been influential. According to *The Drapers' Record* of 1932, only in the 'quieter resorts' was one likely to see men spending 'whole days on the sands attired in shorts only'.[13] Otherwise, the Englishman sitting on the sand in long trousers, lace-up shoes and sometimes even a jacket was visible on most beaches. Similarly, the regulations regarding changing on the beach could also have been the reason why many older women also preferred to sit in their summer frocks, later tucking their skirts into their knickers when they went for a paddle.[14]

Nothing could have been a greater contrast to the glamorous images used by the railway companies to promote seaside travel. Images of bodily perfection being promoted in swimwear advertisements towards the end of the 1930s proved a successful marketing ploy since a quarter of all railway journeys were taken in July and August.[15] As is often so, these posters portrayed clinging costumes on perfect bodies that were impossible to emulate. In reality, the new briefer costumes that were available to women presented distinct modesty problems of their own. The most popular were knitted, usually homemade, but notoriously unreliable even though yarn manufacturers promoted their 'non-stretch' wool. A Worthing visitor remembers costumes knitted for her and her cousin by her aunt: 'They held so much water it was difficult to swim, and when we came ashore we had a plunging neckline down to our ankles.' This was a frequent complaint, together with the smell of the wet wool and the length of time they took to dry.[16]

For middle-aged middle-class women there were always questions of propriety and modesty to be considered. An unmarried 43-year-old social worker from South London admitted that she wore more clothes in the summer months than her 'younger friends': 'I usually wear a vest throughout the year . . . I have a backless sun-suit but do not really feel so comfortable in it as in an ordinary short-sleeved cotton frock as it is not possible to wear my corselettes – or much else under it.'[17]

Magazines and fashion pages of newspapers were always ready with didactic advice on what clothes should be taken on holiday, whether in Britain or abroad. Dress codes could be just as complicated as those for the office or vicar's tea party. A light-hearted column in *The Girls' Favourite* talked of three girls taking their best clothes with them, 'two or three new fluffy frocks' of crêpe-de-Chine, only to find these were too formal for the seaside resort they were visiting. In contrast, another girl

had gone to a very smart boarding house at Brighton . . . and she felt that she did not want to have to worry about her clothes, so she took all washing frocks, and she felt most uncomfortable because she had not an evening frock with her, not even a 'best' frock. The result was the same as in our case – a frantic wire to mother![18]

Fifteen years later, in 1937, *The Lady* was being just as officious in its advice-giving. In an article entitled 'Outfits for Scotland, Spas and the Seaside', it warned readers 'not to make the mistake of going to an elegant place in your second-best, or you will feel obscurely out of it, and envious of other women who fit so well into their sophisticated background'. Places where readers of *The Lady* were told to dress formally were 'all towns (some Englishwomen seem to think that holiday resorts, and foreign towns are not towns at all and dress in peasant cottons with lamentable effect); all bigger places on the French Riviera; all except the very smallest spas; festival centres. . . ; big shoots and house-parties in Scotland'.[19]

The only style of trousers that became mildly acceptable among young middle-class women were 'beach pyjamas'. Lilian May Belben, a shorthand typist, and her sister, Daisy May, both in their early twenties and from Manchester, proudly model beach pyjamas they had made themselves. They wore the tops with cycling shorts as well. (*Greater Manchester County Record Office*)

It is clear from family photograph albums that many women, like older men, were reluctant to relinquish the formality of their town clothing. Yet for young women there was a clear distinction between clothes that could be worn on holiday and ones that 'wouldn't be worn at home'. Mrs E.E. from Pwllheli had a three-piece suit when she was an 18-year-old trainee teacher, comprising 'a top and shorts, and a wrap-round skirt'. She only wore her shorts on the beach, using the wrap-round skirt for to-ing and fro-ing.[20]

Trousers were rarely worn by middle-class women before the Second World War.[21] The only style that was mildly acceptable was beach 'pyjamas' which were popular and fashionable among young women. Photographs of sisters Lilian May, a shorthand typist, and Daisy May Belben, a trainee teacher, both in their early twenties from Manchester, show them both proudly wearing beach pyjamas they had made themselves. They also wore the tops with cycling shorts.[22] Beach pyjamas lived up to their name and were strictly for the seaside only.

THEY SAID THESE BEACH PYJAMAS WOULD LOOK RIPPING ON ME – AND BY GUM, **THEY DO!**

Beach pyjamas lived up to their name and were strictly for the seaside only, but they were still subject to ridicule, as this postcard, sent from Bournemouth to Gillingham in Kent in the early 1930s, shows. Note the male onlookers in jackets that would not be out of place in a city street, though the pale trousers betray their leisure leanings. (*Author's Collection*)

John Lewis, always aware of their customers' middle-class sensibilities, showed a tongue-in-cheek modesty in their promotion of beachwear, in particular shorts, in their June 1932 Special Notice sent out to account customers. An illustration of a tiny boat in the distance is captioned: 'The two people in the little boat are too far away to see distinctly, but they are both wearing the new Flannel Beach Shorts. May we send them on approval? They are 15/11.'[23] Yet again, apart from the 'matelot' trousers and swimwear, the models' outfits would not have looked out of place in any town.

As the annual holiday habit became established in Britain across the working and middle classes, opportunities for sporting activities also increased. The 1920s and 1930s saw a boom in the popularity of many physical activities with new facilities to go with them. The desegregation of beaches and pools and the gradual acceptance of mixed bathing facilities allowed many families to be able to swim together for the first time in public.[24] Other non-competitive activities such as cycling and hiking also became popular among the middle classes. Upwards of half a million people flocked to the countryside every weekend to hike.[25]

Golf also saw a massive growth in popularity in the early part of the twentieth century. It is no coincidence that many golf clubs became established within or close to the new middle-class suburbs of the 1930s. The fact that so many new golf courses were built during the interwar years shows how important the game was to the development of middle-class suburbs.[26]

The French nautical look used to promote this outfit sends the message that in the 1930s trousers for women were both 'foreign' and for holidays alone. (*Wimbledon Lawn Tennis Museum*)

But it was tennis that was key to the social structure of the middle classes in the interwar years. By the 1930s it was reckoned that two million people played tennis – or attempted to.[27] By the early 1920s, for those who could afford it, a private tennis court was undoubtedly a status symbol. For the majority, however, the local tennis club provided a worthy substitute and a social focal point. In 1924 it was said that 'of all the present day games . . . lawn tennis may be considered to have made the biggest strides during the past ten years, and from having been a pastime popular only with leisured people it has become the general favourite of all classes'.[28] By 1926 there were 781 public tennis courts in London parks.[29] Edgware, in North London, had three private tennis clubs by 1931, before the building of the surrounding estates was even finished.[30]

For the majority tennis was an opportunity to socialise and get a little exercise at the same time. Tennis itself was central to the middle-class social scene, not just as a spectator sport but also as an important social activity that underpinned acceptance in local society and acted as a catalyst for social interplay.[31] This was not exclusively a south-east England phenomena. In Liverpool in 1930 over 100,000 people used the public tennis courts.[32]

Social climbing was often a more important aspect of joining a tennis club than the game itself, and even a player who 'might be able to knock spots off the players of [a] club in a game of tennis' might be refused membership if he or she was of 'a certain type, of certain financial standing and vocation'.[33] Serious players looked down on such socially motivated establishments. 'Broadly speaking,' wrote British champion Dorothy Round, 'there are two sorts of tennis clubs. One plays only very mediocre tennis, but it is a wonderful social centre. That is very nice, of course, if you just want a place where you can idle through pleasant afternoons. But it is not really the place to learn how to improve your game.'[34]

DRESSING LIKE A CHAMPION

Tennis also had an inherent language of 'correctness' that maintained certain standards of appearance and decorum.[35] Female tennis stars had a considerable influence on what the young middle-class girl wore on the local tennis court. The greatest name in the 1920s, French-born Suzanne Lenglen, brought a modern style to Wimbledon, which was quickly copied by young girls across the country. Lenglen's style of dress, 'a simple "piqué" dress, or one of drill or white linen, made in the old Grecian style, and fastened at the waist with a ribbon or leather belt',[36] together with a more athletic style of play, led to modesty problems as her knee-

As fashion hemlines dropped in the early 1930s, tennis dresses were becoming impractical again, allowing shorter 'divided' skirts to become acceptable on the tennis court. By the mid-1930s divided skirts worn for tennis increasingly resembled shorts as they were being worn several inches above the knee. (Woman's Magazine, *April 1935*)

length combinations beneath the dress were quite visible. Lenglen's style of play in particular was compared pictorially to various dancing poses in *Woman's Life* magazine.[37] The magazine also offered free patterns for suitable 'tennis knicks':

Dainty garments trimmed with lace do not look quite appropriate for a strenuous game, and in these days when the game is played really hard, lady's undergarments often do not leave much to the imagination, therefore knickers made of silk stockingette seem to be quite the thing.[38]

Not just one pair, however, girls were advised: 'two pairs . . . made just alike . . . the under ones of white jap silk and the top ones of white silk tricot', elasticised at waist and knee'.[39] Alternatively, all-in-one combinations could be worn which were less bulky under the new lightweight tennis dresses.

By the early 1930s everyday skirt lengths were dropping and tennis dresses were beginning to become impractical again. Shorts for women started to make an appearance in fashion magazines undoubtedly through the influence of American films where they could be regularly seen adorning female stars such as Loretta Young and Lyda Roberti. Thus in no longer reflecting current hemline trends tennis wear separated from any semblance of everyday fashion and became true 'sportswear'. By 1934 the divided skirts worn for tennis increasingly resembled shorts as they were being worn several inches above the knee. In the late 1930s advertisements in *Vogue* for ladies' tennis wear from three major sportswear companies all featured shorts.[40] By the outbreak of the Second World War sports outfitters Lillywhite's were confidently able to proclaim to young female tennis players that 'dress is no longer a handicap'.[41]

In contrast, men's tennis wear appeared anachronistic. Even in the 1930s it was a rare sight to see men wearing shorts for tennis. *Punch* picked up on this in 1932 with a double cartoon showing first an Edwardian youth in white breeches mocking his female partner who was weighed down to the ground by her corseted outfit: 'I believe you would have beaten me, Miss Browne, if you were not handicapped by your skirts.' Accompanying it is another sketch of a 1930s 'modern miss' complete with bare arms and shorts, retorting to her partner, 'You'd give me a much better game if you left off those silly trousers.'[42]

But whereas Suzanne Lenglen had been successful in influencing women's sportswear, the leading British players were not merely reluctant but stubbornly refused to deviate from established dress codes on the tennis court. Significantly Fred Perry, who won the Men's Singles Championship at Wimbledon for three consecutive years from 1934, never wore shorts on the Centre Court, preferring to remain with the traditional long 'white' flannels. The son of a Labour MP from Stockport, Perry later admitted that in spite of his unsurpassed success as an English tennis player, he was thought to be 'a rebel from the wrong side of the tennis tramlines . . . not quite the class of chap they *really* want to see winning Wimbledon'.[43] It is somewhat ironic therefore that after Perry's retirement from the tennis circuit he gave his name to one of the most successful ranges of British sportswear in the second half of the twentieth century.

The Men's Dress Reform Party, a short-lived organisation started in 1929, did attempt to encourage male tennis

Joan Hendrick, a secretary from Ealing, West London, shows how quickly tennis styles had changed from the shapeless shift promoted by French star Suzanne Lenglen in the 1920s to the divided skirt and short-sleeved shirt Joan wears on the family tennis court. (*Mr T. Hendrick*)

Most male tennis players stayed with the traditional long white flannels worn with a white shirt, as sported by Dick Williams, seen here with his wife Edna, 'ready for tennis'. Shorts were rarely worn by men for tennis until after the Second World War. (*Mrs A. Sharp*)

players to reject trousers in favour of shorts. They were buoyed by British tennis star 'Bunny' Austin's appearance on the Wimbledon Centre Court in shorts in the early 1930s – the only man to do so.[44] Away from Wimbledon, a few young middle-class men did play tennis in shorts, but they were not commonly worn until after the Second World War. Most players stayed with the traditional white flannels, 'with shirt and socks to match', as worn by Mr L., a 22-year-old student from Nottingham, and Dick Williams, an accountant with the Liverpool Gas

PRE-EMINENT FOR
SPORTS
EQUIPMENT
AND CLOTHING
FOR MEN

With the opening of additional premises at 90-94, Brompton Road, LILI YWHITES now offer the same facilities for the selection of CORRECT SPORTS KIT FOR MEN, with an expert service, at Knightsbridge as at Piccadilly Circus. Every Department is identical at both addresses, and Illustrated Catalogues are available post free on request.

Lillywhites LTD
OF *Piccadilly Circus*
and *Knightsbridge*

In 1937 sportswear store Lillywhites was still suggesting that long trousers were the 'correct sports kit' for men, with shorts being acceptable only on the beach. (*Wimbledon Lawn Tennis Museum*)

Company.[45] Whereas women's tennis clothes were increasingly being influenced by French and American sporting fashions, men's tennis clothes were hidebound by tradition until after the Second World War.

PLAYING THE GAME

Since its inception golf has always been seen as a game for the leisured classes, those with time on their hands and not just the money but also, and more importantly, the connections to gain membership to the best clubs. There were regional differences in the class distinctions on golf courses. Rural areas such as Scotland, traditionally seen as the birthplace of golf, and Wales were able to accommodate all classes of golfers, whereas in areas such as south-east England, where land was at a premium, golf-club entry was controlled far more strictly.[46] In 1890 there were nine golf clubs in and around the London area; by 1909 there were eighty-nine.[47] By the 1920s and 1930s the Prince of Wales's enthusiasm for the game had only enhanced the exclusive image of the sport, making golf-club membership a much sought-after status symbol.

The golf course appears to have been the one place where the middle-class man in particular could relax his innate inhibitions about fashion. Before the First World War golf clothes had been specially made by a man's tailor or adapted from a woman's existing country clothing. Throughout the interwar years specialist clothes for golf were regularly advertised in both the men's and women's press. 'Golf jackets,' it was noted, 'have almost now become a universal fashion. Tens of thousands wear this jacket who never hit a golf ball. This may be taken as a testimonial to the general utility and comfort of the new style.'[48] The comfort was due to a cut which allowed the wide range of movement necessary to swing a golf club.

Knitwear was another area where middle-class men displayed a surprising taste for sartorial differences. So strong was the link between knitwear and the sport that cardigans were often known as 'golfers'.[49] In contrast to most of the other trends in menswear, British golf sweaters were considered too gaudy for American tastes. 'Our golf hose', claimed an advertisement in *Men's Wear* in 1927, 'is worn by the best golfers of the day, who would eschew anything vulgar.'[50] Such 'vulgarity', however, was encouraged by British royalty. The Prince of Wales was famed for his love of the Argyle pattern famously displayed in Sir William Orpen's painting of the Prince, now owned by the Royal & Ancient Golf Club of St Andrews.

Even at a time when plus-fours and patterned knitwear were popular for golf, Sir William Orpen's famous portrait of Edward, Prince of Wales, painted in 1928, shows that Edward's taste in sportswear was more extreme than most. (*Reproduced by kind permission of the Royal and Ancient Golf Club of St Andrews*)

The socks, or rather stockings, required for wear with plus-fours provided a gallery of gaudy colours and patterns, predominated by fancy checks as favoured by the Prince of Wales. There were four pages of golfing socks alone in leading manufacturer I. & R. Morley's catalogues, at prices up to £8 a dozen, while stockings offered the more daring an opportunity to follow royal trends.[51]

In the early 1920s it appears that the importance of wearing the correct garb for golf became increasingly crucial for social acceptance. 'A good deal of importance attaches to the way in which a player dresses for whatever sport he follows,' it was written in 1924, '. . . and golf if played in ordinary city attire would hardly be golf-like.'[52] The game's sartorial codes became progressively more complex. They were ruled both by latent tradition (the Norfolk jacket) and by the contemporary fads and fancies (patterned knitwear) which enhanced class distinctions.

Perhaps because of these complications, and because of the game's attraction to those with social pretensions, golf continuously drew humorous ridicule; the thirty-one short stories by P.G. Wodehouse, which satirise upper-class shenanigans, are perhaps the most famous expression of this. Throughout the 1920s and 1930s golf featured in more *Punch* cartoons than any other sport. The cartoons frequently allude to clothing, but even those that do not provide illuminating insights into the expected stereotypical appearance of such characters as the 'New Rich' golfer, the Northern golfer and the aspiring suburbanite. There were innuendos towards class and regional differences well into the 1930s, applauded by some in the menswear trade press:

> In the North of England they appear to wear more loudly coloured sports clothes than we do in the South, and infinitely more pattern. They are to be congratulated and it is interesting to note the two different trends in taste. In the South at the moment it seems to me that homespuns are leading, whereas in the North saxonies, in checks, and carrying lots of pattern, come first.[53]

Some issues of course decorum were clear-cut. An American golfer pictured on the front page of a British national newspaper playing in his shirtsleeves, would, it

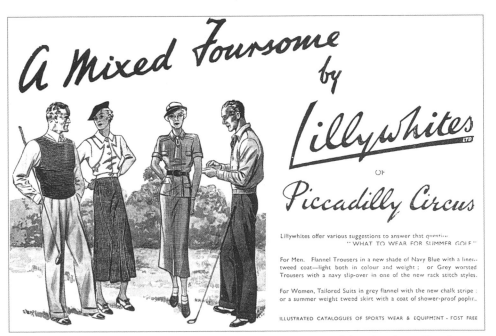

By the mid-1930s most men had adopted the American style of dressing for golf and dispensed with the traditional plus-fours. (*Wimbledon Lawn Tennis Museum*)

Although golf wear for women remained doggedly conventional, Mrs Caulder of Manchester was happy to pose in her local Lafayette studio in 1932 wearing a typical women's knitted golfing outfit and 'co-respondent' golf shoes. (*National Portrait Gallery*)

was said in 1920, 'cause a sensation on British links' although his attire was acknowledged to be 'quite "the thing"' in the United States.[54] Custom thus controlled what men wore on the golf course, and largely what they wore when taking part in any leisure activity.

While most cartoons in *Punch* in the 1930s continued to show golfers dressed in plus-four suits, more often than not this was intended to depict them as fossilised figures out of touch with the latest fashions. By 1938 hardly any men were to be seen playing golf wearing plus-fours. They had become instead the preserve of the country gentleman, more suitable for shooting a brace of pheasants than a round of seventy-two. Most golfers now preferred the casual 'American' look of flannel trousers, soft-collared shirts, ties and tight-fitting sweaters that had been noted a decade earlier.[55]

In contrast, women's golf wear was one area where stolid practicality always came before the whims of fashion. Throughout the interwar period golf for women remained extremely popular although progressively it reflected the semi-segregation of British suburban social life. The formalisation of golf clubs and the time, distance and cost involved in playing the game more and more began to preclude lower-middle-class women from the game as well as younger middle-class women, thus enhancing the homosocial status of the golf club. Nevertheless, by the beginning of 1927 the Ladies' Golf Union had more than a thousand affiliated clubs.[56]

Vogue acknowledged the popularity of the sport among its readers by according it the unique accolade of a regular column on the game itself, rather than just its clothing, in the mid-1920s. Advertisements for beauty products used drawings of young athletic women playing golf to enhance the healthy aspects of their products.[57] Advertisements for the new sportswear shop to be opened in Paris by the couture house Lanvin featured female golfers, confirming the international popularity of the game.[58] There were more advertisements in *Vogue* for women's golf wear during this period than for tennis wear, an acknowledgement of the game's social status.

As a reaction to their hard-won place within the masculinised formal golf-club setting, few women were willing to jeopardise their status by introducing controversial clothes on to the course. In common with almost every other type of sport, women golfers in the late nineteenth and early twentieth centuries had struggled to overcome the constraints of acceptable dress to play the game.[59]

The reality was that, unlike the relaxed social atmosphere of tennis clubs, golf-club regulations restricted playing times not only for women but also for mixed groupings which were (and still are), often disparagingly referred to as 'mixed gruesomes'.[60] Women were also hampered by often hurriedly introduced reactionary golf-club regulations which forbade contemporary fashion details such as decorative pleats, bare legs or short sleeves.[61] They also had to face the hazards of soggy knitted skirts making play impossible, together with the usual jibes in *Punch*.[62]

Photographs of the many middle-class women who played golf in the 1920s show little attempt at stylishness. American *Vogue* dismissively wrote, 'In Britain, most lady golfers continue to appear in crumpled pullovers, shapeless skirts and deplorable hats and shoes.'[63] The majority of players can be seen wearing skirts with deep hand-sewn hems indicating that they adapted existing skirts to cope with the requirements of freedom of movement and protection from weather required for golf. In 1937 Simpson's were advertising golfing suits with trousers for women in *Vogue*: 'These are plaid Scotch tweed . . . and they'll hang as well as your husband's making you the most attractive as well as the most comfortable woman on the course.'[64]

Throughout the 1920s and early 1930s trousers were completely unacceptable for women on the golf course. However, one woman's attempt to introduce trousers for the female golfer has passed into golf folklore. Gloria Minoprio appeared at the English Ladies' Golf Championship held at Westward Ho! in 1933 wearing an outfit of dark navy trousers, polo neck jumper and cap and carrying only one club. In reply, the Ladies' Golf Union said it 'deplored any departure from the traditional costume of the game'. [65] Minoprio failed to change women's attitudes to wearing trousers on the course, however.

While there often appeared to be little difference between the style of American and British team golfers, individual female golfers from abroad appeared glamorous in comparison with their British counterparts. Unlike the more socially competitive world of the male golfer, regional differences among female golfers' clothes were not commented on. Away from the 'holiday golf' outfits worn on the seashore links of Le Touquet, British weather decreed that practicability was the watchword. There is little doubt that tennis encouraged an atmosphere of fun and fashionability, while the world of British ladies' golf promoted only solid respectability.

THE RISE OF THE RAMBLER

In contrast to golf, hiking was the leisure pursuit most closely associated with the lower middle class. However, hiking wear was not noted for its constraint. On 8 October 1934 an irate letter was published in *The Times* from the artist

Away from the socially competitive worlds of golf courses and tennis clubs, shorts for both men and women were more acceptable. Ann Tyler, a shorthand typist from Manchester (middle), poses with friends in 1938 on a tandem, all clearly feeling relaxed and informal – and all wearing shorts. (*Greater Manchester County Record Office*)

W. Russell Flint, deploring 'the spectacle of the country's youths and maidens invading the British countryside each weekend in hideous uniforms'. 'Is hiking so stern a business,' cried Flint, 'that only the ugliest shades of war-time habiliments are considered appropriate?' The debate raged in the letters page of *The Times* for several weeks and extended to include a discussion on the relative merits of men exposing their legs in shorts at all.[66]

The 'youths and maidens' Flint was referring to were part of the enormously popular hiking fraternity in interwar Britain. Hikers, Robert Graves noted in *The Long Weekend*, concurring with Flint, 'adopted a special dress that was almost a uniform'.[67] This consisted, for both sexes, of an open-necked shirt and shorts, both usually of a khaki colour, the traditional colour for country camouflage.[68] However, it could just as easily have been cyclists that Flint was complaining about, another enormously popular weekend activity – or indeed any non-competitive activity that took people out of their homes at weekends or on holidays.

One of the key reasons why khaki shorts became so popular and acceptable to a wide range of British men for weekend wear while in other areas they were rejected, is that, unlike tennis, activities such as hiking, cycling and rambling were not seen as opportunities for sartorial statements or social advancement. On 8 May 1938 Ann Tyler, a shorthand typist from Manchester, posed for a photograph with friends on a tandem, obviously all feeling relaxed and informal – and all wearing shorts.[69]

These shorts were 'unisex' items of clothing and there was certainly a democracy among the walkers particularly that the khaki 'uniform' appeared to enhance. The Ramblers Association, for example, was started by a Communist Party member, Benny Rothman, who promoted public access as being for 'every man'.[70] Bill Jesinger, who joined the Ramblers' Association in the 1930s, recalls members being distinctly lower middle class, 'clerical workers, civil service and that kind of thing'. The unemployed and manual workers were rare. However, in 1932 one man who appeared to be a gentleman when dressed for a ramble turned out to be a steel worker. The surprise was not that a steel worker should be a rambler, 'but only that a rambler who spoke like a gentleman should be a steel-worker'.[71]

Dean Inge, a leading light of the Men's Dress Reform Party, claimed there was a saying during the First World War that 'everyone looks a gentleman in khaki'.[72] While this obviously refers to the supposed democratisation that the military uniform brought with it, there is a ring of truth to the suggestion that even in peacetime the wearing of true khaki colours camouflaged not just the wearer but also the wearer's background. Baden-Powell had given this as a reason for adopting the uniform he did for the boy scouts.[73] He was proud to have his scouts singing songs of dress reform round the campfire, to the tune of 'Men of Harlech':

> What's the good of wearing braces,
> Vests and pants and boots with laces,
> Spats, or hats you buy in places
> Down the Brompton Road?

> What the use of shirts of cotton,
> Studs that always get forgotten?
> These affairs are simply rotten,
> Better far is woad.[74]

Sadly, there is no record of whether any of the young boy scouts had the slightest idea what they were singing about. Nevertheless, the message obviously did get through as these comments from a 32-year-old engineer's draughtsman from Surrey show:

During the 1930s shorts briefly became a 'unisex' item of clothing. Here Mr and Mrs Smith are on a hiking holiday in Devon in 1931; this was a popular lower-middle-class pastime throughout the 1930s. (*Hulton Getty*)

> Having worn shorts for years as a Scout and Scoutmaster I think that shorts are ideal except perhaps in very cold weather – most certainly for summer weather. In brief, I am in favour of bright sporty attire for men and sincerely hope that men's clothes will get more and more like the gay pyjamas they wear (the only colour permitted to men – because nobody except their wives may see it!) and less and less like mourners at a funeral.[75]

In addition to contemporary role models such as Baden-Powell, fictional characters also influenced men's leisurewear. This was a period when the adventure story was emerging from the pages of storybooks on to the cinema screen. Men as well as boys, who had grown up with the stories of G.A. Henty, Rider Haggard and Edgar Wallace, were now able to see their heroes coming to life on the movie screen. Films such as *The Lives of a Bengal Lancer* (1930), *Sanders of the River* (1935) and *Rhodes of Africa* (1936) captured the imagination of the British public. Gary Cooper, star of the US-made *Lives of a Bengal Lancer*, was voted Britain's most popular male film star in 1937.[76]

By wearing versions of their heroes' costumes, which were invariably variations of the tropical outfit, cinema audiences were able to live the celluloid dream, even for just a few hours hiking over the South Downs. It comes as no surprise that many of the male respondents of the Mass-Observation Archive chose khaki shorts as their preferred weekend wear 'for summer cycling and holidays'.[77] One insurance agent from Brighton went so far as to say that he would choose to do [his] work and live [his] life in khaki shorts and an open-necked shirt but BUSINESS demanded that [he] dress well.[78] As Baden-Powell noted, 'for a boy, a uniform is a big attraction, and when it is a dress such as backwoodsmen wear it takes him in imagination to be directly linked up with those frontiersmen who are heroes to him'.[79]

Thus away from home women's sports and leisurewear designs made enormous strides in the 1920s and 1930s and were unrecognisable from the ankle-to-neck modesty of pre-First World War fashion. Men's leisurewear, on the other hand, had moved much more slowly, putting dignity and comfort ahead of modernity. Nevertheless, both laid the ground for post-Second World War improvements as fabric technologies began to revolutionise sportswear for ever.

SIX

Top Hats and Tulle

Ask Robert whether he thinks I better wear my Blue or my Black-and-gold at Lady B's. He says that either will do. Ask if he can remember which one I wore last time. He cannot. Mademoiselle says it was the Blue, and offers to make slight alterations to Black-and-gold which will, she says, render it unrecognisable. I accept, and she cuts large pieces out of the back of it. I say *Pas trop décolletée*, and she replies intelligently *Je comprends, Madame ne désire pas se voir nue au salon.*[1]

E.M. Delafield, *Diary of a Provincial Lady* (1930)

If there is one enduring image of glamour during the interwar years it is that of the debonair dancer, epitomised by Fred Astaire, in his immaculate top hat and tails swirling his partner, Ginger Rogers, around a glittering dance floor. But the reality for most middle-class British men and women was that knowing what was correct to wear for dances, parties, a visit to a theatre or even a restaurant involved a list of dilemmas far removed from the ease and elegance of a Hollywood film star and far more akin to the agonies of E.M. Delafield's Provincial Lady adapting a much-viewed evening dress once again.

Yet the arrival of the movies in Britain did bring an obsession with the glamour of evening wear both in Britain and America, particularly during the 1930s with even the films having titles such as *Evening Clothes*, *The Tragedy of the Dress Suit*, *His Dress Shirt* and most famously the 1935 film starring Astaire and Rogers themselves, *Top Hat*. In the true British style of 'correctness', the obsession was not just confined to the glamour of what was being worn but also concentrated on the minutiae of dress codes surrounding evening clothes in the interwar period. In fact the first scene in *Top Hat* involves an argument between Astaire's British

producer and his valet on the relative merits of a 'square' and a 'butterfly' evening
bow-tie.

Less well-known than Astaire and Rogers but still influential, British role
models such as Jack Buchanan and the aristocratic actress Diana Cooper captured
a home-grown version of glamour that in its way surpassed the American version
for elegance and refinement. Jack Buchanan made his name as the quintessential
man-about-town in his consistently elegant 'top hat and tails' look. Cooper's
refined beauty personified an aristocratic allure that merged with the enchant-
ment of the cinema star.[2]

Thus there was a tussle between the overt glamour of the cinema goddesses,
newly arrived from America, the 'genteel prettiness' of the British stars, and the
enduring elegance of the Parisian model. What was never in dispute was that
throughout the interwar period, although most social events that were held in the
evening required special 'dress clothes', the primary need was for evening clothes
for dances.

STEPPING OUT

The popularity of dancing in the 1920s and 1930s is irrevocably linked with the
growth of commercial music in Britain, particularly after the arrival from
America of ragtime in 1911, the tango in 1912 and then jazz in 1917.[3] In 1919 the
first and most famous palais de dance opened in Hammersmith, to be followed by
Birmingham's palais de dance and dozens more across Britain during the 1920s.[4]
In addition, the relaxation of the licensing laws in 1921 brought in a wave of
nightclubs such as the '43 run by Mrs Meyrick, and the Embassy Club where
'men wore white tie and tails, and the women were in ball gowns designed mostly
by Chanel, Molyneux, Hartnell and Stiebel'.[5]

The popularity of dance music in general was enhanced when the BBC started
broadcasting live music by bandleaders such as Jack Payne and Henry Hall in 1926.
In the 1930s there was a regular 1½-hour dance broadcast every evening.[6] Most
better-class hotels in the major cities also offered tea dances or evening dancing to
small dance groups. Victor Silvester, who originated 'strict tempo' ballroom
dancing (forever associated with the phrasing 'slow, slow, quick, quick, slow' made
famous by his later radio programmes), started by 'partnering any unattached ladies
who [wanted] to dance' at Harrods' tea dances in the early 1920s.[7]

The arrival of dance crazes such as the Charleston and later the foxtrot meant
that new dance steps had to be learned. Dance schools thrived and local

newspapers ran columns of advertisements for dance schools. Victor Silvester charged 15 shillings per lesson at his school in Bond Street, putting him 'among the very top class of dancing schools'.[8] Silvester's book *Modern Ballroom Dancing*, first published in 1928, sold 100,000 copies in the first year.

Dancing was without doubt one of the most important and by far the most popular active leisure pursuit for all classes. However, this did not mean that the 'different social strata danced with each other'.[9] The upper classes restricted themselves to 'clubs, hotels and restaurants' while the working classes enjoyed 'superb facilities for dancing [and] this factor undoubtedly contributed to the situation where skill and grace in ballroom dancing come to be in inverse proportion to social status'.[10]

Commercial dance halls were mostly used by the working classes. The freedom allowed by such 'pay-to-enter' establishments meant they were considered *déclassé* by anyone in the middle classes with social aspirations.[11] Rochdale, for instance, did not get its first purpose-built dance hall until 1934, but before that there were at least six dance venues charging between 1 and 2 shillings for entry.[12] By 1951 there were 450 ballroom dancing halls across the United Kingdom.[13] A 23-year-old salesman from north London found 'public dances suffer from over-crowding . . . women who go dressed as if for the office, wearing shoes fit for hiking and men who go dressed as if for gardening are too common on the ballroom floor'.[14] Among young middle-class women in interwar Liverpool there was 'the ever-present assertion that their dancing did not take them beyond the boundaries of what was considered respectable behaviour within their social group'.[15]

The glamour of the upper–class ball and nightclub circuits and the free-and-easy atmosphere of the local dance hall were both far from the reality of the usual middle-class dance experience. Few middle-class houses were large enough to accommodate dances. Instead, suburban public halls were hired privately for functions such as dances, supper parties, dinners and whist drives, all of which required some form of evening dress. The difference between the type of person who went to public as opposed to private dances was often plain to see, as noted by a 21-year-old clerk from Dewsbury in Yorkshire:

> At the regular dances you will find a much 'rougher' type of person who are used to a bar at the dance hall and the easy familiardys [sic] and easy virtues of the feminine patrons. The reverse to that is at these school and club dances where the ladies are slighty [sic] snobbish and, not in every case, not too good at dancing owing to the fact of not going regular dancing [sic].'[16]

'Ticket-only' affairs were seen as a way to control socially undesirable elements. The snobbery within the middle classes is well exposed in Dorothy Whipple's *High Wages* when the local dignitary's wife is horrified by the arrival of a shop girl, who had been given tickets to a Hospital Ball, and her employers. 'How do tradespeople get the tickets?' she complained. 'I impressed on all salespeople that they must be most careful but . . . the tone, the TONE is lowered year by year.'[17]

While the majority of the middle classes considered pay-to-enter dances socially unacceptable, private functions did not necessarily guarantee a more exciting evening. 'One dance seems very much like another,' observed a 21-year-old clerk from Surrey, 'one wears a dress suit, goes in a crowd of people one likes, has a meal, dances with each other's partners, flirts a bit, drinks a bit more than usual but not to excess (because of getting the car home)'.[18]

Social circles were more controlled at formal dances organised by sports clubs such as tennis and golf clubs, or by an employer's firm. Mr B., a 26-year-old clerk from London, went to about seven or eight dances a year, 'generally on special occasions (coming-of-age, office dance, company's annual "ball", etc).[19] A 23-year-old salesman from North London also mostly went to dances on special occasions, 'Christmas Eve, New Year, St Patrick's or dances in connection with local football and social clubs'.[20]

The middle-class young were well aware that dancing was a 'skill' they needed to learn. If they had not been taught to dance at home or at school, young men particularly had to pay for lessons to improve their social skills. The consequence of not having these skills is summed up by 26-year-old clerk Mr H. of Newport: 'The girls won't look at a fellow unless he is a good dancer . . . some of the unhappiest times in my life have been spent at dances, because I have felt such a fool . . . for two years I went to a dancing class, often paying a guinea for private lessons.'[21]

Although it was not socially acceptable to visit the public dance hall itself – 'the difficulty lies in the type of person that frequents them . . . very loud'[22] – the dancing school at the Locarno in Streatham, South London, was popular with the middle classes. Middle-class girls in their twenties were clear about their reasons for taking classes: 'You never know when you might be wanted for dinners and dances. [It's] socially useful,' said one, and 'the firm's dance is coming off soon and I can't dance', said another.[23] All were in agreement that to be able to dance was 'a social necessity'.

At the apex of the social scale, aristocratic soirées were organised within a close-knit circle of the country's most eminent families. For the upper middle classes as well, private dances and balls were an essential part of a social life which also revolved around family, friends and acceptable acquaintances. The grander hotels in Oxford and Cambridge as well as in smart seaside towns would organise regular dances with live bands.[24] 'I'd rather sooner go to a few decent [dances] than a lot of cheap "do's",' stated Miss H., a 23-year-old shorthand typist from Liverpool. 'The dances I attend most are rugger club dances and similar functions, where I know a good number of the people, or at any rate what they'll be like.'[25]

Occasionally, the lower middle classes did pay to go to dances but even in 1939 there was some disquiet about the cheaper public dances, as explained by an 18-year-old girl student from Romford in Essex: 'The other day I went to a "bob hop". My friends were shocked . . . you musn't [sic] really go to a dance cheaper than 3/6.'[26]

With dance halls, where dress regulations were more relaxed, ruled out on grounds of respectability, it is not surprising that 'Flannel' dances appeared to be popular among the young. 'Flannel' or 'flannel-and-muslin' dances allowed the wearing of lounge suits and cotton dresses so the formalities of evening dress were dispensed with both for the young men and the girls. Taken a stage further, the '*bal musette*' was a form of fancy dress dance where the girls had to wear a blouse and a skirt and the men working clothes with 'neck crops' or scarves. The idea had been brought over from France and was liked by the 43-year-old civil servant from Forest Hill who claimed it had the benefits of a full fancy dress without the complications, and in addition, 'achieved the purpose of such a dance at the same time, i.e. the forgetting of dignity'.[27] The popularity of fancy dress as a whole during the early twentieth century may well have been in part a reaction to the constrictions of evening dress.

Towards the end of the 1930s there was a distinct move towards a democratisation which the dance bandleaders with their large record sales and radio broadcasts encouraged. Ambrose, who led a band at the Mayfair hotel popular with 'the society crowd' including royalty, was acutely aware of this:

> We ruined it for ourselves. For 5½ years we had a regular Saturday night broadcast. We used to attract people from the provinces, not the hoi polloi, but nice people. It was their big night out. But, unfortunately, it drove away the other people – high society – away. We were over-popular.[28]

With all social classes now basically dancing the same steps, 'any social cachet . . . applie[d] only to *where* one dance[d] and not *what* or *how*'.[29]

DRESSING FOR THE OCCASION

In addition to dances, all social events, such as trips to the theatre, dinner parties and, for a sophisticated few, visits to nightclubs, involved a ritual of dressing. The nuances of male evening wear during the interwar years were as highly categorised as an army officer's battery of uniforms. Writer Bryan Magee remembers seeing his father put on his white tie and tails to go to formal freemason dinners in the West End, epitomising for him 'a certain attitude to going out: in those days everyone used to dress up a bit when they went out, whatever the occasion'.[30]

While novelists such as E.F. Benson could make jokes about what a man might be expected to wear, with his heroine Lucia's ruling of 'Hitum', 'Titum' and 'Scrub', for the aspiring middle-class man this was no laughing matter. 'Hitum' indicated white tie and tails, Titum, a black tie and dinner jacket, and Scrub, morning dress.[31] Benson's heroine Lucia would add these words to her invitation cards to indicate the dress requirements for her parties. No man wanted to risk

THE BRITISH CHARACTER.
IMPORTANCE OF NOT BEING AN ALIEN

Men's evening dress was a minefield of social *faux pas*. No man wanted to risk being likened to the poor foreigner who stands like a lone pine tree in a forest of elegant oaks in trousers that are too short and obviously the 'wrong' style of evening dress. (Punch, *15 April 1936 © Punch Ltd*)

Points to Watch in

EVENING CLOTHES

THE WAISTCOAT LINE
Care should be taken to see that the waistcoat does not come below the lower edge of the jacket front. It is usually best to fit both jacket and waistcoat on together when buying.

THE JACKET
If the scye is cut too deep it will be found that arm movement lifts the jacket side out of place. This is a fault that is not only undesirable at the time, but which will soon spoil the set of the jacket permanently. The dinner jacket or tail jacket shoulder should be kept as natural as possible, any necessary squaring being done by tailoring rather than padding.

COLLAR AND TIE
The proportions of the tie and collar should be conformed both to each other and to the wearer's features. If the collar wing is bold the tie should be wide in proportion.

TROUSERS
The cut of dress trousers is most important, both on account of the short tail jacket and also of dancing movement. A well cut trouser should show no drag creases when the leg is moved forward.

BACK OF COLLAR
The dress collar should set parallel to the line of the jacket collar at the back. The cut of the jacket collar should be specially watched to see that it does not stand away from the neck.

SHOES
The shoe must be light in weight, preferably in patent leather. A laced and not a court shoe is correct. It may be plain or with toecap.

THE HIP LINE
It is essential to keep the slim hip line to a dinner jacket. The whole effect is easily spoiled by carrying things in the side pockets sufficient to cause a bulge.

There was no shortage of advice from tailors on the finer points of men's dress clothes though few of their clients would have lived up to these idealised images. (Man and His Clothes, *January 1933, LD51, by permission of the British Library*) being associated with Pont's cartoon from his famous series on 'The British Character', entitled 'Importance of Not Being An Alien'.[32] The poor foreigner in question stands like a lone pine tree in a forest of elegant oaks in trousers that are too short and what is obviously the wrong waistcoat.

Another famous cartoonist of the period, 'Fougasse', captured the agonies of turning up in the wrong outfit in his cartoon entitled 'When we long for an earthquake'. Its caption, 'I know nothing more awful than turning up at a function in fancy dress when it isn't a fancy dress function after all – except, of course turning up in the wrong kit,' touches on the deep embarrassment and social derision associated with wearing incorrect clothing at social events.[33]

In 1929 a menswear magazine noted firmly that 'improper attire makes one miserable'.[34] Seven years earlier, an editorial in *The Times* had called for the dress codes of evening wear to be reappraised. The dictum 'don't bother to dress' had fitted in with wartime conditions when there was rarely the time or opportunity to change into evening dress. However, just as the relaxation of day clothing as a reaction to four years in uniform for many men was seen as a dangerous slide towards degeneracy, so there was a call for the rules for evening wear to be tightened up as well:

There is a crying need, for men especially, of a good, rigid rule . . . A man is dependent, not only for his being well dressed; but for the far more important social quality of feeling well dressed upon nothing so much as the fitness (which is more to him even than the fit) of his clothes. Not what he wears, but when he wears it is at once his social cachet and his comfort.[35]

Man and His Clothes claimed that before the First World War evening dress was 'confined to the upper set, but it is now common property'.[36] This was in part due to the enormous increase in the popularity of dancing. The upper middle class, however, was used to wearing a selection of evening dress outfits for a variety of occasions in addition to balls and dances, such as theatres and dining out.

For adult men, formal evening occasions required a tailcoat or 'dress coat', a white waistcoat, a white, hand-tied bow-tie and a stiff shirt with wings. Even in their own homes, the upper middle classes in particular invariably changed for dinner, the men donning dinner or velvet smoking jackets with stiff-fronted shirts depending on who was dining with them in the house.[37] Not until the mid- to late-1930s did it become acceptable to discard the stiff, winged-collared shirts when at home.[38]

THE BRITISH CHARACTER.
"ADAPTABILITY TO FOREIGN CONDITIONS."

Pont lampoons the upper-middle-class ritual of putting on evening dress even in the furthest corners of Britain's rapidly shrinking empire. Along with a rubber of bridge and an after-dinner cigar, these features of 'The British Character' would have been familiar to many *Punch* readers. (Punch, *4 April 1934 © Punch Ltd*)

Whereas the lounge suit was worn for many lower-class dance halls, dress clothes were the norm among the middle classes by the mid-1920s. It was a brave man who was prepared to go against these rituals. A 43-year-old civil servant from Forest Hill remembered 'a staff affair' at a large London hotel: 'the dance was evening dress optional [but] as is usual in such cases, not half a dozen brave men turned up in lounge suits'.[39] Even the dance manuals prescribed what should be worn on the dance floor – tails for most evening functions, a dinner jacket only if the occasion was 'quite informal'. When in doubt, it advised, go in tails.[40]

The dress rules of such occasions were in-bred from an early age with young men of sixteen regularly wearing dress clothes to private dances.[41] Osbert Lancaster recalled a visit to the theatre to see *No, No, Nanette*:

Where the audience was studded with our school mates of whom we made a careful count of those who were not, as we were, in dinner jackets and cast

From an early age young upper–middle-class men such as Mrs Blomfield's elder son from London would have owned a set of dress clothes. Unlike his younger brother, he is clearly quite at ease with such formality. (*National Portrait Gallery*)

envious eyes at the few, all members of the fast set in Hodgesonites and ostentatiously smoking, who were in tails and were undoubtedly going on to the Berkeley or the Embassy [a fashionable nightclub], which we were not.[42]

While there was little superficial difference between the outfits of the young and those of the more mature man, *Men's Wear* recognised that the younger man was more likely to be fashion-conscious while the older man would favour a more subdued look as reflected in an older-style collar or tie.[43] In the early 1930s miniature bow-ties and large winged collars were briefly popular with trend-setting young men. However, when these exaggerated styles were taken up by musicians in dance bands, they were quickly dropped in favour of more traditional styles, 'the kind you see Prince George wearing'.[44] The double collar was still considered anathema by well-dressed men, as was the ready-made bow, although there is evidence that thousands were sold.[45]

In a similar vein, in the late 1920s the double-breasted dinner jacket was no longer seen as respectable once it was noticed being worn by 'certain West End male choruses'.[46] *Man and His Clothes* ran a series on 'Points to Watch in Evening Clothes', giving little reassurance to men who were even expected to make sure that the proportions of the tie and collar should be 'conformed both to each other and to the wearer's features'.[47]

In the best circles a man was not only expected to wear the right clothes but also to have bought them at one of a handful of 'right' shops as well.[48] Improvements in mechanised tailoring techniques were slowly bringing down prices but the dinner jacket still remained an investment purchase. Luckily, evening wear was the least susceptible to changes in fashion. While trouser widths might change for the upper-class undergraduate, for most men the evening suit they acquired in 1920 would not have looked greatly out of place in 1939.[49]

Dress suits were sometimes seen as something of an heirloom that could be passed down to the male members of the family, much to the embarrassment of the young. In 1939 a 35-year-old solicitor from Leeds remembered his first dance being spoilt by the fact that he had had to wear what he considered 'a very old-fashioned dinner jacket suit discarded by an elder member of the family'.[50]

Men's evening dress resisted most attempts at reform. In 1929 the Men's Dress Reform Party, under the aegis of Dr Arthur Jordan, vainly tried to persuade the Englishman to reject his stiff evening collar and tails in favour of a soft open-necked shirt and breeches for evening wear.[51] As early as 1920, a Mr Harry Parkes also suggested reforming men's evening wear by the introduction of more colourful waistcoats. Mr Parkes never achieved the publicity that the MDRP were to get nine years later but he received a sympathetic hearing from tailors anxious to improve their takings.[52]

Of all the ideas that the MDRP put forward, its proposed changes in evening dress were the most widely ridiculed and its attempts to overthrow such a pinnacle of British male dignity were doomed to failure.[53] The MDRP also suffered from its association with the bohemian 'Chelsea' set who were also constantly derided by the establishment press.[54] The only success that Dr Jordan had was to convince Sir Henry Wood and Dr Adrian Boult that the male players in the BBC Promenade Orchestra could wear in the summer, from the early 1930s onwards, a black Palm-Beach jacket and a soft white shirt with attached collar. 'They are glad,' reported Dr Jordan in *The Times*, 'to be spared the heavy coat and "boiled" shirt and collar of conventional evening dress.'[55]

For most social occasions, however, dignity was paramount. The Englishman had a reputation for wearing 'his formal clothes in a manner that cannot be quite achieved by others' – a jingoistic jibe at other nations' attempts to emulate *Le Style Anglais*.[56] There was no shortage of advice on hand from tailors and outfitters to guide a man through the maze of black and white evening wear. Throughout the 1930s Austin Reed produced a series of booklets for their customers including one on 'Evening Wear' and another on 'Dress Clothes', which detailed the high standards expected of anyone wearing 'dress clothes'.[57]

White waistcoats worn with a dinner jacket were not in good taste, black being always preferable. The only time when a black waistcoat might be worn with tails was in the case of mourning as on the death of George V; while it might have been acceptable on the continent, it was not in 1920s and 1930s London.[58] Accessories mattered as well. Even the Prince of Wales found himself being castigated by his father for not wearing white gloves at a ball.[59] Shoes were to be laced patent leather which could not be worn at any other time other than with evening wear.[60] Woe betide the man who turned up at an event wearing the wrong tie. The ultimate *faux pas* was the ready-made evening bow with its metal buckle showing at the back of the collar.[61] It was better to come armed as *Punch* cartoonist Fougasse's imaginary guest with an armful of both black and white ties and waistcoats and check with the maid before entering the establishment.[62]

OPTIMISM IS NOT ENOUGH

When ordering new dress clothes a man expects them not to depart by a hair's breadth from those standards which are implied by the very words "dress clothes." But he cannot be certain until the garments are finished and ready for him to wear.

It is on this unassailable fact that the "New Tailoring" bases its claim for the most serious consideration. Immediately you are completely satisfied on every point —quality of cloth; excellence of tailoring; correctness of style; perfection of fit—then, but not until then, the "New Tailoring" presents dress clothes ready for you to wear.

This method has appealed very widely to men who realise that— in dress clothes, at least—optimism is not enough.

Dress Coat - 7 gns.
Dinner Jacket
    4½ and 6 gns.
Waistcoat - - 30/-
Trousers - - 45/-
Any garment can be purchased separately and matched at any future time.

THE "NEW TAILORING"
—the fit is assured when you choose clothes instead of cloth

AUSTIN REED'S
of REGENT STREET

Ten "New Tailoring" Centres:
WEST END: 103-113 Regent Street   24 Coventry Street   CITY: 13 Fenchurch Street
Also at Glasgow, Birmingham, Liverpool, Manchester, Sheffield, Leeds and Bristol

Correctness in evening wear was one of the most important of interwar dress codes. In an advertisement in 1929 menswear retailer Austin Reed offered its clients dress clothes that did not 'depart by a hair's breadth from those standards which are implied by the very words "dress clothes"'. (Tatler, *11 December 1929, LD171, by permission of the British Library*)

"I SAY, QUICK—IS IT BLACK TIE OR WHITE?"

Turning up incorrectly dressed at a 'do' guaranteed social embarrassment so knowing the right dress code for evening wear was even more important for men once the black tie and dinner jacket became accepted for less formal occasions. (Punch, *31 May 1933* © *Punch Ltd*)

SARTORIAL STYLE IN THE STALLS

The other evening entertainment popular with the middle classes was the theatre, in spite of the encroaching spread of the cinema. There was a variety of revues, farces and classical productions in the West End in the 1930s, with playwrights such as Noel Coward, Terence Rattigan and Ivor Novello producing some of their best-known works. These were aimed at a middle-class audience and Rattigan later admitted he had in his mind an imaginary 'Aunt Edna', a 'nice, respectable, middle-class, middle-aged maiden lady with time on her hands and money to help her pass it, who resides in a West Kensington hotel', as the type of person who would enjoy his work.[63]

The influx of middle-class theatregoers meant that the Edwardian tradition of those with seats in the stalls wearing evening dress struggled to continue. This was exposed in a series of correspondence in *The Times* in 1932. The upper classes felt their territory was being encroached upon by, as one correspondent wrote, 'middle-class theatre-goers' not willing or able to 'conform with [the] social customs of another class with which they have little in common'.[64] It was

By 1932 readers of *The Times* felt that standards of dress at the theatre were falling. Few were as elegant as this first-night audience of a new play called *Little Catherine* at the Phoenix Theatre in London in 1931. (*Hulton Getty*)

brought to the attention of readers of *The Times* by an actor, Eric Maturin, who had noticed, over the footlights, the number of men in the audience not wearing evening dress. 'It is surely rather annoying,' he wrote,

> for any who have paid for their stalls in a theatre and have taken the trouble to don evening dress, for their comfort and in consideration for those sitting next to them, to find themselves seated next to persons still wearing the same clothes they have worked in all through the day. Anyone who can afford the price of a stall is sure to possess evening dress in some form or other, and one does not feel one is allowed the benefits and privileges of being a stallholder unless some sort of regulation is in force with regard to wearing of evening dress.[65]

In defence of the middle-class man, another writer replies, 'It seems quite unreasonable to expect the man in the street when he pays 12s 6d for a stall to incur the additional trouble and expense involved (as any honest suburbanite can affirm) by the assumption of the ugly and inconvenient livery of the prosperous diner-out.'[66]

Yet another correspondent, also calling herself a 'suburban theatregoer', praised the more relaxed style of dress worn at theatres on the continent which she felt was 'more delightful . . . and sincere'.[67] A correspondent from Perthshire admitted that he had arrived at the Whitehall Theatre 'not suitably clad but . . . reassured that it did not matter . . . I must admit that I was the only man in the stalls that night dressed in a grey tweed suit . . . it may be some small comfort to Mr Maturin to know that I felt rather uncomfortable before the performance began – a fitting subject for Mr H.M. Bateman.'[68] H.M. Bateman's famous series of cartoons entitled, 'The Man Who . . .' focused on the social embarrassment that could befall the Englishman who stepped out of line.

This lowering of standards was seen as the thin end of the wedge by one correspondent who felt the stalls were being invaded by couples whose 'general appearance and behaviour wrote them down as something a good deal less than decent middle class'.[69] The social significance of the play itself was also dragged into the argument:

Why is the worst dressing usually found at Shakespearian productions? Mr. Shaw's patrons are almost as carelessly dressed . . . he has, of course, a certain smartly attired following among the middle-aged and the youthful *intelligentsia* but there is always a big proportion of 'tweedy' patrons which would horrify the 'immaculate'.[70]

Playwrights Frederick Lonsdale and W. Somerset Maugham were said to have a good influence on the dress of their audiences, as did musical comedy and revue. The best-dressed audiences were to be found at the opera although 'Strauss seems to be sure of a better dressed following than Wagner'.[71]

Restaurants were a similarly sticky area. *Punch* took the view that diners-out often gave themselves away by their dress, the white-tie man meriting a vintage bottle of Chambertin, the black-tie wearer a bottle of Graves and the customer in a lounge suit merely a half-bottle of red.[72] A joke of the 1920s derived from the shabby dress clothes worn in restaurants which meant that the waiters looked more distinguished than the guests.[73]

VELVETS AND TULLE

In contrast, for many women, especially young women, dressing up for the evening was 'half the fun':

> Getting one's frock ready, wondering whether you should have your hair done, or whether it'll stick up by itself, hoping it won't be wet, or cold, for that matter, for even if you go by car it's generally pretty draughty. It always strikes me as particularly odd that in the middle of winter it is considered necessary to divest oneself of practically all one's clothing, in order to go out at night. However, it's all part of the game . . . having arrived at the appointed place, we at once repair to the cloakroom, where we powder our noses afresh. (Quite unnecessary, but still everyone else is doing the same.)[74]

Without doubt the glamour of the movie screen captured the imagination of working-class girls throughout the interwar years. However, women from the middle classes were more likely to admire the elegant dress styles of actresses such as Lady Diana Cooper or Adrienne Allen, star in the 1930s of Noel Coward's *Private Lives*, who traditionally followed the trends from Paris rather than Hollywood. They looked for reassurance to their own stars of theatre and screen.

Two top British female film stars, Gracie Fields and Jessie Matthews, regularly jostled with each other in the popularity polls.[75] The cinema press said of Gracie Fields in the 1930s that 'women adored her because they shared her dress sense so there was no envious wish-fulfilment' – a significant comment as it confirms the rejection of the 'glamour' so much associated with Hollywood stars – even among working-class women who were her main fans.[76] For some, it was her lack of glamour that made her stand out, as a contemporary comment shows:

> In the cinemas there is an absence of healthy amusement, there is too much sex-appeal: but in the performance of Gracie Fields we get a breath of fresh air and an opportunity for some real laughter. This all helps to keep the right spirit of England together – clean living, with a total absence of anything bordering on the unnatural.[77]

British viewers, particularly women, appeared to want their heroines to be 'innocent . . . and asexual'.[78] Jessie Matthews undoubtedly fitted this bill. She was 'tops' with a 'wistful and winsome femininity'.[79] Anna Neagle, another highly popular star, also represented the 'quintessential English lady'. They both combined a 'genteel prettiness' with a non-threatening allure. In 1937 Matthews was rated Britain's favourite film star, coming seventh behind such famous names as Norma Shearer and Greta Garbo.[80] The popularity of Matthews and Neagle implies this 'genteel prettiness' was just as acceptable as Hollywood's often-blatant sexual glamour.

The first dance was a rite of passage for many young women – and with it came the attendant agonies and ecstasies of finding something to wear. The first third of Rosamund Lehmann's novel *Invitation to the Waltz* focussed on just that task and the pleasures and perils of having a length of flame-coloured silk made up by a local dressmaker.[81] The reality was not so different. Going to the unromantic-sounding Guild of Insurance Officials' dance in 1921 involved three months of preparation for 19-year-old undergraduate Miss O. from Glasgow, who 'haunted the shop windows for ideas on how to look Parisian on a very small sum'.[82]

For women, the vagaries of fashion, particularly skirt lengths and bare backs, loomed over their purchases. There was no greater solecism than arriving at an event wearing an inappropriate outfit, as 38-year-old Miss S. from Croydon remembered: 'I had a very cheap dress of violent mauve which I saw was all wrong as soon as I got there.'[83] There was no better transformation for a woman than being able to wear the 'right' dress. Borrowing heavily from Shaw's *Pygmalion*, Gracie Fields in *Sally in our Alley*, invited to sing at an upper-class party, is 'elevated' into high society by the hostess putting her into a backless evening dress.[84]

Evening wear was always an expensive item. Jenifer Wayne, who grew up in South London between the wars, remembers purchasing her first 'bought' evening dress for her final school dance as the defining moment in her youth: 'solid purple taffeta; ruching; gathering; yards of bias-cut skirt; stiffened epaulettes tapered to a point . . . artificial Parma violets tucked in the bosom [which] my mother tore . . . out and substituted [with] a hand-made ruffle of shaded violet ribbon'. Bought with – and by – her mother from Chiesman's in Lewisham, it forever represented for Wayne the moment when she 'grew up'.[85] Eileen Elias, the daughter of a medical researcher from Peckham, had similar memories. As a young girl she window-shopped for the 'real dance dress . . . an apricot dance dress, dusky brown with a tulle overshirt or beautiful floating panels, a waist low on the hips, and a spray of artificial roses trailing down to the hem . . . only 3 guineas, to transform yourself into a different person'.[86]

Although the fashion was for low-backed dresses in the 1930s, the practicalities of supporting the bosom precluded dramatically low backs for many. Compromises were frequently made, as demonstrated here by secretary Ann Tyler, showing off her plum-coloured, crimped chiffon dress in the late 1930s. (*Greater Manchester County Record Office*)

Like Wayne and Elias, most middle-class girls relied on their mothers to buy their dresses. This came with the added factor of influence on their choice. Not all young girls were lucky enough to have their mother's financial support. Mrs M., a 23-year-old housewife from Richmond in Surrey, was bitterly disappointed when, as a teenager, her mother refused to buy her a new dress for a dance. 'My mother will never know how intensely I hated her when she pompously remarked that my best green silk frock was perfectly suitable.'[87]

The number of evening gowns that a woman owned was primarily governed by her class and income. In 1925 Lady Beatrice O'Brien claimed she had had fourteen evening frocks destroyed in a fire.[88] Within that number it was likely that there were dresses for different levels of formality. Variations in formality could be confusing if one were an outsider in terms of either class or country. A contemporary editorial in *The Times* argued that there were 'no border-line cases in a wardrobe of ancient etiquette', as they termed the selection of a British lady's evening outfits. 'To each of these belonged a special costume as precise in its detail as the differing uniforms of a soldier.'[89]

A woman returning to Britain from the Malay States wrote to *Vogue* in 1929 admitting she felt out of touch and did not know what was currently correct wear for visiting a restaurant or when one wore 'a pukka evening dress'. *Vogue* advised her to have some sleeveless black lace dresses with matching cardigan coats made as they were 'very much worn by well-dressed women for dining in public places this season'. In addition, she should wear her 'important' evening dresses when being 'entertained at a private house and at any dinner at a small restaurant' adding that 'if they are not too formal' she could wear them at nightclubs.[90]

On the whole women could make the transition from day wear to evening wear more easily than men could. Some fashion companies capitalised on the fact that by the mid-1920s many more middle- and lower-middle-class young women were now working and found it impossible to change several times a day.[91] Suits called 'transformations' allowed the wearer to shed or add an item enabling 'the smart individual to be correctly garbed on all occasions throughout the day, and even for a restaurant dinner, a theatre, or informal dance'.[92] There was a fashion for a 'cinema frock' in the early 1930s. '[This] frock', it was claimed, 'has a shorter skirt than the formal evening gown, and is frivolous and charming . . . usually having a little coat or decorative cape, which when removed allows of its use as a restaurant or dinner frock.'[93]

At whatever level of social activity, the importance of the occasion was always emphasised and the underlying message from women's magazines was one of correctness:

Do not let the question of clothes worry you, and remember that it is better to be too simply dressed than the opposite. If your young man comes from a family that is rather higher in the social scale than you are, it won't matter at all if you have only a semi-evening dress for dinner, so long as it is a pretty one. Far better to wear it than to produce something unsuitable, bought for the occasion and a thousand times better than appearing in an evening gown when your new family are accustomed only to changing into simple frocks.[94]

The actress Beatrice Lillie, advised the girl with a small dress allowance to 'have a simple evening dress, as well cut as she can afford, with plain court shoes to tone, no cheap buckles to spoil the effect, and taupe colour fine gauge silk stockings'.[95] However, even by 1936 it was still being suggested in dance manuals that a woman needed at least three different types of dance dress:

For family or quite informal dances, almost any style of light dance frock will be suitable. For semi-formal occasions, a rather more elaborate dress will be desirable; while for formal or important dances, full evening dress should be worn.[96]

In reality, most middle-class women were far more likely to have possessed only one evening dress. A knitted suit could be bought for only 12 shillings 11 pence in the 1930s, while an evening dress cost several pounds, making it a major purchase which had to be made to last once bought.[97] Among the upper classes, it was the norm to spend between £12 and £14 on a ball dress, an expenditure far beyond the reach of most middle-class girls. Many women probably coped in the same way as 26-year-old housewife Mrs B. from Dorking in Surrey: 'I keep my best dress for about three months for parties, or a special occasion like a wedding, or a surprise invitation. After three months or so, the best becomes second-best and is worn on such occasions as going out to tea [or] a day in town.'[98]

Many readers of E.M. Delafield's *Diary of a Provincial Lady* would have identified with and sympathised with the protagonist's attempts to revamp one of her two evening dresses seen regularly by all her neighbours at Lady Boxe's dinners.[99] The importance of this issue is confirmed by Mrs T.R., an undergraduate at Cambridge in the late 1930s:

But, I mean, you did mind about evening . . . you know, you really *did* wear evening dresses; if you went to a dance, let alone a May Week ball, you know, it was really important, you couldn't wear the same one too often in the same sort of place . . . I mean like in Gloucestershire I could have worn the same dress year in, year out . . . But at Cambridge and in London . . . I tried always not to wear the same thing to the same type of event. But you could spin it out to about a dozen times I should think.[100]

The two major fashion interventions, which had definite social implications on dress code judgements for evening wear, were the dropping of hemlines and the exposure of backs in the late 1920s and early 1930s. For those left behind, either because of their pocket or their youth, not being up to the minute in terms of fashion could cause acute embarrassment and accentuate social differences, as 24-year-old Miss F. from Hampstead, who worked for the Education Department of the BBC, remembered:

My cousins had become really wealthy. I never knew any of their friends of whom the dances chiefly composed . . . The youths – of 16, 17 and 18 – always wore evening dress, which used to scare me, because I wasn't used to it . . . the dresses of the maidens were always more expensive, more fashionable than mine; it was at the time when evening dresses were becoming long again and there was great variation from year to year. My dresses were always too girlish. As a result, I used to sit in corners a lot of the time and imagine I couldn't dance.[101]

A 23-year-old housewife from Richmond had been extremely annoyed with her mother when, as a 16 year-old, she was made to wear a silk day dress instead of being bought a new 'dance frock':

It scarcely reached below my knees; and no flights of imagination could carry it to the fashionable ankle-length then in favour. However, I ultimately became resigned to the green frock and armed with a pair of silk shoes that I had left from my sister's wedding the year before . . . [thought] perhaps my dress wouldn't look so out of place, after all . . . a renewed gust of loathing overtook me

as I entered and beheld the dresses of everyone present. They all seemed to have a dance frock designed to the height of fashion but me, I thought, and I hurriedly determined to sit out for the whole evening in order not to expose it.[102]

THE HOUR-GLASS OF FASHION.
Girl (meeting friend). "I SAY, A LONG FROCK! I'D NO IDEA IT WAS SO LATE IN THE AFTERNOON."

As skirts became long again and legs were once more covered in the evening, dresses with plunging backs became fashionable. Men could be taken aback by this fashion. Mr L.W., a young

Many women changed two or three times a day depending on their social diaries, especially since by the start of the 1930s knee-length skirts were no longer acceptable for evening wear. (Punch, *4 June 1930 © Punch Ltd*)

newsagent from West Hartlepool, was rather surprised at his first dance, 'during a ladies' call when, on being asked to dance by a rather attractive young lady . . . found that to put my right hand in the correct position (as taught) that it meant putting it on her bare back owing to her dress being rather low.' Not surprisingly, he commented, 'things went much better after this dance . . .'.[103]

These fluctuations in women's evening wear were the constant butt of the *Punch* cartoonist, with jokes such as the 'horrible nightmare of a lady who dreams that she has gone to a ball in her night-gown and found herself shockingly overdressed'.[104] Into the 1930s the fashion for low-backed dresses regularly featured on the pages of *Punch*. The vogue for finding 'new bits to show' was seen by some to mirror the more relaxed fashions on the beach but also reflected the lure of cinema-screen glamour. In reality, the practicalities of supporting the bosom precluded dramatically low backs and compromises were usually made.

After marriage, modesty and suitability became the primary concerns for women. Fluctuations in hemlines caused few problems to the stalwart ladies of the middle classes. Fashionable trends were no longer an issue. As John Lewis advised its account customers in 1932, 'evening gowns are still instep length. For the present, at all events, we are not parting with the dignity they give us.'[105]

Most women drew on this new-found veil of modesty reluctantly. Many of the Mass-Observation married female respondents admitted that they loved dancing but hardly ever had the chance to since their marriages. Mrs B. of Dorking,

Movie-star glamour was often a long way from the reality of most women's evening dress choices. Mrs Tweedale, wife of an industrial factory owner from Manchester, maintains the high degree of respectability expected of a woman of her age and social position. (*National Portrait Gallery*)

Department stores proudly advertised designer copies such as an evening gown inspired by Mainbocher, the Paris-based American designer who dressed Wallis Simpson, later the Duchess of Windsor. 'You have to see the front and back views . . . to appreciate the triumphant daring of encrusting navy blue panels in bold Picasso fashion on white'. (*John Lewis Partnership Archive*)

aged 26, retained a wistful enthusiasm for such socialising. She was slightly luckier than most and gave her reasons with refreshing honesty:

> I love to go to dances and before I was married I went to as many as I possibly could – I suppose about 20 a year. . . . Now I go to as many as I can persuade my husband to attend, i.e. about 5 a year . . . My thoughts, when not engaged in probing into other people's minds out of curiosity and interest, are about other women's clothes, make-up, attractiveness, skill in dancing, and their partners if attractive or of unusual interest. Chiefly the women though.[106]

Mrs B.R., a 36-year-old London housewife, said dancing and reading were her main pleasures when she was young and at Oxford. Since her marriage she had only been to four dances and plaintively noted that she had not danced with anyone who really enjoyed dancing 'for the last 14 years'.[107]

Later in life mothers were sometimes able to achieve a vicarious pleasure from accompanying their daughters to dances.[108] Among the middle classes there may well have been an element of chaperoning in this together with the fact that locally-organised dances often included the whole family. Some, like 50-year-old Mrs C. from Laindon in Essex, were happier to see dancing as predominantly a youthful pleasure and dressed accordingly: 'I do not go to dances, only to Church Socials where there is usually a little dancing of the go-as-you-please sort to a small band. Here there is no dressing up . . . Only a girl or two might come in a dance frock. We older ones go in something warm and ordinary.'[109]

It was not just the 'older ones' who went for something warm. While the glamour of evening wear was in the eye of the beholder, often for the wearer it was less comfortable, especially in chilly British ballrooms. The skimpy pen-and-ink sketches of glamorous women's evening creations in the magazines belied what most women, even the young ones, wore under their dresses. In addition to the ubiquitous change of shoes, women often carried a change of warm underwear with them for the journey home. This would be in addition to what they were already wearing.[110] 'Much underwear, "in case I caught a chill",' remarked a 21-year-old female bank clerk from Twickenham.[111] A 42-year-old writer looked back to her first dance when she wore 'soft cotton combinations and heavy white cotton knickers and of course a petticoat . . . my mother was bothered at my inability to wear proper stays with bones and said that no nice man liked dancing with a stayless girl'.[112]

Similarly evening wear required new beauty rituals which brought their own problems. Miss P., a 30-year-old secretary from Hillingdon in Surrey, arrived at a friend's Christmas dance in 'a new dress, oyster colour with a bit of blue embroidery down the front. It had no sleeves, and I was very conscious of this as I had shaved my arms for the first time and they tickled.'[113] Others were not so particular, as a 42-year-old housewife from West London noticed at a 'trade dinner' she had been to where 'some of the women had shaved their eyebrows and drawn black lines on their foreheads [but] one of those . . . had not shaved her armpits'.[114]

While it was possible to buy the latest styles in evening dresses ready-made by the 1920s, the cost of a fashionable dress was still out of the range of many women. Cheaper evening dresses were sneeringly called 'guinea gowns'.[115] Manufacturers blatantly advertised the inspiration of their evening gowns. John Lewis featured 'Helga. Copy Mainbocher', quoting *Vogue*'s praise of the original: 'You have to see the front and back views . . . to appreciate the triumphant daring of encrusting navy blue panels in bold Picasso fashion on white . . . it is fitted above the waist and free below, in the way all new evening dresses should be.'[116] Mainbocher, best known for dressing Wallis Simpson, both before and after her marriage to Edward VIII, was American by birth but had chosen to base himself in Paris.

The dresses worn by movie stars in the dance epics of the 1930s were the stuff of dreams for young working-class girls[117] but the version of glamour that came out of Hollywood had less appeal for the English middle-class woman. While there is a grain of truth in saying that 'theirs was more the culture of the playing field than the culture of the dance hall,'[118] there is no doubt that, unless money was no object, interwar evening wear was bound up by notions of modesty and respectability, and of all clothing needed the most attention to detail.

SEVEN

Everything to Match

Never wear an outfit until you have collected everything, yes everything, to go with it – hat, shoes, gloves, handbag, scarf and even a special umbrella to match.[1]

Miss Modern (1936)

The advice from *Miss Modern* magazine in 1936 was clearly aimed at young women, but for men and women alike, young and old, accessories completed an ensemble yet their importance was often out of proportion to their size. They were frequently vital emblems of correctness and respectability. Seemingly minor items such as gloves, ties, braces or hats, if incorrectly chosen or worn, had clear social significance and could betray a person's lack of breeding.

Accessories can generally be divided into those that can be justified on the grounds of necessity and those that can be seen only as fashion items. A few, such as hats and gloves, fall between two stools; they were often needed but, for women, they were fashion items in their own right. As broadcaster René Cutforth pointed out, they comprised 'a whole armoury of paraphernalia, cufflinks, cigarette holders, cigarette cases, studs and tie pins . . . and most of these gadgets were counters in the class game'.[2] They were items that Mr D., a 27-year-old insurance agent from Hove, with typical middle-class reserve of the period, termed 'anything unnecessary in dress'.[3]

THE TIES THAT BOUND

There was one accessory that men could not avoid wearing and that was the tie. To do so was to be associated with the plebeian collarless worker. For the middle classes there is little doubt that P.G. Wodehouse's Jeeves was correct when he stated that 'there is no time . . . at which ties do not matter'.[4] While ties were often seen as tyrannical objects, associated with the strangulating stiffness of collars, the British male of all classes was extremely reluctant to relinquish them even at leisure.[5]

For the man from the upper middle classes in particular, the tie was part of the coded language of his social group. In the wardrobe of every upper-middle-class man would have been at least one striped tie denoting the key rites of passage to his current social position – public school, regiment/ship, sports club, gentlemen's club – all were represented by prescribed sets of coloured stripes. Mr B., a 27-year-old undergraduate, owned only two ties. Significantly one was the 'club stripe of a club I belong to and [the other] one quiet blue – worn alternatively'.[6] Another Mr B., Stanley Baldwin, although his son insisted he did not 'dress to impress [and] would never wear his old school tie', did admit that he relished 'wearing the yellow, red and black striped tie of the I Zingari Cricket Club when out of London'.[7] This exclusive club, formed in 1845, boasted one of the first recorded 'striped' ties.

The fashion for wearing ties with affiliations started in earnest at the turn of the century. The majority of British public schools established their striped-tie colours in the Edwardian era, and they were often linked to the establishment of 'Old Boys' societies. This was the period when the majority of the regimental, school and university tie designs were registered with a few select companies such as T.A.M. Lewin of Jermyn Street which had been established in 1898. Those who had not already done so created their designs in the 1920s and 1930s.

A tie manufacturer's pattern book of the period shows 183 different combinations of silk stripes, ranging from No. 1, the Guards (maroon and navy), to No. 183, the Royal Corps of Signals (pale blue and green with a narrow navy stripe). In between were other military organisations and Old Boys clubs such as the Old Carthusians of Charterhouse public school (navy with narrow grey and maroon stripes) and the Old Bedfordians (navy and grey).[8]

From the 1930s many public schools such as Sherborne and Berkhampstead had 'country' and 'city' colours, particularly when the original colour schemes were bold. The 'city' version would have smaller, more discreet stripes on a black or navy background.[9] Subtle variations were also available. Lewin's designed a tie for those who went to school at Harrow and then on to Christ's College, Cambridge, combining the colours of both school and university college. In addition, firms like Lewin's and Benson & Clegg produced ties with crests, bow-ties, blazer badges, hat bands, cufflinks, cravats and scarf squares all with the appropriate colour or crest. Ties with crests on were rare during this period and did not become popular until after the Second World War, possibly connected with the large number of ex-service organisations which chose symbolic regimental emblems for their crests in preference to stripes in the late 1940s and 1950s.

In 1968 it was still possible for dress historian James Laver to categorise 750 different ties with club, school or career associations from sporting clubs to the Inns of Court.[10] Thus by the late 1930s the middle-class man would have had a small but distinct choice of ties to wear signalling to others his educational background, social standing and sporting interests.

To the untutored eye many of the patterns seem indistinguishable but this was the most classic and subtle form of social exclusion. With the lounge suit becoming more universal, the upper middle classes clung tenaciously to any distinguishing factors that could maintain the class divide. The presumption of any man stupid enough to wear a tie to which he was not entitled naturally earned him social disapproval. In 1925 Ernest Hemingway spotted F. Scott Fitzgerald in Paris wearing a Guards tie with the distinctive – and distinguished – navy and maroon stripe. He claimed to have bought it in Rome.[11]

In the 1930s *Apparel Arts*, an American menswear trade magazine, published an article detailing the thirty major British regimental colours.[12] The Guards tie was a style that had sold 'like hot cakes' in America once Edward, Prince of Wales, who of course was entitled to, was seen wearing it. In Britain *Punch* pointed out the humour of all and sundry being able to buy 'club' ties in a poem entitled 'Gents' Smart Neck-wear. Lines inspired by the spectacle of a number of club-ties in the windows of a sixpenny "cash-and-carry" store':

> How deep a debt we owe to Mr Woolworth
> (I speak in tropes: his rule is strictly cash),
> Who for our humble sixpence gives such full worth,
> Enabling one and all to cut a dash
> (It matters not with howsoever thick a mist
> Obscurity enwraps their earlier years)
> Either as Old Etonian or Wykehamist
> On Britain's proms and piers!

> Incogniti, Crusaders, Bacchanalians,
> See how they flaunt their richly-blended hues!
> Hawks, Butterflies, Authentics, Old Borstalians,
> I Zingari – you've only got to choose;
> No need to face the hazard of rejection
> Or year by year to pay immoderate subs;
> At sixpence each you have a wide selection
> Of all the smartest clubs.[13]

In 1933 dress historian Doris Langley Moore confirmed the truth behind this poem and showed how easily the naive shopper could be ensnared:

> In a certain 'mammoth store' we saw a counter covered with ties, tobacco pouches, and other articles, made up in well-known combinations of colours, and hanging about them a show card bearing these words: 'School and Club Colours – Always Fashionable.' And there we observed a number of men innocently *choosing* their stripes.[14] (Original italics.)

Even in the early 1950s, when George Thomas took his seat as a young Labour MP in the House of Commons, he was accosted by a Conservative Chief Whip who accused him of wearing an Old Etonian tie. Thomas, unabashed, assured him he had bought it from a Co-operative Society store in his Welsh constituency of Tonypandy.[15] Mindful of this sort of confusion, a few organisations insisted on identification before purchase. Ogden's, official suppliers to the Sir Joseph Williamson's Mathematical School, Rochester, Kent, would only sell to registered names.[16]

For those excluded from this 'club tie' coterie, which meant the majority of lower-middle-class men, their main concern was maintaining an image of respectability through the appearance and cleanliness of their shirt collars. 'Sonny' Farebrother, a character in Anthony Powell's *A Dance to the Music of Time*, hoped to make his fortune with a machine to turn stiff collars so that both sides could be used, thus 'reduc[ing] laundry bills by fifty per cent'.[17] The failure of his machine was matched only by the disgust of his snobbish friends at such a suggestion.

During the 1930s men in the middle classes had a choice of collar style for day wear. However, the older generation were reluctant to relinquish the formality of the pre-First World War era and many retained the winged collar. This

Stiff collars looked dated by the 1930s but the older generation were reluctant to give up a look to which they felt accustomed as shown by two generations of the Bunce family from north London. The *pater familias*, complete with hat in hand (standing, right), prefers a more traditional look to his middle-aged sons. (*Mrs E. Baxendale*)

encouraged a look of *gravitas* they were unwilling to part with. Younger men tended to stay with the separate stiff collar throughout the 1930s for reasons mainly of economy rather than comfort. It was cheaper to launder a collar rather than a complete shirt. The shirt with an attached collar was acceptable for informal wear and was quickly taken up by the young in preference to the stiff collars their fathers preferred. A popular style had long points which were secured under the tie knot with a gold pin. 'It was a social error,' recalls broadcaster René Cutforth, 'if this tiepin had a twisted bar or a round bar or a silver bar: it must be flat and gold.'[18]

Whatever the style, clean collars were imperative, dirty collars suggesting a lack of respectability, a cliché going back to the eighteenth century at the very least. The older generation were not about to abandon a look to which they were accustomed, despite the acknowledged discomfort of the starched collar. In many ways, just as the corset had given women a bearing that was easily visible and definable, so the stiff collar gave a man a sense of uprightness which could be equated with dignity. Certainly anything less would not be considered except by a younger generation.

The abolition of the stiff collar was one of the main proposals in the 'manifesto' of the Men's Dress Reform Party when it was established in 1929. They were not the first to tackle this issue in the 1920s. In 1926 the Anti-Collar League had met in Paris. They knew they wanted to abolish the starched collar but, according to press reports, could not agree on what to have as a substitute.[19] The MDRP in contrast wanted to replace the collar with a fixed or 'soft' collar to be worn without a tie. The question of doing away with stiff collars for men was also fundamental to their ethos. By advocating the abandonment of not just separate and stiffened collars but also ties as well, they alienated many men.

Ten years later, in 1939, a military man from Eastbourne, Sussex, admitted that the use of 'loose collars' would be more hygienic but insisted that 'the weight of conservative opinion' against this meant that he did not 'consider the question one to be pursued'.[20] It was the younger generation who were taking the lead as usual. A 22-year-old bank clerk from Wiltshire was typical in not wearing stiff collars, 'a departure', he admitted, 'from my father's tradition'.[21]

THE PATH TO RESPECTABILITY

The pressure on women was to obtain matching accessories and in particular shoes and bags. The language of shoes ('well-heeled', 'down at heel') amply conveys the importance of footwear as an indicator of status. 'A lady', said *Miss Modern* in 1936, 'used to be known, and recognised as such, by her neatly-shod, well-bred feet. The young woman of to-day has not forgotten this axiom, and that tap-tap of her heels beats a tattoo of chic.'[22]

Shoes were regularly sent to the menders and repair costs were an important economic consideration. As with the main wardrobe purchases, it was the lower income families who had to spend proportionally more money on repairs, not just on their clothes but on their shoes as well. Lower-middle-class families were also spending twice as much proportionally of their income on shoe buying.[23] However, the poor quality of cheaper shoes showed that it was a false economy. Mrs B., a 26-year-old housewife from Dorking in Surrey, explained why:

> I like to spend as much as I can possibly afford on shoes. . . . I spend anything from 1 *gn* to 3 *gns* on a pair. The cheaper ones definitely are not an economy to me as I find that they lose their shape in about a month, while the more

There is no need for colour in
H.M. Bateman's cartoon since the
expression on the face of the snooty butler
says it all. The poor man has just realised
he is wearing 'brown in town' – an
unforgivable social solecism at the time.
(*Estate of H.M. Bateman*)

expensive shoes last almost for ever.
My cheap shoes last six to nine
months with care, but the dearer
ones last easily two years and still
keep their shape and to their dying
day look 'good'.[24]

Not even a Savile Row suit could
protect the owner from comment if
with it he was wearing the incorrect
shoes. The most well-known *faux pas* of this period was that of wearing brown
boots or shoes with a dark town suit – 'never brown in town'. To wear brown for a
formal occasion was to show disrespect, as had been immortalised by the 1910
music hall song 'Brahn Boots', later popularised by Stanley Holloway in 1940:
'And we could 'ear the neighbours all remark/"What, 'im chief mourner? Wot a
blooming lark!/"Why 'e looks more like a Bookmaker's clerk . . . In brahn
boots!"'[25]

Here is a classic example of how a seemingly innocent and necessary basic item
of clothing could place the wearer in a social minefield. Similarly, there was no
need for colour in H.M. Bateman's cartoon, 'The Wrong Shoes', since it was
clear that the mortified man lacked the *savoir faire* to realise that he had worn the
wrong colour of shoes.[26] Even in 2002 David Beckham, England's football
captain, who had recently been voted one of Britain's best-dressed men, was
criticised in the press for selecting brown shoes to be worn with blue suits for the
England squad formal uniform.

Sometimes an item's decline down the social scale can be charted as it became
unacceptable to each successive social rank. An example of the occasional
inevitability of the trickle-down of fashion is the theme of the 1922 *Punch*
cartoon, 'the downward spread of the spats habit'. The text reads that while spats

had been considered 'becoming in the case of the Chief, permissible in the junior partner and perhaps to be tolerated in a confidential clerk', when the office boy takes to wearing them, asks *Punch*, 'who knows where it will end?'[27]

By the late 1920s *Punch* associated spats with caddish behaviour using a seaside landlady in a cartoon to say, after an unsatisfactory experience with a flashily-dressed lodger, 'A white spat may often 'ide the cloven 'oof.'[28] Less than ten years later spats were included in a list of things a 23-year-old printer from Worthing particularly classed as 'vulgar' – a list that included lavender suits, double-breasted waistcoats, lemon kid gloves, bowler hats, and showy and prosperous-looking overcoats'.[29] Once items were no longer exclusively worn by the upper classes, it was often seen as pretentious and 'vulgar' for someone of a lower class to wear them.

For men in particular, accessories could convey messages about sexuality. The combination of brown and suede in shoes was associated with, as Robert Graves noted, the 'Pansy' or 'homosexual beauty'.[30] Worn with flannel trousers since the 1920s, by the mid-1930s brown suede shoes were only just acceptable for casual wear within the middle classes. Mrs R., an undergraduate at Cambridge in the late 1930s, remembers suede shoes being controversial: 'But I knew lots of people who did wear them. They were . . . I think they were probably looked down on by the dons if you know what I mean.'[31]

Just as for men, coloured shoes for women could be seen as social mistakes. Black was not to be worn in the country.[32] During the 1930s shoes made of two tones of leather, one light, one dark, and worn by both men and women, were known as 'divorce court' or 'co-respondent' shoes. It was well known that Wallis Simpson wore them but it would have been considered extremely daring for a middle-class British girl to do the same. Mrs R., an MP's daughter from Gloucestershire, remembers 'two-coloured shoes, you know, they were known as co-respondent shoes, everyone knew that. I mean you wouldn't dream of them. Or if you did, you were not quite our class dear, which was, NQOCD. Isn't that awful? That was said sometimes.'[33]

HAND IN GLOVE

For women, gloves were seen as a necessity throughout the middle classes. There is no doubt that this was a hangover from the centuries-old ideals of aristocratic gentility, together with Victorian respectability when the gloved hand became the mark of a lady who had no need to work.[34] From the early twentieth century the practicalities of modern living, travelling on public transport and later the increased popularity and availability of car driving, only served to emphasise the expediency of gloves for all women. In 1923 the firm of Atherton & Clothier, based in Woodstock, Oxfordshire, were producing 6,000 pairs of gloves a week, of which 200 were hand-sewn chamois gloves.[35]

The usefulness of gloves did nothing to lessen their importance as a social statement either. Far from becoming more democratic, gloves became a mark of social standing with spotlessly clean white kid gloves being at the top of the status tree. White gloves rarely regained their purity after washing and few women could afford the extravagance of Nancy Astor, who sent hers to the cleaners after only one wearing.[36] As *The Girls' Favourite* pointed out, 'White gloves that *aren't* white do spoil the general appearance of a smart girl, don't they?'[37]

For the majority of women white gloves were a luxury kept for best. Female university students at Bedford College, London, had to wear white gloves with their academic dress on public occasions though there is little photographic evidence that they wore them willingly at any other time.[38] For the most part, leather gloves in a variety of more practical colours were the accepted choice. Woollen gloves were not acceptable other than for sporting or country wear. 'Good gloves, nicely fitted, are the best economy in all ways, for neatness and daintiness in detail are the primary considerations that must be ever present in the mind of all women striving towards Success through Dress!'[39]

Not surprisingly, Mass-Observation found in 1939 that gloves were worn less by younger women than by those over thirty who did not work, suggesting that it was older women who were anxious to utilise this symbol of gentility.[40] Gloves were put on before leaving the house but few women went to the extremes of a schoolmaster's wife in 1924 who retained the Victorian habit of keeping her gloves on when visiting for tea.[41] Nevertheless, gloves were seen as 'the hall-marks of refined apparel'.[42] The girls of the Merchant Taylors' School in Crosby, for example, were told they must wear their gloves on the way home 'so as not to be mistaken for council school children'.[43]

The necessity for gloves had certainly not lessened by the end of the 1930s. Even the reduction of hat-wearing did not diminish the popularity of gloves for women. Glove historian C. Cody Collins has attempted to explain why this was so. 'Gloves', Collins stated in 1947, are 'of paramount importance to that instinctive feeling of a completed costume and are a signature of social standards.'[44] In a list of hat and glove purchases in Bolton in 1939, some women are listed as not wearing hats but there is no such entry for gloves.[45] Gloves were an integral part of any outfit and it was desirable that they matched other accessories such as shoes and bags.

With the need not just for quantity but also for quality in gloves, they were listed as often being given or received as presents.[46] In 1934 gloves were advertised at Christmas as 'gifts that are absolutely certain of success'.[47] The majority of female Mass-Observation respondents wore gloves year round for going out of the house, some even for work.[48] A teenage student from Romford, Essex, who admitted she did not wear them, says that most of her friends did because they did not feel dressed without them.[49] Gloves were not always worn willingly, however. The feeling among many Mass-Observation respondents was that one had to wear them otherwise other people would think one was not 'dressed'.[50] As with hats, the idea that gloves were an essential social accessory for women was still widespread well into the 1950s.[51]

HATS OFF!

In contrast, the choosing and wearing of hats initially did not seem so fraught with anxiety and social brinkmanship. Indeed, the most common visual cliché of the interwar years is the inevitability of hat-wearing among both men and women. It is presumed that men of all classes willingly wore hats whenever they were out of doors, whether it was a trilby, a top hat or a flat cap. But since the eighteenth century and before, men's hats had been part of a code of etiquette unique to an item of clothing.[52]

Hats were still seen as an essential prop of street etiquette for the man from the middle and upper classes who cared about decorum. To fail to acknowledge status distinctions by dress and gesture was disrespectful, and therefore anathema to the respectable persona so many of them were trying to present. Young men brought up in an upper-middle-class family would have been initiated into the complicated rituals of hat lifting from their youth.

For those less sure of the social rites involved, there was no shortage of published advice. The following extract published in 1937 shows by its length how complicated the rituals were to those unsure of themselves. While hat honour may have been second nature to many men, to the uninitiated it was a social minefield:

It is not necessary for you to raise your hat if you see a lady of your acquaintance in a public vehicle in which you are also a passenger. A little smile or nod is sufficient. Otherwise, you should always raise your hat when meeting a lady whom you know. If the lady is a close friend, raise your hat immediately she gets near; but if you do not know her very well, you should wait until she acknowledges your presence before raising your hat. You should also raise your hat when meeting a male friend accompanied by a lady, whether you know the lady or not, when walking with a lady who meets someone she knows, and when walking with a man who has occasion to raise his hat. To raise one's hat, however, does not constitute an introduction. If, for example, when walking with a friend you meet an acquaintance of his and raise your hat, you should make no sign if you meet the lady again when alone – unless she should happen to smile or bow. . . . While there is no need for a sweeping movement like that of the cavalier of other days, do not go to the other extreme and simply touch the brim with your forefinger, as many men have a habit of doing in these days. Raise the hat just clear of the head for a moment, that is the correct procedure.[53]

It comes as no surprise that this is taken from a revised version of an etiquette manual for men first published in 1902. What is surprising is that while changes had been made to various other sections, this particular section remained essentially the same from 1902 to 1937.

It was a recognised problem that the man who went hatless was in danger of not being able to 'make his most courteous gesture to a woman'. Writing to *The Times* in 1934 under the heading 'Polite Though Hatless', Mr Roberts of Bristol was 'unrepentant about [his] sartorial deficiency' but anxious to find an alternative gesture of courtesy.[54] A reply from Mr Stuart Jervis of London suggested such an alternative:

I have been hatless for years . . . I used to smile (I hope) charmingly, and incline my head, in what I can only describe as a lingering, and slightly fond, manner. The success almost dazzled me. I could almost hear the ladies say, "Ah! An eccentric. But what manners." But now (*eheu fugaces*) [Alas! Our fleeting years pass away] I am older, still hatless, and rather fat. But the method still works. A smile, an inclination of the head, . . . at least I am not mistaken for a Fascist by the passers-by.[55]

The debate on hatlessness centred on etiquette. The confusion of a vicar from Moretonhampstead exposed the complications of hat lore in the pages of

The Times in 1929. It shows that not only was hat honour directed at women but also that there was a complicated hierarchy of professional men to be acknowledged as well:

> I cannot keep my hat on in a bank, though I know my courtesy is often mistaken by my young friends for eccentricity, not to say insanity. It dates from my undergraduate days at Oxford, when none but a 'bounder' would have done it. The reason, as I understood it, was that a banker is not a tradesman but a professional man. Even now I suppose, hats come off in a doctor's consulting room, or a lawyer's office. What has the poor banker done, that he should be insulted?[56]

It is not surprising that the older generation were reluctant to give up wearing a hat, while the less deferential younger generation were more relaxed about it. After the First World War there was an anxiety in the industry that men were leaving off their hats in an effort to appear more relaxed.[57] There was a mild resurgence in hat-wearing in the late 1920s, caused mainly by the variety of hats now needed to suit different social occasions. For the majority of middle-aged men one or two hats would have been all they needed – or wanted. Some men, said the *Hatter's Gazette*, were 'so conservative in their tastes that they would dread the change from a bowler to a soft felt as they would dread the migration from their native haunts to an unexplored territory'.[58]

Newspaper photographs from the 1920s and 1930s suggest that the majority of men wore hats of varying styles whenever they were out of doors. Yet closer inspection reveals another story. By the end of the 1920s there were already murmurs of discontent among the hatting trade that 'hatlessness' was again affecting their business. Such was the concern that hat manufacturers and wholesalers refused to see travelling salesmen who were hatless.[59] Among the trade journals, retailers were shown medical propaganda from America, which was intended to be sent to schools, pointing out the supposed health risks of going hatless.

The trade suspected that the hatless movement was led by a younger generation not willing to follow the formality of their fathers. They also tried to suggest that hatless men were 'inclined towards loose morality, criminal tendencies, suicide and revolutionary activity'.[60] Since this was at a time when the Men's Dress Reform Party was saying that hat-wearing was unhealthy, it was not difficult for the trade press to point out the eccentricity of the MDRP to further its own cause.

In addition, there were regular debates in the trade press on the correct way to tilt one's hat, if at all. The tilt at which a man wore his hat was of consequence. Commenting on the film *Cavalcade*, made in America but supposedly set in Britain, a correspondent to *The Times* said the film's one flaw was the men's hats, especially in the crowd scenes, since 'Englishmen don't wear their hats like that.'[61] Pushed over to the right, the wearer looked like 'a rowdy' or someone 'presiding at a coconut shy'. Tilted back, one could look like 'Mr Alfred Jones, of Peckham, in a punt with his braces on,' or in other words like a working-class man at leisure. The worst was to tilt to the left when one would lose 'social status completely [and] become a mental deficient'.[62]

The main worry for the hat trade was obviously that many men were disregarding etiquette altogether and leaving off hats. In an article in *Punch* entitled 'My Hat!', the author confessed to hating hats. While he could see they had their uses in wartime, 'in the civilised times of peace it cannot be denied that the principal end of a gentleman's hat is to be taken off to ladies'.[63] This, he felt, could not justify the prolonged use of an item of clothing.

A more fortuitous linkage was the one that developed between the cinema and the hat industry. Battersby's, leading men's hat manufacturers, realised that the 'hatless' problem was coming from the younger generation. 'The hat Father wants is not the one that his son is likely to wear,' they claimed.[64] The customer they were losing was the sixteen-to-twenty-five year old whose 'principal form of

With hat sales falling in the early 1930s, the hat trade was grateful for the opportunity to promote hat-wearing through film star role models such as Paul Muni. (*Hulton Getty*)

relaxation [was] taking his girl to the "talkies", and without his hat he [felt] sporty and bold, and perhaps a bit dashing'.[65] This young man, they assumed, identified with the characters he admired on the screen – 'perhaps, that exclusive product of Hollywood, the "Tough Guy"'. In response to this, Battersby's produced a lower priced hat called the 'Big Shot'. To judge from the press coverage, the hat appears to have been a success, selling 100,000 in eight months.[66] The 'Big Shot' was followed by the 'Tiger Rag' named after the bandleader Harry Roy, and then the 'Alex James'.[67]

Nevertheless, it was still an uphill struggle to persuade young men to buy these hats since many of them were rejecting not just the styling of hats but also the hat etiquette followed by their fathers. It is significant that hats such as the 'Big Shot' were aimed at the young or working man from the lower middle classes. The more solid older man would have shunned such a raffish look as bordering on the 'spiv', on a par with the brown bowlers worn by 'street-corner bookmakers'.[68] Instead, the trade press tried to appeal to a man's dignity by pointing out the status he might lose by going out hatless. For example, if a man did not keep his hat on in a department store, claimed the *Manchester Evening Chronicle*, he was in danger of being mistaken for a floor walker.[69] *Men's Wear Organiser* used the accusation of meanness to try to shame men into buying a new hat to replace one that perhaps they had used for anything up to twenty years.[70]

In 1935, in an effort to attract publicity, a hatting firm in Luton – the 'boater borough' – invited French film star Maurice Chevalier, known for wearing straw hats, to the town to receive a donation of presentation boaters. The visit was a huge success in terms of publicity since thousands of town residents, many of whom would have worked locally in the hatting industry, turned out to see him.[71] However, a photograph of the crowd shows that even in this hatting town at least half the men, mainly young, are not wearing hats.

By 1939 the hat trade had to try harder than ever to maintain sales by pursuing blatant links with the cinema. 'Tie Up with the Films' headlined a feature in the *Hatter's Gazette* showing photographs of Adolphe Menjou and other well-known actors wearing various styles of soft-brimmed hats.[72] They were fighting a losing battle against the tide of men who preferred to be hatless whether for expense, status or fashion. The decline of hat-wearing is confirmed by the attitude of the respondents of the Mass-Observation directives. It is hard to find a man who has something positive to say about wearing hats. Conversely, they are eager and proud to state that they do not wear a hat at all, except for two men who only wore one in the rain.[73] Hatlessness was becoming a sign of male daring.

The *Hatter's Gazette* was right to be concerned since informal head-count surveys during a snowstorm in London in January 1939 show that 23 per cent of the men seen were hatless. Perhaps even more surprising were the results of similar surveys from the hatting centres of the north of England. Male hatlessness was at 14 per cent in Stockport and 20 per cent in Manchester.[74] A final blow came when the War Office issued a photograph of a hatless man in July 1939 representing the militiaman's off-duty uniform.[75] Under the heading, 'Were they going to send them out like this?', the hat trade complained bitterly. As an afterthought, the War Office, somewhat surprisingly, added a beret to the outfit. However, the damage had already been done and hat-wearing would never return to the levels of the 1920s.

A FEATHER IN HER CAP

The trade in women's hats in contrast was robust between the wars, millinery still being a high-fashion accessory. The relatively low cost of a hat compared with that of the complete outfit allowed women to update their look for a moderate expenditure. The popularity of women's hats waxed and waned depending on hairstyles. In 1926 the *Luton News* claimed the town, the centre of Britain's hat-making industry, had been 'made rich by shingling'. The need for a pull-on hat that did not have to be pinned had 'banished unemployment from Luton'.[76] Removing hats in public, however, meant exposing squashed or untidy hair. Such exposures were especially tricky for middle-class women involved in public speaking:

> Some of the early Labour women leaders, and particularly the younger generation of bobbed-headed enthusiasts, solved the hat question economically. Their first act on mounting a platform was to discard their headgear. Many of the advanced feminists also follow this practice. Some, for instance, even in a public restaurant at lunch-time, almost invariably remove their hats. The 'hatless' vogue on the platform, of course, involves additional care of the coiffure. . . . The platform speaker can gain assurance by the knowledge that she is wearing the correct hat.[77]

Most women solved the squashed-hair problem by not removing their hats in public places. However, in general women were not subject to the same demanding hat etiquette as men. Women's hats did not have to be removed for any social

THE BRITISH CHARACTER.
ABSENCE OF DECISION

Women's hat–buying habits were the constant butt of jokes but hats were a relatively cheap way of enlivening much–worn outfits and remained a popular accessory for women until after the Second World War. (Punch, *13 October 1937 © Punch Ltd*)

acknowledgements and generally remained in place once they were outside and in public places such as shops and tearooms.

How to cope with hats was to prove an issue for the first female Members of Parliament. Male MPs were not allowed to wear hats inside the House of Commons unless they wished to make a point of order, although they needed to have one with them to reserve their seat. Female MPs were exempt from the rule such was the almost biblical strength of feeling that women ought to have their heads covered on public occasions.

Women's supposedly frivolous attitude to hats was the constant butt of cartoons. While acknowledged as a social necessity, hats appeared to incorporate all the weaknesses of the female gender: extravagance, frivolity and indecision. Some women regarded hats not as something frivolous but as a necessity which was often a nuisance to buy. A politician's daughter from Gloucestershire only ever wore the one hat she owned in London and never during her time as an undergraduate at Cambridge.[78]

Gloves and hats were vital social accessories for women throughout the interwar period. However, while hats remained firmly in place during social outings, it was increasingly unusual to keep one's gloves on indoors although they would always be close at hand. (*Hulton Getty*)

There appears to have been a more relaxed atmosphere at Cambridge, in contrast to the all-female Bedford College in the heart of London's Regent's Park, where students were not allowed to leave the college grounds without a hat.[79] A non-hat-wearing school teacher in 1930 was warned that she would not be recommended for promotion unless she took to wearing a hat. With the scarcity of jobs, she resigned herself to knitting a tam o'shanter to wear.[80] A 37-year-old nurse from Chester admits buying one hat that suited her for winter and wearing it 'until it drops to bits'.[81]

These women's rates of hat buying were well below average since according to Mass-Observation by 1939 'Mrs Everywoman' was buying 2.7 hats a year.[82] The *Daily Mail* doubled this figure, telling its readers that 'five times a year (on average) every wife goes home with a smile and hatbox in the hope of pleasantly surprising her husband with the honeyed words, "Do you like me in *this* model, dear?"' The paper acknowledged that there was a percentage of what manufacturers termed 'open air' girls who did not wear hats except on special occasions. 'This habit (or lack of habit)' was said to be on the increase especially in the north of England, for some unexplained reason. The hat trade did not, the paper said, regard this as widespread enough to be menacing.[83]

However, by the mid-1930s the press local to the centre of the hat-manufacturing trade in Luton were giving the clear impression that it *was* a problem. Hatting factories posted notices requiring all employees to enter the premises wearing some form of headgear. 'We weren't allowed in the factory without a hat on – take it off when you get round the corner maybe – but you had to wear a hat . . . it was just as simple as that.'[84]

The older generation of women remained solidly loyal to everyday hat-wearing until well into the 1950s.[85] Indeed, it was one of the last vestiges of pre-war respectability to disappear, along with the City gentleman's rolled umbrella and bowler hat.

EIGHT

Radicals, Bohemians and Dandies

He was tall, slim, rather swarthy, with large saucy eyes. The rest of us wore rough tweeds and brogues. He had on a smooth chocolate-brown suit with loud white stripes, suede shoes, a large bow-tie and he drew off yellow, wash-leather gloves as he came into the room; part Gallic, part Yankee, part, perhaps, Jew; wholly exotic.[1]

Evelyn Waugh, Brideshead Revisited (1949)

Evelyn Waugh looked to his friend Brian Christian de Claiborne Howard, the American-born but Eton-educated poet, for his description of Anthony Blanche in *Brideshead Revisited*. Howard was unusual in being both foreign and openly homosexual, 'the "aesthete" *par excellence*, a byword for iniquity from Cherwell Edge to Somerville'.[2] He was also, not surprisingly, a rarity in the interwar years and belonged with those individuals and groups who 'stood out from the crowd' because of their style of dress.[3]

People who break the rules are often self-conscious about the effect their clothes have on others. The motives for their individuality are various. Some choose to step outside the mainstream of British dress codes in order to draw attention to themselves for political or artistic reasons. Others have no ideological motive other than not to conform to the norm. There is also a third group who see themselves as fashion groundbreakers, adopting individual styles and then rejecting them as soon as they become acceptable to the majority.

THE RISE AND FALL OF 'RATIONAL' DRESS

The idea of 'anti-fashion' in one form or another was not new in the 1920s. For women in particular, the greatest organised rebellion against 'fashionable' clothing had been at its apex in the second half of the nineteenth century. The Rational Dress Society, founded in 1881, was a coordinated attempt by a group of British women to reject what was seen as the unhealthy corseted style of the time.[4] They wished to replace this style not just with looser, more flowing garments but also with fabrics that were promoted as being healthier for the skin. Drawing on classical styling, these dresses became a 'fashion' themselves and were worn by women across the classes who enjoyed the artistic implications of style.[5] A testament to their success is the number of designs produced and marketed by the London department store Liberty's, the leading proponent of 'artistic' dress.[6]

As in America, the Rational Dress Society's promotion of trousered or 'bifurcated' garments was not successful. Just as Amelia Bloomer had failed to get American women to accept her version of the Turkish tunic dress, so later attempts to promote any form of 'trouser' for British women were ignored before the twentieth century. Nevertheless, throughout the nineteenth century there had always been individual women who wore tailored jackets in a masculine style particularly for country wear and sports such as archery, hunting and bicycling. By the turn of the century it was acceptable for the top half of women's dress to follow a 'mannish' style in Britain as long as the 'feminine' skirt was retained below.[7]

There was no male counterpart to the Rational Dress Society during the nineteenth century. Attempts to change men's clothing were slow and rarely successful. In America as well any hint of change was not well received.[8] The main instigator of revolutionary ideas in menswear was Dr Jaeger, who propounded the benefits of wearing wool next to the skin and emphasised the health aspects of 'sanitary' dress. Dr Jaeger's best-known supporter was the Irish dramatist and socialist supporter, George Bernard Shaw. Shaw's costume usually consisted of a brown country-style tweed suit wherever he went which became 'a part of his personality'.[9]

By the end of the nineteenth century there was a move to 'politicise' items of clothing of both men and women. Although the wearing of party colours during elections was nothing new in British history, it was new for socialists in particular to 'wear their hearts on their sleeves' and proclaim their politics through their dress on an everyday basis. Though without a formal 'uniform' as such, socialists were a group often defined by their clothing or at least by an item of clothing. Keir Hardie, Britain's first socialist MP, clung to his working-man's hat when entering the House of Commons for the first time in 1892. This apocryphal 'cloth cap' was in fact a tweed deerstalker. Nevertheless, the cloth cap and the red tie were the socialist badges of the late nineteenth-century man.[10]

For women, by the turn of the century 'socialist' gowns had developed from the original Pre-Raphaelite dress of soft pleats from the neck downwards.[11] Significantly, it was not a style taken up by the Suffragettes in their fight for the vote in the early twentieth century.[12] Rather than rejecting mainstream fashions, the Women's Social & Political Union encouraged its members to maintain a fashionable, feminine look. Recognising early on in their campaign that the women's appearance could and would be used as a propaganda weapon against them, the WSPU went out of its way to highlight its members' femininity to counteract damaging counter-information. Although the Suffragettes had no formal association with the socialist parties of that period, many of them wore 'socialist' dress but this was because of the links with lifestyle ideals rather than mainstream politics.[13]

The Bohemian style was well established in London before the First World War.[14] The Bohemian was thought of as disowning fashion and embracing 'anti-fashion'. However, it was not as straightforward as that. There is a long tradition of professional artists, of both the visual and written arts, affirming their position by their chosen costume. The Romantic Poets and the Pre-Raphaelite Brother-hood of the nineteenth century, for example, developed a distinctive look unique to themselves. By the early twentieth century, the British artist Augustus John took pride in bringing his family up to wear loose flowing gowns and open-necked shirts.[15]

In contrast to those who rejected mainstream fashion, there were also those who adopted fashion to the extent of 'dandyism'. Oscar Wilde, whose wife Constance was a founder member of the Rational Dress Society, was a well-known exponent of this style of dress. However, dress historian James Laver puts Wilde's friend and contemporary Max Beerbohm a step ahead even of Wilde. In Beerbohm's own words, 'the true dandy must always love contemporary costume', whereas Wilde's style of dress harked back to a more romantic era.[16]

'BOYETTES' AND BOYISHNESS

During the 1920s two groups of young people dominated the popular press, 'flappers' and young male undergraduates at the country's top universities. In the post-war period there was exaggerated anxiety about the increasing emancipation of women, culminating with the giving of the vote to all women aged 21 or over in 1928. After the furore surrounding the 1928 election died down, so press interest in young women as 'flappers' evaporated.[17] Yet 'flappers' were instantly recognisable as much by the clothes they wore as by the politics and morals they were supposed to have.

Young women were in a 'no-win' situation. If they dressed in the latest feminine fashions, sporting short skirts, lipstick and rouge, they were accused by the older generation of being immoral. However, if they veered towards another popular fashion, the flat-chested cropped-hair look, they were accused of being 'mannish' by the press.

The link between the two fashions was the new hairstyle, which the media feared gave young women a 'boyish' look. Inspired by the publication of Victor Margueritte's novel *Le Garçonnette* ('The Bachelor Girl'), women, first in France and then in Britain, were quick to copy the heroine and cut their hair short. This is an almost unique instance where a hairstyle combined with new dress fashions to produce an influential 'look'. The *mode à la garçonne* drew women of all classes out of the boudoir and into the more public space of the hairdressing salon.[18] That it was young women who were adopting the new hair and dress styles only added to the concerns of that champion of morals, the *Daily Mail*. In 1927 it railed against such fashions:

> The 'Boyette' has been increasingly prevalent this Easter at southern resorts where a year ago one saw only occasional specimens of this very latest type of the young emancipated female . . . The Boyette not only crops her hair close like a boy but she dresses in every way as a boy. Sometimes she wears a sports jacket and flannel 'bags'; more generally, she favours a kind of Norfolk suit. Nearly always she goes hatless. In age she appears to be in the last years of flapperdom and her ambition is to look as much like a boy as possible; but little feminine mannerisms disclose her sex and show her to be just a healthy, high-spirited young hoyden amusing herself by a masquerade that is harmless enough, though some people may disapprove of it as ultra-tomboyish. What they think does not trouble the Boyette; she wears her boy's suit with a jaunty unselfconsciousness and revels in the freedom of movement it gives her for cycling, golf, and walking. A point of interest to eugenists is that the Boyette has a finer physique than the average boy of her age. One thing that betrays her is that she cannot manage her cigarette like a boy.[19]

This sort of diatribe comes as no surprise from a paper such as the *Daily Mail* in the year before the first fully emancipated election. In terms of fashion and body shape, the flapper was definitely seen as different and not just in Britain. The 'Tables of Size Specifications' of a 1928 guide to American fashions list 'Misses' Regular Sizes, Juniors' Special Sizes, and Flappers' Special Sizes'. Whereas the Misses' size 14 is a shapely 34½, 25, 36 inches, and the Juniors' size 13 is 34, 26, 36 inches, the 'Flappers' size 14 is a more androgynous 33½, 29, 35 in.[20]

Novelist Barbara Cartland classed herself as a flapper in her youth. She noted that in the upper-middle-class circles in which she grew up, before 1914 the term merely meant 'an adolescent who was old enough to wear her hair tied with a large bow at the back'. The war changed this, and in 1919 and 1920 Cartland defined the flapper as 'a high-spirited girl who typified the Modern Miss'.[21] She suggested other more emotional explanations for the changing look of young women:

> The reason my generation bobbed and shingled their hair, flattened their bosoms and lowered their waists, was not that we wanted to be masculine, but that we didn't want to be emotional. War widows, many of them still wearing crepe and widows' weeds in the Victorian tradition, had full bosoms, full skirts and fluffed-out hair. To shingle was to cut loose from the maternal pattern; it was an anti-sentiment symbol, not an anti-feminine one.[22]

Contemporary dress historian Doris Langley Moore also dismissed any lesbian overtones in 'mannish dress'. 'Women have nearly always been supposed to be on the verge of taking to definitely male attire, but they have never done so yet, and it is quite unlikely that they ever will.'[23]

There is little doubt that the nervousness surrounding the popularity of mannish dress was exacerbated by the publicity surrounding a handful of women who publicly took the final step of wearing a tailored man's suit with trousers, shirt, tie and sometimes even a man's hat. Of these, the best known was Radclyffe Hall. Through her classic work of lesbian literature *The Well of Loneliness* (1928), and her public displays of 'mannish' dress, she became infamous during the late 1920s. She was not the only woman to dress in such a masculine style but few did it in such a public way. The impression she left in her wake was that she wore men's full evening dress. In fact, she always wore a black skirt with a striped braid down the side similar to a man's evening suit trouser. Hall wore with it a male dinner jacket, black bow-tie and monocle which did nothing to detract from the masculine impression she wished to give.

The fashion for short hair and masculine clothes provoked outrage in the press, which railed against the 'boyette' look. Nevertheless, some women such as Miss Magee clearly relished the chance to pose in men's clothes. (*National Portrait Gallery*)

Although lesbianism was not technically a crime, there was still a veil of secrecy surrounding lesbian relationships such as those of Vita Sackville-West and Virginia Woolf, which were only known about among an intimate circle of friends. Yet under the cloak of marriage and country living, many lesbian women were no doubt able, as Sackville-West was, to wear menswear such as jodhpurs without drawing undue attention to themselves. Sackville-West remembers the freedom she felt on first wearing such clothes in 1918. 'I had just got clothes like the women-on-the-land were wearing, and in the unaccustomed freedom of breeches and gaiters I went into wild spirits; I ran, I shouted, I jumped, I climbed, vaulted over gates, I felt like a schoolboy let out on a holiday.'[24]

'VARSITY TROUSERS'

The closest male equivalent to the 'flapper' was the male Oxbridge under-graduate. These men also spawned a short-lived fashion that will forever be associated with the 1920s, 'Oxford Bags'. The origins of the trousers are disputed although Harold Acton claims them as his invention in his *Memoirs of an Aesthete*.[25] He remembered that on his arrival at Oxford he

> bought a grey bowler, wore a stock and let my side-whiskers flourish. Instead of the wasp-waisted suits with pagoda shoulders and tight trousers affected by the dandies, I wore jackets with broad lapels and broad pleated trousers. The latter got broader and broader. Eventually they were imitated and were generally referred to as 'Oxford bags'.[26]

Worn by male undergraduates at the country's main universities, they were an extreme example of the influence that wealthy young men with an interest in fashion could have. Although a pair was seen within the Royal Enclosure in the mid-1920s, they were a brief trend that only lasted two years.[27] *Punch* was quick to suggest that the 'trickle-down' effect signalled their demise – in other words once they were adopted by the 'masses', the upper-class elite no longer wanted to wear them. It is more likely that the impracticalities of such a wide trouser sounded their

ANOTHER BLOW FOR OXFORD.

Punch implies that the 'trickle-down' effect signalled the demise of Oxford bags, but it is more likely that the impracticalities of such a wide trouser sounded their death-knell even before the delivery boy started wearing them. (Punch, *22 April 1925 © Punch Ltd*)

death-knell. They did, however, have an influence on men's trouser widths in general, which have never returned to the narrowness of the pre-war period.[28]

By the mid-1930s Oxbridge university students as a group had lost any influence that they might have had on men's fashions. This change in undergraduate clothing habits was part of a wider move away from the more extreme fashions of the 'Bright Young Things' of the mid-1920s and towards the standard leisure clothes of the middle-class man. An item in *The Times* suggested that 'an old pair of flannel trousers and a sports coat seemed to constitute the wardrobe of the undergraduate [in 1935] whereas years ago the young members of the University were regarded as the arbiters of fashion and were invariably well turned out'.[29] A 43-year-old writer from London noted in 1937 that 'so far as I can see the younger set are definitely more careless about clothing, preferring comfort to swank and are, even, too unceremonious. I have not come across the "dandy" or "dude" while, when I was a boy, I knew several fellows who had say forty or fifty neckties.'[30]

There are two key reasons for the disappearance of the 'varsity' youth as a fashion symbol. First, there had been, as occasionally happens, a particularly 'glittering' group of 'aesthetes' at both Oxford and Cambridge during the 1920s, glittering in terms both of their talent and of their dress sense. John Betjeman, writing in 1938, said that these aesthetes had previously been

> easily recognisable for their long hair or odd clothes. With the advent of left-wing politics into modern verse, the aesthete has slightly changed his appearance. He is a little scrubby-looking nowadays; his tie alone flames out. Where in old days he was keen on food and affected an interest in wine, he is now more keen about a good hike or bicycle ride with a friend or a long draught of beer among the workers.[31]

This may well be an exaggeration but just as the spending excesses of the 1980s 'yuppies' were seen as unfashionable and inappropriate after the financial upheavals of the 1990s, so in the 1930s the excesses of the 'Beautiful Young Things' were out of place in a country divided by economic depression. This was coupled with a move towards the acceptability of 'leisurewear' for men in general.

DANDIES

In the 1920s there was at Oxford a clique of young men whose interest in clothes went much further than the 'average' undergraduate's. According to Robert

Graves, several of these 'Beautiful Young Things' were frequently 'punished' for such an interest by the 'hearties', those sporting undergraduates with little interest in anything other than the games field.[32] Graves names no names but this group included Harold Acton and Oliver Messel, who were matched at Cambridge by outrageous dressers like Cecil Beaton and Stephen Tennant. Although their homosexuality was not openly acknowledged, they were known by outsiders to be 'dandy-aesthetes'.

Visions of the dandy-aesthete are probably mostly clearly remembered from the literature which came out of the period. In addition to Waugh's use of his friend Brian Howard as an 'aesthetic' role model, the description of Cedric in Nancy Mitford's *Love in a Cold Climate* is based on Mitford's friend and upper-middle-class eccentric Stephen Tennant's appearance.[33] 'He was a tall, thin young man, supple as a girl, dressed in a rather bright blue suit; his hair was the gold of a brass bed-knob, and his insect appearance came from the fact that the upper part of the face was concealed by blue goggles set in gold rims quite an inch thick.'[34]

Cecil Beaton, seen in his kitchen in 1934, shows he cared little for traditional menswear styling at the time. However, for a homosexual of this period it was only safe to wear more 'outrageous' outfits in one's own home or those of a small circle of trusted friends. (*Hulton Getty*)

Harold Acton, son of an Anglo-Italian father and a wealthy American mother, epitomised the homosexual man who worshipped at the altar of beauty, be it a Renaissance painting or a spotted cravat. Acton had no problem with appearing different from those around him, indeed he took a pride in it. 'The label of aesthete has clung to me since I left school. I am aware of its ludicrous connotations in England, owing to the late Victorian movement which parodied and falsified its meaning. . . . It is undeniable, however, that I love beauty.'[35]

Without the classical background of Acton but with just as keen an interest in beauty, middle-class Cecil Beaton walked a tightrope between permissible eccentricity and outright theatricality during the late 1920s and 1930s. Photographs of him at home in his kitchen show that he cared little for current styling. For a homosexual of this period, it was only safe to wear more 'outrageous' outfits in one's own home and those of a small circle of trusted friends.

Only among the more literary upper classes did the homosexual man find it possible to adopt a more colourful dress code. There was little acceptance lower down the social scale. Middle-class gay men in particular sought 'invisibility' through clothing to avoid any notoriety. This was a situation that did not change significantly until the repeal of the homosexuality laws in 1967.[36]

Unacceptable items of clothing were not always used as sexual signals; they might also indicate possible criminal connections. It was generally supposed that a lower-class man who wore anything other than the accepted standard 'uniform' way of dressing was a person of dubious character. Lower-middle-class men had to be extremely careful what accessories they wore, otherwise they might suffer the double indictment of vulgarity and effeminacy.

Jewellery for men was immediately suspect although a wedding ring (and possibly a signet ring) was permissible.[37] In the upper middle classes a signet ring, usually bearing a family crest, was acceptable for men, while lower down the social scale 'pinkie' rings could be an indicator of homosexuality. Large rings gave the impression that 'the wearer wishes to draw attention to him or herself, or to their wealth or position'.[38] A 22-year-old engineer from south London felt it denoted 'a pansy'.[39]

For a man who was interested in clothes, even the choice of socks, ties and handkerchiefs could provoke accusations of effeminacy. As Noel Coward pointed out to Cecil Beaton in 1930,

Your sleeves are too tight, your voice is too high and too precise. You mustn't do it. It closes so many doors . . . It's hard, I know. One would like to indulge one's own taste. I myself dearly love a good match, yet I know it is overdoing it to wear tie, socks and handkerchief of the same colour. I take ruthless stock of myself in the mirror before going out.[40]

In contrast to the way women were encouraged to co-ordinate their outfits with accessories, for a man to do so was not a good idea. One Mass-Observation respondent, a 26-year-old cost clerk from Newport in Wales, liked to match all his accessories to the colour of his suit although he knew it was 'suspect'. He insisted that he 'most decidedly [didn't] want to look like a band-box. I want to feel comfortable, and to look smart, without being "dressy".'[41] A 34-year-old north London book-keeper noted that the trick was to look 'neat' and in 'good taste' without appearing too expensively or over-dressed, which equated with being seen as being 'pansy-ish'.[42] The problem was, according to Quentin Crisp, that

the men of the twenties search themselves for vestiges of effeminacy as though for lice. They did not worry about their characters but about their hair and their clothes. Their predicament was that they must never be caught worrying about either. I once heard a slightly dandified friend of my brother say, 'People are always accusing me of taking care of my appearance.'[43]

While 'dandyism' was abhorred by the middle classes, it did not always denote homosexuality. The dandy of the 1920s and 1930s was most likely to be a heterosexual displaying an un-British passion for clothes. They were also mostly likely to be 'gentlemen by birth'.[44] Famous examples would be Edward, Prince of Wales, later King Edward VIII, and Conservative MP and baronet's son, Anthony Eden.

Eden's interest in clothes was seen as 'feminine rather than effeminate' and marked him out from his fellow cabinet members who, on the whole, showed a marked indifference to the sartorial elegance of well-groomed clothes. His detractors, including many in his own party, were less kind and it did him few favours in political circles that 'women and haberdashers swooned as he passed'.[45] Among the general public his reputation as something of a dandy could have been seen to border on effeminacy, a trait which would not have endeared him to the average middle-class Englishman. Ultimately, his vanity was seen as a mark of weakness, as demonstrated by the disparaging nicknames his colleagues gave him, including 'Miss England' and 'Robert Taylor', a handsome film star of the time.[46]

A self-confessed lover of fine clothes, Edward VIII was the archetypal dandy, a trait not generally admired among the more staid middle classes. (*Author's Collection*)

In any other man the Prince of Wales's interest in his wardrobe might well have been seen as a mark of effeminacy rather than a boost for British clothing companies. The trade magazines suggest that Edward may have encouraged sales of certain items of menswear by constantly setting the latest fashion styles.[47] However, in reality his appeal to the average middle-class man was limited because his style was just too colourful. Medical researcher's daughter Eileen Elias, who grew up in south-east London, remembers her young brother Aubrey 'particularly admir[ing] the Prince's plus-fours' but in general those around her thought 'he dressed too casually'.[48]

The prince's self-confessed dandyism started when he was at Oxford, he later admitted. 'All my life, hitherto, I had been fretting against the constrictions of dress which reflected my family's world of rigid social convention. It was my impulse, whenever I found myself alone, to remove my coat, rip off my tie, loosen my collar and roll up my sleeves.'[49] However, it was what Edward put on rather than what he took off that led to his reputation as a dandy – a reputation that stayed with him for the rest of his life.

With my father, it was not so much a discussion as to who he considered to be well or badly dressed; it was more usually a diatribe against anyone who

dressed differently from himself. Those who did he called 'cads'. Unfortunately, the 'cads' were the majority of my generation, by the time I grew up, and
I was, of course, one of them. Being my father's eldest son, I bore the brunt of
his criticism.[50]

Reactionary George V may have been but there is no doubt that the Prince of Wales
gave him what he must have felt was acute provocation. The 'majority of [his]
generation' were not wearing the same clothes as the Prince of Wales. Edward's
extreme taste in sportswear in the late 1920s, for example, was definitely not
standard golf-club wear. That many of his outfits were considered too eccentric for
the average British male was later confirmed by the then Duke of Windsor himself.
He was well aware that he was photographed on every occasion with 'an especial
eye' for what he was wearing and for a more adventurous American market.[51]
Edward's obsession with clothes is confirmed by the fact that when writing his
personal memoirs, he devoted a third of the chapters to family opinions on clothes,
clothes he bought, clothes he had had made and all the minutiae of his wardrobe
which most British men would probably still find astounding.[52]

BOHEMIAN STYLE

If there was any continuity in terms of anti-fashion, it was among the Bohemians
of Britain's art world. There was a whole clutch of young artists who basked in
the reflected glory of society figures such as Augustus John and Walter Sickert,
who were both by the 1920s 'grand masters' of the art world. Both were known
for their eccentric dress sense. John was an established and successful portrait
painter hounded by society hostesses.[53] It won him no fans in Romford, however,
where a young student noted that her mother held him up as an example of
decadence: 'just think of it – a red suit, with a green silk scarf, . . . and earrings!'[54]
Sickert, also at the peak of his career, could afford to adapt fashion to his own
style. He was particularly fond of sporting a tailcoat suit in a check more usually
seen in caricatures of bookmakers.[55]

To judge from the cartoons that appear during this period, no society party was
complete without a Bohemian or two on the guest list. The press looked on these
artists as 'pretenders', society hangers-on who used the Bohemian costume as an
entry ticket to Chelsea society. Writer Ethel Mannin, who came from a lower-
middle-class background, describes in her memoirs of the 1920s the group she
mixed in: 'We . . . were young, artistic, unconventional, and in general, what we

" HEARD OF ANYONE CALLED BARCHESTER-CHOLMONDELY-SMYTHE HERE? SWINE WEARS A TIE."

Among the 'Chelsea' set, those who did not join in with the informality of the society art world and its relaxed dress codes were easy targets for ridicule. (Punch, *7 March 1937* © *Punch Ltd*)

liked to called "Bohemian".' She, and many of her friends, belonged to a club in Soho call the Ham Bone Club. Jacob Epstein, the sculptor, was also a member: 'writers, artists, theatrical people paid a guinea-a-year subscription; business men two or three – as was right and proper'.[56]

Punch particularly enjoyed poking fun at society hostesses who accepted all dress codes in order to acquire the obligatory Chelsea artist at their party.[57] A few years later, those who did not join in with the informality of the society art world were also ridiculed.[58] A 1937 *Punch* cartoon of a Chelsea studio party features an angry bearded Bohemian demanding of his *outré* cigarette-smoking, trousered hostess, 'Heard of anyone called Barchester-Cholmondely-Smythe here? Swine wears a tie.'[59]

Outside Chelsea and Fitzrovia the Bohemian style fared less well. Writer Arthur Calder Marshall recalls a poet living in the village of Steyning in West Sussex where he grew up:

To his clothes he paid as little attention as to his person. Although this was a time for plus-fours and beltless sports-coats, the people of Steyning would have accepted the knickerbockers and Norfolk jacket, if he or his wife had made some attempt to patch them up. This was the supreme outrage. The gentry would have accepted a starving poet, living for his art, if he only had washed. They would have pardoned his dirt and tatters, if only he had seemed ashamed of them. But the air of arrogance was more than they could bear.[60]

A 23-year-old shorthand typist from Liverpool was wary of any man who looked as though he might be guilty of 'posing'. 'I know a young man who is an artist, and he persists in wearing his hair long and wearing loud ties, and another fellow who is a photographer, and he affects green velvet trousers.'[61] She did not

THE BRITISH CHARACTER

IMPORTANCE OF NOT BEING INTELLECTUAL

One thing worse than being a foreigner among the British middle classes was being a thinker. His beard and scowl hint at this unwelcome guest's intellectual leanings but his dark, shabby clothes confirm them. (Punch, *6 January 1937 © Punch Ltd*)

approve. A few, like this young male ballet dancer from London, made a conscious decision to dress differently. As he explains, 'my reasons for attending to my appearance are mainly that I like to be noticed and desire to appear superior or unusual'.[62]

However, being an artist was one thing, being an intellectual was quite another. Thinkers were perceived as far more of a threat in less liberal middle-class milieus, as shown by Pont's cartoon, 'Importance of not being intellectual'.[63] Part of Pont's famous 'British Character' series which appeared in *Punch* throughout the 1930s, it pinpointed the middle-class fear of anyone who used their mind. He demonstrated also that there was a perceived way of dressing associated with intellectualism. Mr T., a 24-year-old journalist from Battersea, who owned only brown suits and a dinner jacket, felt if he had been 'asked to wear something which, in [his] opinion, made [him] look immensely intellectual and Left Wing, [he] should probably do it proudly, if self-consciously'.[64] Unfortunately he did not itemise the garments that would have made him look 'immensely intellectual' but cartoons such as Pont's left little doubt as to what was perceived as an intellectual 'uniform' and it usually included a beard and a dark-coloured shirt.

Writers of the period frequently sported tweed jackets, hand-knitted waistcoat vests, checked shirts and a badly knotted tie. This disregard for conventional dressing shows a clear desire to 'advertise' their status as budding authors and intellectuals. Although at first glance carelessness seems a necessary requisite, one aspiring intellectual 22-year-old youth from London admits that there was some conscious calculation in presenting oneself. 'In myself I like to appear well dressed but would prefer to be quietly noticeable than obviously well dressed. On an informal occasion I would rather wear green corduroys than a check lounge suit.'[65]

Right at the peak of the artistic and academic group was what Noel Annan termed the 'intellectual aristocracy' of Britain, a web of families related through work and interest but most importantly through class and marriage.[66] A mixture of artists and writers, these people enjoyed a more genuinely Bohemian lifestyle than the pretend artists of the Chelsea drawing-rooms, albeit they were often supported by family wealth. Yet they are rarely to be seen sporting a beard, a cravat or any of *Punch*'s prerequisites for the caricature Bohemian.

What does distinguish most of this group, which reached far beyond the exclusive Bloomsbury Group, is a distinct lack of interest in the care of their clothes. Particularly in the 1920s, they adopted a far more casual style than was acceptable in the upper-middle-class society from which they came. Many of them coupled this

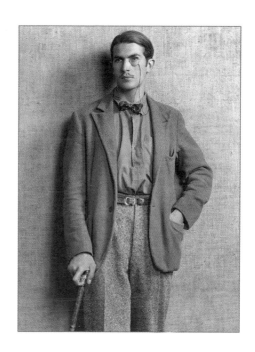

Artist's son R. Briton Riviere proudly wears his coloured shirt and bow-tie with a less than immaculate jacket and trousers, proclaiming his own artistic and intellectual credentials. (*National Portrait Gallery*)

with a total disregard for what were seen as the 'niceties' of the time, such as sharp creases in the trouser leg and daily clean collars. Virginia Nicholson affectionately described the daily dress of her father, potter Quentin Bell, son of Bloomsbury artist Vanessa Bell, who had dressed in a similar way since his youth in the 1920s:

> His checked trousers, carelessly fastened, his shabby clay-covered jerseys, their sleeves unravelling and burnt in places by dropping ash from his pipe . . . his cheerful ties donned with a blithe disregard for their state of cleanliness or harmony with whatever frayed shirt he had put on that morning, his comfortable old slip-on sandals, his unkempt beard – all betray the Bohemian artist that, in his sympathies, he felt himself to be.[67]

The women among this 'intellectual aristocracy' follow one of two paths. Those involved in the visual arts stand out as having had no apparent interest in contemporary fashions. In wearing versions of the 'artistic' dress of the turn of the century, there is something curiously 'old-fashioned' about the style of these women. By the 1930s they would have been considered middle-aged or 'matronly' in any other social group, yet women frequently stay with a style that they adopted when they were young. Gwen Raverat, granddaughter of Charles

Darwin, and at the heart of Noel Annan's 'intellectual aristocracy', refused ever to wear a bra and was so uninterested in fashion that she reputedly wore one dress all winter and another in the summer.[68]

Nevertheless, there is a hidden message here that shows that 'fashion', or developments in the commercial world of dress, had little effect on what these women wore. This was different from the attitude of women such as arts society hostess Lady Ottoline Morrell and poet Edith Sitwell.[69] These women were also not in the least bit interested in mainstream fashion but instead developed striking individual styles, which took account of their unconventional physical looks. Sitwell, in particular, made a conscious decision, encouraged by her brother, to reject 'fashion' in order to create a visual artistic persona.[70] However, this required a confidence in one's class, talent and, in particular, sexuality that hardly any women possessed. More artistic women in the middle classes would have empathised with the sentiments of Miss G., a commercial artist from the home counties, who was happy for her clothes 'to be amusing, and not go on for ever, and I don't like to choose a colour just because it is serviceable'.[71]

'BRIGHTER COLOURS IN MEN'S FASHIONS'

So-called Bohemian fashions were endemic among the artistic communities of Chelsea and Fitzrovia, several of which were involved in the Men's Dress Reform Party. The party attempted to extend many of the Bohemian ideals of late nineteenth-century aesthetic dress for men, such as loose, open-necked shirts, on the grounds that they were healthier than stiff collars and three-piece suits. In addition, they tried to encourage the wearing of shorts for everyday wear, including office work. However, the party overlooked one of the key factors in men's choice of clothes which was the dignity that they could confer – a vital consideration to the aspiring middle-class solicitor or banker.[72] Shorts were hardly acceptable on the tennis court so on the High Street they could make you a laughing-stock.[73] Mr B., a 20-year-old student, admitted that 'whenever possible I wear an open-necked shirt, shorts and sandals'. He would have preferred 'a little more colour' but did not want 'to walk about like a carnival exhibit'.[74]

The Men's Dress Reform Party was not the first to try to change men's attitudes to the way they dressed in the twentieth century.[75] There had been an earlier attempt at men's dress reform in 1920. It was started by Mr Harry Parkes, who is reported in the menswear press to have held public meetings calling for 'Brighter Colours in Men's Fashions'.

The latest advocate of dress reform seems to think that we want to get more life and colour into our garments in order to 'shed the sunshine of gladness upon a shell-shocked world.'. . . Mr. Parkes hopes to enlist the aid of some thousands of young sportsmen – 'clean-living sportsmen and gentlemen' he insists – to carry the leaven of reform among us so that 'we shall quietly exchange our drabness for a world of colour and sunshine'.[76]

Mr Parkes was ahead of his time but by 1927 fashion had made the changes for him, with the men's fashion press acknowledging the 'Bolder Colours [Now] Preferred' in coloured shirts. 'This change in shirt fashions', *Men's Wear* admitted with an element of exaggeration, 'is one of the most remarkable developments which have ever taken place in the trade.'[77] Sculptor Eric Gill would have agreed. In a short work published in 1931, he outlined his own views on dress reform: 'The idea that women should be "beautiful" and men have "character", the idea that beauty is effeminate and colour in men's clothes a sign of decadence – all these things are the nearest thing to complete nonsense.'[78] Eight years later such changes were only just becoming acceptable among the lower middle class who, as these comments by a 22-year-old bank clerk from Wiltshire show, were reluctant to adopt a fashion trend until it was in common use: 'I do not invariably wear a white collar, but have a good few coloured shirts with collars to match . . . it only came about because I happened to notice other people wearing coloured collars.'[79]

One campaign to hijack coloured shirts for political ends did damage the reputation of the coloured shirt well into the end of the twentieth century. Oswald Mosley, originator of the British Union of Fascists, introduced the uniform of a black shirt to his organisation as a symbol of fascism, of authority and significantly, he thought, of classlessness. 'In the Blackshirt,' Mosley later wrote, 'all men are the same, whether millionaire or on the dole.'[80] Its failure was later acknowledged by Mosley who realised that the overt military appearance of the shirt was a mistake. It certainly contributed to the banning of paramilitary uniforms by a Public Order Act in 1936.

Mosley later claimed that the black shirt on its own would have been preferable.[81] This is confirmed by its initial popular appeal. When Lord Rothermere, owner of the *Daily Mail*, urged support for Mosley at the outset of his campaign, journalists working on the paper happily wore black shirts to work since they were 'a fashionable thing'.[82] However, their popularity soon diminished as the implications of Mosley's manifesto became clear. As the *Mail*'s news editor put it, 'the black shirts are in the wash and the colour is running very fast'.[83]

With shorts for men strictly for the beach or countryside rambles, it is little wonder that this supporter of the Men's Dress Reform Party won few converts on his stroll down London's Strand in July 1930. (*Hulton Getty*)

Mosley had his own image problems. A socialite in the 1920s and later an MP, he was seen as 'a perpetual affront to conventional politicians – the overwhelming majority', and condemned by 'his unparliamentary good looks suggestive of the dark passionate, Byronic gentleman-villain of the melodrama'.[84] Although it was acceptable for film stars to have such looks, government stalwarts should not. 'The real trouble with Sir Oswald Mosley,' wrote MP Ellen Wilkinson, was that he had the 'sort of good looks that are a positive disadvantage to a man . . . he looks so like a cinema sheik'.[85]

It is difficult to assess the feelings of Mosley's followers towards their 'uniform'. Other small political group leaders such as Major C.H. Douglas of the Social Credit Party, forerunner of the Green Party, and James Maxton of the Independent Labour Party had tried briefly to use colour to mark out their supporters, Douglas, not surprisingly, with green shirts, Maxton with red. Despite its gradual insinuation into fashionable circles, such blatant use of colour was still unacceptable. By the 1930s, particularly after the banning of paramilitary uniforms, the red tie of the socialists was mostly worn only at weekends, supporters being concerned lest they prejudiced their employment chances.[86]

There is no doubt that any coloured items were worn with conscious forethought at all times. When Labour MP John Parker was seeking election in the staunchly socialist area of east London, he deliberately wore an open-necked red shirt for a social outing in the summer of 1935 and remembers his outfit 'was a great success!'[87] *Punch*, as usual, saw the humour of such gestures, and featured a cartoon of a girl questioning the taste of her young man. 'But darling, you've chosen a reddish tie. Do you really like that?' To which he replies, 'Not particularly, but I'm terribly pleased with the way the Government is behaving.'[88]

While the obvious association to be made with socialism and the colour red is through the 'red flag' of communism, there is another more obscure clothing connection with politics. The black polo-neck sweater was an item of menswear that by the end of the 1930s was becoming increasingly identifiable with left-wing politics. Yet again, here was a seemingly innocent piece of knitwear that was associated with homosexuals. '[They] were abandoned by normal men shortly after they had been introduced, simply because they were seen on many who were known to be unmanly,' wrote Doris Langley Moore in 1929.[89] This was confirmed by Noel Coward, who pointed out to Cecil Beaton in 1930 that 'a polo jumper . . . exposes one to danger'.[90] Nevertheless, many left-wingers, less concerned with public opinion than those in mainstream politics, were happy to be seen wearing them at least in a leisure environment.

On the whole there was almost an obligation on the most left-wing supporters to proclaim their politics through their dress. Mr G. stated that 'as a proud member of the Communist Party of G.B.,' he felt, 'shame in admitting that I am definitely conservative in matters of male fashion'.[91] A disdain for sartorial elegance was thought to be a key requisite for showing one's left-wing qualifications. This meant that anyone with the look of a left-winger might be labelled as such. George Orwell quotes the dismissive aside of a commercial traveller on a bus in Letchworth to two elderly men in tight khaki shorts – 'Socialists'!'[92] Class was not so easy to disguise, however, as Orwell noted of the old Etonian communist who 'would [have been] ready to die on the barricades, in theory anyway, but you notice that he still [left] his bottom waistcoat button undone'.[93]

Conclusion

This book opened with a quotation from Rose Macaulay's novel of 1928, *Keeping Up Appearances*. In it, Macaulay's heroine Daisy wonders if she will ever be able to play the game of living sartorially, 'a complex and many-changing business . . . at it from morning until night, in order not to risk being caught in the wrong clothes'.[1] The middle classes were particularly anxious about the social stigma that might attach to them if they did not follow the dictates of interwar dress code. The analysis of those who did break the rules gives some indication of the price to be paid, from mild social embarrassment to ostracisation by family and friends.

The concept of image is a modern one, but presentation of self through clothes is age-old. The dress codes of a particular era have always illuminated the social anxieties and cultural divisions within that society. Although class divisions appeared to be as strong as ever in interwar England, the level of anxiety shown about dress codes reflects a more general insecurity felt by a country still deeply shocked by a devastating world war and concerned about high unemployment and world events. If the middle classes felt that they had no control over these wider issues, it gave them some reassurance to feel that they did have control over the minor details.

Self-judgement is a vital key to class definition. A man might consider himself to have achieved upper-middle-class status by education or occupation but being seen wearing braces in the garden told another story to his neighbours. Middle-class society in the interwar years was increasingly self-monitoring in a way that previous eras were not. Golf clubs, tennis clubs, Rotary clubs – all involved forms of selection to weed out undesirables. 'Old Boys' organisations had done this since childhood. These organisations grew and thrived during the interwar period so that by 1939 they were part of the fabric of middle-class identity.

Given the porous nature of the middle classes, there were inevitably overlaps, families elevated by education or marriage, or lowered by finances. Anxiety about the rules of etiquette and dress codes was especially marked among the lower-middle classes. Whereas the upper-middle classes saw such rules as part of their everyday lives, the lower-middle classes, less socially confident, were always concerned to be seen to do what was 'correct'. The key matter of social anxiety was less obvious among the working and upper classes than within the middle classes.

In any discussion about the styles of the 1920s and 1930s questions are inevitably asked about differences before and after the First World War. Class divisions were highly visible during the Edwardian and previous periods. Therefore, it is not a new story that emerges in the 1920s and 1930s but rather one of change and growing uncertainty. In the early 1920s attitudes were surprisingly relaxed about the variety of clothing that could be worn by a man for work. Yet by the end of the 1930s there was a uniformity among men that paints a dull picture in comparison. This reflected both changing fashions and fears about job insecurity. While they were willing to embrace the changes brought about by improved housing and some consumer durables, the middle classes were steadfastly reactionary in their attitudes to dress correctness.

The steady flow of mass-produced goods, particularly of men's suits and women's frocks in the 1930s, made a variety of clothes more readily available both to the lower-middle and working classes. The upper-middle and upper classes remained largely untouched by mass production because they had financial access to high-quality merchandise and custom-made clothes. They could clearly be distinguished from the lower classes. In contrast, the middle classes were unsettled by a new world in which, according to the press, every man could look good in a 'fifty-shilling' suit or a woman in a 'guinea' gown.

The burgeoning new tailoring businesses, far from encouraging individuality, ironically appear to have spawned an anonymous uniformity across the classes that was much less apparent before the First World War. One must not overstate the monotony of men's fashions, however: for younger men in particular there could be a touch of modernity about, say, the cut of a ready-made suit which distinguished its wearer.

While middle-class women supposedly had more choice in what they were able to wear for work, they were still subject to constraints of modesty and decorum. The story is one of stability but nevertheless reflects the increased number of women working since before the First World War, even given the restrictions of the various marriage bars. Overall, however, from the female MP to the teacher, sobriety was recommended and in general adhered to. Yet lower down the social and employment scale, girls were also expected to be ornamental. Terms such as 'shabby', 'garish' and 'ill-dressed', in contrast to 'trim', 'spruce' and 'neat', spotlight the difficult balancing act that young women in particular had to cope with in offsetting fashion desires against office decorum.

Most middle-class men trod an even more traditional path. They appeared to accept the monotony of the clothes they wore for work. Within the lower middle-classes men saw this as the accepted price for job security. This attitude even increases in the 1930s leaving the workplace untouched by the spirit of 'modernity' encouraged by some retailers. Those professionals who dealt with the public, such as doctors, solicitors and bank managers, used their dress to maintain respect for themselves from their clients/patients and to distinguish themselves from the lesser levels of the professions.

Rules about clothes were rarely necessary within organisations since peer and superiors' approval or rather disapproval was enough of a controlling factor. Those who worked for themselves, from the entrepreneur down to the small shopkeeper, were able to be more relaxed about their codes of dress. Older men were the most reluctant to make any changes to their working wardrobes. As Flugel pointed out, men's office clothing allowed few outlets for personal vanity among men.[2]

There were also many ambiguities and contradictions regarding dress within the home. While men could wear leisurewear around the house if they chose to do so, especially at weekends, lower-middle-class women in particular often saw the clothes they wore in their homes as 'workwear', a reflection of the increased emphasis on all things domestic (though such work was not valued as unpaid employment).

Whereas men were allowed a degree of relaxation within their own homes, women felt they were constantly on show once the front door was open. Any form of socialising even with neighbours required high standards of respectable dress. Cosmetics were a rare instance where something became an accepted part of the contemporary dress codes so relatively quickly that to do without powder and lipstick by 1939 was as much of a 'poor show' as to use it at all in the 1920s.

Individuality was not admired. Overt interest in clothes by men was construed as a sign of homosexuality, still a criminal offence. Women were less readily condemned for an interest in fashion, indeed, businesses such as magazine publishing and retailing thrived during this period on encouraging such 'frivolity'. Yet even fashion-conscious middle-class women were nervous of embracing the new, particularly in the workplace and domestic space. Only away from the home, during leisure activities or on holiday, did young middle-class women feel relaxed enough to wear newer more emancipated fashions such as shorts and trousers.

Towards the end of the 1930s there is a growing contrast between the attitudes of young adults in their late teens and early twenties and those of their middle-aged parents. A 23-year-old young man from Chelmsford complains that 'the older generations' [sic] idea of being well-dressed is one of conformity – neatness and tidiness in an accepted style'.[3] Here the conflict between tradition and modernity is at its most potent, as an 18-year-old boy from Leicester explained: 'They not only want to dress well themselves, but since I'm of their family, they expect me to. Which I object to . . . and I really don't want to. But they insist that in their seeing I should be what they call respectable – the whole thing is based on a class consciousness of what people will think.'[4]

Young men such as these liked to think that they were more adventurous than their fathers by not wearing a hat or a stiff collar, or by preferring a sports jacket and open-necked shirt to a formal suit. These may appear today to be minor alterations but at a time when dress codes were so rigid even small deviations were significant. The slow speed of adoption of more informal leisurewear by younger men indicates that the influence of American movie images of a more casual glamour was limited.

In contrast, there were significant differences in the attitude towards leisure clothes between those who grew up before the First World War and those after. The older generation were the most reluctant to alter their way of dressing to suit either fashion or place. Tradition came before comfort, with a marked reluctance towards change. There was a resistance towards anything too 'new', together with a clinging to the reassurance of the familiar.

Young women also showed generational differences. For a young nurse from Cheshire 'smartness' was more important than the 'neatness' that ruled her mother's wardrobe.[5] It was not until the 1960s that adult and youth styles clashed head-on but the seeds were there even before the Second World War.

There was a clear correlation between the popularity of certain sports and leisure activities and the development of leisurewear for both men and women. Role models from sports such as tennis influenced changes in everyday fashion styles especially for women. Group activities such as hiking encouraged the wearing of shorts and shirts previously only seen on the sports field.

By 1939 the younger generations among the middle classes were enjoying the availability of a wider range of leisure clothes. Holidays in particular were a time when younger men and women felt able to relax in 'free-and-easy garb'. A 24-year-old journalist from London summed up the situation by describing his parents' attitude to clothes:

> They wouldn't dare to be seen anywhere in shorts, open-neck shirts, bathing trunks or any sensible garment of pleasant bright colour. They must stick to their drab colours whatever the occasion and put on plenty of good woollen underclothes. They may look respectable, but they would look much nicer if they were decently comfortable.[6]

Nevertheless, getting leisure clothes right was important whatever the age of the wearer. The middle-class young were often keen to try out more colour and adopt the 'sporting look' exhibited on the cinema screen by glamorous American film stars radiating health, beauty and modernity. However, there was still the constraint of respectability holding them back from anything 'vulgar'.

Older middle-class women were more reactionary in their attitudes to changing leisure fashions. As for men, comfort and tradition were paramount and modesty and respectability reigned supreme. As in other areas of dress, the middle classes were the last to embrace new fashions, insisting on maintaining codes of decorum even when their toes were touching the sea.

Working-class girls made no secret of the effect of their screen heroines on their dress desires. In contrast, middle-class women were still more influenced by Paris and royalty than by movie stars. The evidence is that they too were interested in fashion but were constrained by the desire for respectability. Women from the upper classes could indulge in fashion to a far greater extent because of their higher incomes as well as their greater self-confidence. But however many or few outfits a middle-class woman might own, she had to be careful about the purchase of every item.

Far from being a simple choice of one suit versus another, or whether to acquire a pretty frock, the choice of 'dress clothes' during the interwar period was particularly fraught with social nuances. This diminished some of the supposed pleasure in social events for the wearers. Whereas working-class young adults felt dancing gave them a sense of freedom and glamour, few middle-class men admitted to being at ease in whatever version of the dress clothes uniform they had to wear.

For men the 1930s in particular were not a time for experimentation, but rather of just getting things right, not taking any risks and most importantly not standing out. Dress clothes were a necessary evil that they were nevertheless reluctant to discard. They grudgingly bore the expense involved in kitting themselves out with 'dress clothes' following the ritual of formalities lest they be considered an outsider. This attitude hardly varied among men from one end of Britain to the other. The average middle-class Englishman was quite happy to leave the immaculate image of evening glamour to screen dance heroes such as Astaire and Buchanan.

For women the choices were more complex. Female evening wear has always been a 'high-fashion' area where economy tends to be ignored in an attempt to be seen to be up-to-date. In addition, there was pleasure in the colours and textures of the luxury fabrics used for evening dresses. In contrast to men, women did want to stand out in a way that showed that they were economically secure enough to be fashionable without being vulgar. It says a great deal for the British vision of glamour that by the end of the 1930s the actresses Jessie Matthews and Anna Neagle were the closest Britain had to screen sirens with their girl-next-door version of glamour complete with frothy dresses and fluffy hair.[7]

However much she enjoyed dressing up, the English middle-class woman never looked completely relaxed with such a display of ostentatious luxury as her American or continental counterparts. This was only in part because evening wear was an expensive luxury. While young working-class girls looked to Hollywood for guidance, middle-class women still drew their inspiration from the solid sensible evening wear worn by their queen. It was certainly true that 'make-up, cinema and dance halls were not part of a middle-class culture *before* they were used by working-class girls and boys'.[8]

In response to the growth of mass-produced suits and frocks, middle-class men and women looked for other ways to define themselves in terms of visible self-presentation. They turned increasingly to smaller items of clothing such as ties, hats and gloves as signifiers of status. The stripe of a tie, the cleanliness of a pair of white gloves, the lift of a hat, had less to do with money than with 'correctness'. They took these details to new extremes, not of fashion, which had happened more colourfully in the past, but of social significance.

There were various accessories that were crucial to a person's overall appearance and the persona he or she wanted to present. One ill-chosen piece could make or break an outfit. They were the keys to correctness and clues to class distinction. A club tie could say a great deal about a man's position in society regardless of whether or not his suit had come from Savile Row. Similarly if a woman's shoes were down at heel, it would matter little which shop they had come from originally.

Almost all groups within the middle classes are united in enforcing rigid codes of behaviour, however unwillingly. These are not the codes of the high Edwardian period, however. By the 1930s the subtlety of the striped tie had replaced the flashiness of the silk cravat and brought such symbols of status within the reach of a far wider social network.

What these items, hats, gloves, and ties in particular, gave the middle classes was a feeling of security. They stand out as emblems of the conformity of this period. A middle-class professional man could feel safe wearing his old school tie knowing there was no risk of offending anyone with an unsuitable pattern which might be thought 'flashy' or 'effeminate'. There was the added bonus that he might even impress a colleague or acquaintance with such a tie. Ever anxious to maintain a respectable exterior, a man chose his hat as an essential tool of social discourse and only rarely a fashion item. It helped him maintain a barrier not only from the rain but also from those he did not wish to acknowledge.

The reverence in which certain items are held belies the rise of informality in the 1930s. They are the symbols of the formality of dress and etiquette. Yet they were being gradually eroded by a younger, slightly more adventurous generation. If an item such as a hat has to be worn to satisfy social standards, there will always be those who rebel against such strictures. The growing number of young within the 'hatless' brigade shows that this symbol of middle-class respectability was being threatened, perhaps anticipating the 'youth' revolution in clothing of the 1960s.

The vogue for 'hatlessness' was seen as an insidious rebellion. Without a hat, a man could no longer follow the complicated canons of hat etiquette, which was increasingly being seen as antiquated. Just as the non-conformists of the eighteenth century rejected hats, so young men in the interwar years were able to extricate themselves from the complications of hat lore. This trend began much earlier than had previously been thought.

For the middle-class woman, accessories were a way of presenting a respectable yet fashionable front. It was often a nuisance to have to squash one's hair by wearing a hat, an economic strain to have well-heeled shoes and an effort to have not just a pair but also a clean pair of gloves. Yet most women felt it was a small price to pay for the seal of respectability and would have been horrified to have done without them. Young women were for the most part happy to wear hats in particular, since a new hat was still a relatively cheap way of enlivening an outfit.

The two interwar decades show a hardening in attitudes towards anything out of the norm. The vocabulary of the period could be damning. Words such as 'pansy', 'effeminate', 'mannish', 'vulgar' and 'band-box' immediately classified the wearer according to his or her sexuality and class. Such words rarely appeared in the tailoring and women's magazines eager to promote mainstream fashions but to judge from the comments of the Mass-Observation respondents were in regular use in conversation when making judgemental statements about others.

There is a marked contrast between the sexes in terms of those who stood out from the crowd, particularly in the 1930s. There was no female upper-class equivalent to the dandy or the aesthete, other than a handful of well-known individuals. When the vogue for 'mannish' fashions disappeared in the early 1930s, the only female rebels were those few women who were part of the Bohemian art scene. For men, however, it was different. When the smallest of dress items could cause comment – 'noticeable tiepins, buttonholes, any handker-chiefs showing in pocket near lapel'[9] – to wear a whole outfit that went fully against the norm was asking for attention.

The political scene was so tense by the 1930s that clothing colours took on new, more sinister meanings and Mosley's influence banished the black shirt as a fashion item until well into the second half of the twentieth century. Left-wing intellectuals, too, became more marginalised as they moved away from the artistic Bohemian style of dress towards a version of the standardised male dress, recognisable still but subtly different. While most claimed to have no interest in clothes, there was a statement to be made and the corduroy suit made it.

Middle-class men and women who mixed with the upper classes, especially in Bohemian society, found that, not surprisingly, the true aristocracy had a unique social confidence. This allowed more freedom and relaxation in their attitude to dress if they so chose than would have been considered permissible among, say, the middle-class members of the Stourbridge Rotary Club, conscious of their hard-won status within the local community. Similarly, while many working-class men and women took a pride in displaying long-saved-for 'Sunday best' outfits, this was increasingly looked down upon by a middle class who felt themselves to be above such pretensions.

Similarly, what was acceptable in a high-society drawing-room in Chelsea would have been looked at askance in a suburban living-room in Stockport. Many of the upper classes were more relaxed in their attitudes towards those who preferred to dress on the margins of fashion. In experimenting with dress, Bohemians, dandies and aesthetes were all pushing fashion to its limits. If these men and women happened to come from the middle classes, as did Cecil Beaton and Noel Coward for example, they found far more acceptance away from the class they were brought up in and among those who were more secure in their social groups. Beaton confessed that he became detached from his parents as his success grew and was ashamed of their 'suburban' connections when they fell on hard times. 'How remote I was now from the struggling middle-class family,' he admitted.[10] Estrangement was often the price to be paid for non-conformity.

Degrees of formality differed depending on space and context. Areas of work, home, leisure and formal entertainment all demanded their own sets of rules for both men and women. London was not just the fashion centre of England but also a place where one dressed appropriately to visit. There were regional differences as well as a town and country divide. Public spaces, whether in cities or suburbs, golf courses or tearooms, theatres or the workplace, all called for clearly defined dress codes for both men and women. There is even a definite feeling that a shopping expedition outside one's neighbourhood involved a degree of 'dressing up'.

Clothes as material items have many roles to play. They serve not just as body coverers but also as signifiers of gender and sexuality, taste and cultural differences. The middle classes saw themselves as guardians of respectability in interwar England. 'Correct' clothing acted in much the same way as a uniform and gave the security of belonging to the wearer. This was memorably summed up by the Yorkshire housewife who felt self-conscious unless she was dressed 'suitably for the occasion': 'When I know I look "right" I can forget myself.'[11] Without a thorough knowledge of the dress codes of the time, that was a luxury few could – or would – afford.

Notes

Introduction

1. R. Macaulay, *Keeping Up Appearances* (Collins, 1928, repr. Methuen, 1986), p. 63.
2. R. Cutforth, *Later Than We Thought. A Portrait of The Thirties* (Newton Abbot, David & Charles, 1976), pp. 34–7.
3. M.-O. A., D.R. 1211 reply to June 1939 directive.
4. T. Jeffery, 'A Place in the Nation: The Lower Middle Class in England', in R. Koshar (ed.), *Splintered classes. Politics and the lower middle classes in interwar Europe* (New York, Holmes & Meier, 1990), p. 71.
5. C. White, *Women's Magazines 1693–1968* (Michael Joseph, 1978), p. 117.
6. R. Lewis and A. Maude, *The English Middle Classes* (Phoenix, 1949), p. 13.
7. H. Perkin, *The Rise of Professional Society. England since 1880* (Routledge, 1989, repr. 2002), p. 96.
8. R. Samuel, 'The middle class between the wars: part three', *New Socialist*, May/June 1983, p. 29.
9. A. Jackson, *The Middle Class 1900–1945* (Nairn, David St John Thomas, 1991), p. 12.
10. R. Samuel, 'The middle class between the wars: part one' (*New Socialist* Jan/Feb 1983), p. 30.
11. Lewis and Maude, *English Middle Classes*, p. 20.
12. D.H. Aldcroft, *The Inter-war Economy: Britain 1919–1939* (Batsford, 1973), p. 352.
13. J.B. Priestley, *English Journey* (Heinemann, 1934; repr. Mandarin, 1996); R. Graves and A. Hodge, *The Long Weekend* (Faber & Faber, 1940, repr. Abacus, 1995).
14. Priestley, *English Journey*, pp. 4–5.
15. A.M. Carr-Saunders, and D. Caradog Jones, *A survey of the social structure of England and Wales, as illustrated by statistics* (Oxford, Clarendon Press, 1938), p. 62.
16. J. Laver, *Taste and Fashion* (Harrap, 1931, repr. 1945), p. 104.
17. E. Wilson, *Adorned in Dreams. Fashion and Modernity* (Berkeley, University of California Press, 1985), p. 160.
18. Samuel, 'The middle class: part three', p. 29.
19. Samuel, 'The middle class: part three', p. 29.
20. Wilson, *Adorned in Dreams*, pp. 149–50.
21. C. Breward, *The Culture of Fashion. A new history of fashionable dress* (Manchester, Manchester University Press), p. 183.

22. A. de la Haye, 'The Dissemination of Design from Haute Couture to Fashionable Ready-to-wear during the 1920s', *Textile History* 24, 1 (1993), pp. 40–2.

23. A. Holdsworth, *Out of the Doll's House: The Story of Women in the Twentieth Century* (BBC Books, 1988), p. 159.

24. T. Polhemus and L. Procter, *Fashion & anti-fashion: an anthropology of clothing and adornment* (Thames & Hudson, 1978), p. 69.

25. I. Goffman, *The Presentation of Self in Everyday Life* (Penguin, 1959, repr. 1990), p. 28.

26. *Daily Mail*, 8 February 1936.

27. Quoted in A. Ribeiro, *Dress and Morality* (Batsford, 1986), p. 159.

28. J.M. Heimann, *The Most Offending Soul Alive. Tom Harrisson and his Remarkable Life* (Honolulu, University of Hawaii Press, 1999, repr. Aurum, 2002), p. 129.

29. D. Bloome et al., *Reading Mass-Observation Writing. Theoretical and Methodological Issues in Researching the Mass-Observation Archive* (Brighton, University of Sussex Library, 1993), p. 3.

30. C. Horwood, '"Keeping Up Appearances": Clothes, Class and Culture, 1918–1939', Ph.D., Royal Holloway, University of London (2003).

31. G.B. Shaw, *Man and Superman* (Constable, 1903), p. 325.

1. *Shopping for Status*

1. *Vogue*, January 1931, p. 53.

2. L.E. Neal, *Retailing and the Public* (Allen & Unwin, 1933).

3. J.B. Jefferys, *Retail Trading in Britain 1850–1950* (Cambridge, Cambridge University Press), p. 61.

4. Jefferys, *Retail Trading*, p. 62.

5. Neal, *Retailing*, pp. 43 and 47.

6. Jefferys, *Retail Trading*, p. 78.

7. Jefferys, *Retail Trading*, p. 329.

8. M. Corina, *Fine Silks and Oak Counters. Debenhams 1778–1978* (Hutchinson Benham, 1978), p. 111.

9. Corina, *Fine Silks*, p. 121.

10. History of Advertising Trust/SEL/813.

11. D. Wainwright, *The British Tradition. Simpson – a World of Style* (Quiller Press, 1996), p. 30.

12. B. Lancaster, *The Department Store. A Social History* (Leicester University Press), p. 102; Corina, *Fine Silks*, p. 117.

13. E. Whiteing, *Anyone for Tennis?' Growing up in Wallington between the wars* (Sutton, Sutton Libraries, 1979), p. 35.

14. History of Advertising Trust/SEL/1223.

15. Neal, *Retailing*, p. 23.

16. Whiteing, *Anyone for Tennis?*, p. 30.

17. History of Advertising Trust/SEL/322/1933.

18. John Lewis Partnership Archive, 18, memo dated 2 September 1932.

19. John Lewis Paterniship Archive, 118, memo dated 6 June 1932.

20. Lancaster, *Department Store*, p. 86.

21. Neal, *Retailing*, p. 12.

22. History of Advertising Trust/CA/1/3.

23. History of Advertising Trust/CA/1/4; History of Advertising Trust/CA/1/3.

24. History of Advertising Trust/CA/1/4; History of Advertising Trust/CA/1/3.

25. History of Advertising Trust/CA/1/9; History of Advertising Trust/CA/1/16.

26. *The Statistical Review of Press Advertising*, II, 2, January 1934, pp. 118–19; IV, 1, October 1935, p. 139.

27. Lancaster, *Department Store*, p. 90.

28. D.W. Peel, *A Garden In The Sky. The Story of Barkers of Kensington 1870–1957* (W.H. Allen, 1960), p. 80.

29. A. Adburgham, *Shops and Shopping 1800–1914. Where, and in What Manner the Well-dressed Englishwoman Bought her Clothes* (George Allen & Unwin, 1964), pp. 281–2.

30. Interview with Mrs J.B.

31. Oxfordshire County Record Office, B7/N/9.

32. J. Benson, *The Rise of Consumer Society in Britain 1880–1980* (Longman, 1994), pp. 206–7.

33. W. Bland, 'Fashion for Pleasure', *Costume* 12 (1978), p. 95.

34. L. Goldman, *Oh What a Lovely Shore! Brighton in the Twenties through the Eyes of a Schoolboy* (Brighton, L. Goldman, 1999), p. 98.

35. Whiteing, *Anyone for Tennis*, pp. 37–8.

36. Oxfordshire County Record Office, B17/c/1.

37. Interview with Mrs T.R.

38. A. Wise, 'Dressmaking in Worthing', *Costume* 32 (1998), p. 82.

39. Lewes U3A Oral History Group, *Lewes Remembers Shops and Shopping* (Lewes, Lewes U3A Publications, 1999), p. 54.

40. Jefferys, *Retail Trade*, p. 334.

41. Wise, 'Dressmaking', p. 84.

42. Goldman, *Oh What a Lovely Shore!*, p. 37.

43. D. Whipple, *High Wages* (John Murray, 1930, repr. New York, Harmondsworth, 1946).

44. Whipple, *High Wages*, pp. 115–16.

45. E. Newby, *Something Wholesale. My Life and Times in the Rag Trade* (Secker & Warburg, 1962, repr. Picador, 1985).

46. Newby, *Something Wholesale*, p. 171.

47. H. Levy, *The Shops of Britain* (Kegan Paul, Trench, Trubner & Co., 1947), p. 84.

48. Goldman, *Oh What a Lovely Shore!*, p. 101.

49. C. Langhamer, *Women's leisure in England 1920–1960* (Manchester, Manchester University Press, 2000), p. 40.

50. M.-O. A., D.R. 1559 reply to April 1939 directive.

51. M.-O. A., T.C. 18/2/F.

52. M.-O. A., D.R. 1077 reply to May 1939 directive.

53. L. Goldman, *Brighton Beach to Bengal Bay* (Brighton, L. Goldman, 1999), p. 35.

54. J. Wayne, *The Purple Dress: growing up in the thirties* (Gollancz, 1979), p. 42.

55. Goldman, *Oh What a Lovely Shore!*, p. 103.

56. M.-O. A., D.R. 1032 reply to May 1939 directive.

57. Royal Holloway, University of London, Bedford Centre for the History of Women Archive RHC RF131/7, M. Pike, *Social Life at Royal Holloway College 1887–1939*, Part II, p. 212.

58. M.-O. A., D.R. 1559 reply to April 1939 directive.

59. Interview with Mrs E.E.

60. M.-O. A., D.R. 1289 reply to June 1939 directive.

61. White, *Women's Magazines*, pp. 94–5.

62. Mass-Observation, *Browns of Chester. Portrait of a Shop 1780–1946* (Lindsay Drummond, 1947), p. 200.

63. Aldcroft, *Inter-War Economy*, p. 352.
64. P. Massey, 'The expenditure of 1,360 British middle-class households in 1938–39', *Journal of the Royal Statistical Society*, CV, part 3 (1942), pp. 159–85.
65. Massey, 'Expenditure', pp. 159–85.
66. K. Bill, 'Clothing Expenditure by a Woman in the Early 1920s', *Costume*, 21 (1993), pp. 57–8.
67. E.M. Delafield, *The Diary of a Provincial Lady* (1930, repr. Virago, 1985), pp. 9–10.
68. J. Robson, 'The role of clothing and fashion in the household budget and popular culture, Britain, 1919–1949', D.Phil. Oxford (1998), pp. 97–8.
69. *The Lady*, 2 January 1936, p. 35.
70. *The Lady*, 9 January 1936, p. 72.
71. *The Lady*, 9 July 1936, p. 93.
72. *The Lady*, 19 March 1936, p. 490.
73. *The Lady*, 3 July 1913, p. 50.
74. *The Lady*, 30 January 1919, p. 111.
75. *The Lady*, 1 October 1925, Supplement, p. VI.
76. *The Lady*, 7 February 1939, Supplement, p. III.
77. *The Lady*, 9 March 1939, Supplement, p. II.
78. *The Lady*, 21 January 1932, Supplement, p. II.
79. *The Lady*, 3 January 1929, Supplement, inside front cover.
80. Victoria & Albert Museum Archive, AAD/1989/8/2/1.
81. V. & A. M.A. AAD/1989/8/1/180.
82. V. & A. M.A. AAD/1989/8/1/167.
83. Delafield, *Diary of a Provincial Lady*, pp. 44–5.
84. V. & A. M.A. AAD/1989/8/1/32; AAD/1989/8/1/116.
85. V. & A. M.A. AAD/1989/8/1/124–7.
86. A. Briggs, *Friends of the People: The Centenary History of Lewis's* (Batsford, 1956), p. 129.
87. Briggs, 'Friends of the People', p. 89.
88. Interview with Mrs E.E.
89. Interview with Mrs S.R.
90. Interview with Mrs S.R.
91. Oxfordshire County Record Office, B17/F10/1 (Jan 1933–Feb 1937); B17/F10/2 (March 1937–Dec 1941).
92. *Vogue*, January 1931, p. 53.
93. *Sartorial Gazette*, October 1929, p. 479; December 1934, p. 546; *Style Guide* (1935), 1, p. 55.
94. E. Sigsworth, *Montague Burton. The tailor of taste* (Manchester, Manchester University Press, 1990), p. 51.
95. *Men's Wear*, 2 July 1921, p. 16.
96. *Sartorial Gazette*, January 1935, p. 16.
97. M.-O. A., D.R. 1590 reply to May 1939 directive.
98. B. Ritchie, *A Touch of Class. The Story of Austin Reed* (James & James, 1990), p. 56.
99. P. Byrde, *The Male Image. Men's Fashion in England 1300–1970* (Batsford, 1979), p. 1.
100. *Men's Wear*, 7 October 1922, p. 7.
101. Briggs, *Friends of the People*, p. 153.
102. M.-O. A., D.R. 1225 reply to May 1939 directive.
103. M.-O. A., D.R. 1291 reply to April 1939 directive.
104. M.-O. A., D.R. 1318 reply to April 1939 directive.
105. Levy, *Shops of Britain* p. 87.
106. Jefferys, *Retail Trade*, p. 315.
107. M.-O. A., F.R. A17 (Clothes), p.18.
108. Jefferys, *Retail Trade*, p. 300.
109. Lewes OHG, *Lewes Remembers Shops*, p. 57.

110. Sigsworth, *Montague Burton*, pp. 42–3.

111. E. Campbell, *Can I Help You, Sir?* (Peter Davies, 1939), p. 250.

112. Campbell, *Can I Help You, Sir?*, p. 254.

113. Ritchie, *A Touch of Class*, p. 47.

114. Sigsworth, *Montague Burton*, p. 46; K. Honeyman, 'Montague Burton Ltd: The creators of well-dressed men', in J. Chartres and K. Honeyman (eds), *Leeds city business 1893–1993* (Leeds, University of Leeds, 1993), p. 207.

115. M.-O. A., F.R. A17 (Clothes), p. 16.

116. Simpson's Archive, Guardbook 1 'B'.

117. Sigsworth, *Montague Burton*, p. 50.

118. M.-O. A., F.R. A17 (Clothes), p. 17.

119. Jefferys, *Retail Trade*, p. 303.

120. Ritchie, *A Touch of Class*, p. 44.

121. D. Caradog Jones, 'Cost of Living of a Sample of Middle-class Families' in *Journal of the Royal Statistical Society*, IV, 1928, p. 471.

122. *The Tatler*, 11 December 1929, p. xxix.

123. D. Lockwood, *The Blackcoated Worker. A Study in Class Consciousness* (George Allen & Unwin, 1958, repr. Oxford, Clarendon, 1989), p. 45.

124. Campbell, *Can I Help You Sir?*, p. 167.

125. Interview with Mr M.M.

126. Campbell, *Can I Help You Sir?*, p. 166.

127. W. Tute, *The Grey Top Hat. The Story of Moss Bros of Covent Garden* (Cassell, 1961), pp. 58–9.

128. Campbell, *Can I Help You Sir?*, p. 173.

2. Black Coats and White Collars

1. M.-O. A., D.R. 1216 reply to May 1939 directive.

2. *Sartorial Gazette*, October 1925, p. 443.

3. Aldcroft, *Inter-War Economy*, p. 352.

4. Jeffery, *A Place in the Nation*, p. 83.

5. J.G. Marley and H. Campion, 'Changes in Salaries in Great Britain, 1924–1939', *Journal of the Royal Statistical Society* IV (1940), p. 531.

6. H.L. Smith, *The New Survey of London Life and Labour, III, Survey of Social Conditions (I) The Eastern Area* (1932), Appendix 1, p. 416.

7. C.R. Hewitt, *Towards my Neighbour: The Social Influence of the Rotary Club Movement in Great Britain & Ireland* (Rotary International Association of Great Britain and Ireland, 1950), p. 3.

8. Hewitt, *Towards my Neighbour*, p. 11.

9. L.J. Shaw, *The Rotary Club of Poole, Dorset* (Poole, Rotary Club of Poole, 1973), p. 4.

10. Hewitt, *Towards my Neighbour*, p. 11.

11. H.J. Haden, *The Rotary Club of Stourbridge 1922–1972. The Golden Jubilee History of Stourbridge Rotary Club* (Stourbridge, 1973), between pp. 16 and 17.

12. F. Mort, *Cultures of Consumption. Masculinities and Social Space in late twentieth-century Britain* (Routledge, 1996), p. 137.

13. Caradog Jones, 'Cost of Living', pp. 463–502; Massey, 'Expenditure', pp. 159–85.

14. M.-O. A., D.R. 1415 reply to May 1939 directive.

15. M.-O. A., D.R. 1456 reply to May 1939 directive.

16. M.-O. A., D.R. 1264 reply to May 1939 directive.

17. Sartorial Gazette, May 1933, p. 203.

18. M.-O. A., D.R. 1194 reply to May 1939 directive.

19. M.-O. A., D.R. 1508.1 reply to May 1939 directive.

20. M.-O. A., D.R. 1130 reply to June 1939 directive.

21. Newby, *Something Wholesale*, p. 45.

22. E.J. Howard, *Slipstream. A Memoir* (Macmillan, 2002), p. 14.

23. R. Cobb, *Still Life. Sketches from a Tunbridge Wells Childhood* (Chatto & Windus, 1983), p. 141.

24. *Man and His Clothes*, January 1927, p. 7.

25. S. Nicholas, 'The Construction of a National Identity: Stanley Baldwin, "Englishness" and the Mass Media in Inter-war Britain', in M. Francis and I. Zweiniger-Bargielowska (eds), *The Conservatives and British Society, 1880–1990* (Cardiff, University of Wales Press, 1996), p. 140.

26. A.W. Baldwin, *My Father: The True Story* (George Allen & Unwin, 1955), p. 140.

27. D. Judd, *Radical Joe. A Life of Joseph Chamberlain* (Cardiff, University of Wales Press, 1993), p. 265.

28. A. Marwick, *Class. Image and Reality in Britain, France and the USA since 1930* (Collins, 1980), p. 88.

29. *Sartorial Gazette*, February 1934, p. 82.

30. *Manchester Evening News*, 9 November 1938.

31. *Bradford Times & Argus*, 4 May 1935.

32. T.S. Eliot, 'The Wasteland' (1922), in H. Gardner (ed.), *New Oxford Book of English Verse 1250–1950* (Oxford, Oxford University Press, 1972), p. 84.

33. P. Corfield, *Power and the Professions in Britain 1700–1850* (Routledge, 1995), p. 32.

34. A.M. Carr-Saunders, and D. Caradog Jones, *A survey of the social structure of England and Wales, as illustrated by statistics* (Oxford, Clarendon Press, 1938), p. 64.

35. A.M. Carr-Saunders, and D. Caradog Jones, *A survey of the social structure of England and Wales, as illustrated by statistics* (Humphrey Milford, 1928), p. 69.

36. Perkin, *Rise of Professional Society*, pp. 116–17.

37. Samuel, 'The middle class, part one', p. 30.

38. C. Breward, *The Hidden Consumer. Masculinities, fashion and city life 1860–1914* (Manchester, Manchester University Press, 1999), pp. 76–7.

39. Letter from Mr J.T. Hendrick, 31 March 2000.

40. M.-O. A., D.R. 1178 reply to April 1939 directive.

41. *Style Guide* (1935), 1 sec., p. 59.

42. *Style Guide*, December 1934, p. 546.

43. *Style Guide*, June 1933, p. 277.

44. M.-O. A., D.R. 1411 reply to May 1939 directive.

45. I am grateful to his son Professor T.P. Barwise of London Business School for this information.

46. M. Berg, *A woman in history. Eileen Power, 1889–1940* (Cambridge, Cambridge University Press, 1996), p. 153.

47. N. Robinson, *The Royal Society Catalogue of Portraits* (Royal Society, 1980), p. 178.

48. J. Brown, *Lutyens and the Edwardians* (Viking, 1996), plate 11, between pp. 84 and 85.

49. W. Blunt, *Married to A Single Life. An Autobiography 1901–1938* (Salisbury, Michael Russell, 1983), p. 141.
50. M.-O. A., D.R. 1435 reply to April 1939 directive.
51. M.-O. A., D.R. 1425 reply to April 1939 directive.
52. B. Magee, *Clouds of Glory. A Hoxton Childhood* (Jonathan Cape, 2003), p. 178.
53. M.-O. A., T.C. 18/1/C.
54. M.-O. A., D.R. 1435, D.R. 1507 replies to April 1939 directive.
55. L. Ugolini, 'Clothes and the Modern Man in 1930s Oxford', *Fashion Theory* 4, 4, 2000, p. 440.
56. C. Breward, 'Men, fashion and luxury, 1870–1914,' in A. de la Haye and E. Wilson (eds), *Defining Dress. Dress as object, meaning and identity* (Manchester, Manchester University Press, 1999), p. 52.
57. Lockwood, *Blackcoated Worker*, p. 45.
58. R. McKibbin, *Classes and Cultures. England 1918–1951* (Oxford, Oxford University Press, 1998), p. 45.
59. F.D. Klingender, *The Condition of Clerical Labour in Britain* (Martin Laurence, 1935), pp. 79–80.
60. M.-O. A., T.C. 18/1/C.
61. M.-O. A., D.R. 1207, reply to April 1939 directive.
62. M.-O. A., T.C. 18/1/C.
63. John Lewis Partnership Archive, 3004/p.
64. *Sartorial Gazette*, January 1929, p. 12; July 1934, p. 309.
65. M.-O. A., T.C. 18/1/C.
66. M.-O. A., T.C. 18/1/C.
67. M.-O. A., T.C. 18/1/C.
68. Lockwood, *Blackcoated Worker*, p. 122.
69. *Sartorial Gazette*, August 1930, p. 360.
70. M.-O. A., D.R. 1459 reply to April 1939 directive.
71. M.-O. A., D.R. 1427 reply to May 1939 directive.
72. J. Flugel, *The Psychology of Clothes* (Hogarth Press, 1930), p. 113.
73. J. Flugel, *Men and Their Motives* (Kegan Paul, Trench, Trubner, 1934), p. 65.

3. Business Girls and Office Dresses

1. Victoria & Albert Museum Archive, aad 1995/10/2 *Daily Mirror*, 18 February 1935.
2. J. Lewis, *Women in England, 1870–1950* (Hemel Hempstead, Harvester Wheatsheaf, 1984), p. 152.
3. L. Davidoff and B. Westover, '"From Queen Victoria to the Jazz Age": Women's World in England, 1880–1939', in L. Davidoff and B. Westover (eds), *Our Work, Our Lives, Our Words* (Basingstoke, Macmillan Educational, 1986), p. 28.
4. S. Alexander, 'Men's Fears and Women's Work: Responses to Unemployment in London Between the Wars', *Gender and History* 12, 2 (2000), p. 417.
5. K. Sanderson, '"A Pension to Look Forward to . . . ?": Women Civil Service Clerks in London, 1925–1939', in Davidoff and Westover, *Our Work*, p. 151.
6. Lockwood, *Blackcoated Worker*, p. 91.
7. Lockwood, *Blackcoated Worker*, p. 122.
8. Carr-Saunders and Caradog Jones, *Survey* (1928), p. 68; Carr-Saunders and Caradog Jones, *Survey* (1938), p. 65.

9. C. Dyhouse, *Feminism and the family in England 1880–1939* (Oxford, Blackwell, 1989), p. 64.

10. *Girls' Favourite*, 27 May 1922, p. 400.

11. T. Davy, '"A Cissy Job for Men; a Nice Job for Girls": Women Shorthand Typists in London, 1900–1939', in Davidoff and Westover, *Our Work*, p. 129.

12. *Miss Modern*, October 1930, p. 30.

13. M. Ryan, *Office Training for Girls* (Pitman, 1933), p. 134.

14. *Girls' Favourite*, 9 December 1922, p. 451.

15. M.-O. A., D.R. 1178 reply to May 1939 directive.

16. *Girls' Favourite*, 1 April 1922, p. 194.

17. *Miss Modern*, January 1932, p. 9.

18. Lockwood, *Blackcoated Worker*, p. 45.

19. *Daily Mail*, 19 November 1927.

20. Marley, 'Changes in Salaries', pp. 530–1.

21. R. Bowlby, 'The Cost of Living of Girls Professionally Employed in the County of London', *Economic Journal* 4 (1934), pp. 328–33.

22. Whiteing, 'Anyone', p. 59.

23. M.-O. A., D.R. 1085, reply to June 1939 directive.

24. H.L. Smith, *The New Survey of London Life and Leisure, V, London Industries II* (London School of Economics and Political Science, 1931), p. 195.

25. Smith, *New Survey*, V, II, p. 180.

26. M.-O. A. T.C. 18/1/C.

27. F. Donaldson, *Child of the Twenties* (Weidenfeld & Nicolson, 1959, repr. 1986), p. 134.

28. *Miss Modern*, February 1936, p. 32.

29. *Miss Modern*, November 1932, p. 20.

30. Victoria & Albert Museum Archive, aad/1995/10/2; *Daily Mirror*, 18 February 1935.

31. *Miss Modern*, October 1930, p. 42.

32. M.-O. A., D.R. 1040 reply to May 1939 directive.

33. *Girls' Favourite*, 27 June 1922, p. 400.

34. M.-O. A., T.C. 18/1/C.

35. M.-O. A., T.C. 18/1/C.

36. Sanderson, 'A Pension to look forward to', p. 152.

37. Marley, 'Changes in Salaries', p. 527.

38. M. Pugh, *Women and the Women's Movement in Britain 1914–1939* (Basingstoke, Macmillan, 1992), p. 192.

39. C. Sykes, *Nancy: the life of Lady Astor* (Panther, 1972), p. 202.

40. J. Fox, *The Langhorne Sisters* (Granta, 1999), p. 319.

41. *Drapers' Record*, 12 July 1930, p. 57.

42. Davidoff and Westover, 'From Queen Victoria', p. 10.

43. A. Vickery, 'Golden Age to Separate Spheres: A Review of the Categories and Chronology of English Women's History,' *Historical Journal* 36, 2 (1993), p. 413.

44. Quoted in R. Macaulay, *Life Among the English* (Collins, 1942), p. 21.

45. A.S. Williams, *Ladies of Influence. Women of the Elite in Interwar Britain* (Allen Lane, 2000), p. 46.

46. M.-O. A., D.R. 1068 reply to April 1939 directive.

47. M.-O. A., D.R. 1534 reply to April 1939 directive.

48. E. Campbell, *Can I Help You, Madam?* (Cobden-Sanderson, 1938), p. 104.

49. D. Beddoe, *Back to Home and Duty. Women Between the Wars 1918–1939* (Pandora, 1989), p. 77.

50. J. Gathorne-Hardy, *The Public School Phenomenon* (Hodder & Stoughton, 1977), p. 243.
51. S. Harrop, *The Merchant Taylors' School for Girls, Crosby. One hundred years of achievement 1888–1988* (Liverpool, Liverpool University Press, 1988), p. 105.
52. Harrop, *Merchant Taylors'*, p. 105.
53. A. Brazil, *Joan's Best Chum* (Blackie & Co., 1926), frontispiece.
54. Harrop, *Merchant Taylors'*, pp. 84–5.
55. Harrop, *Merchant Taylors'*, pp. 84–5.
56. M.-O. A., D.R. 1581 reply to May 1939 directive.
57. E. Edwards, *Women in teacher training colleges, 1900–1960* (2000), p. 41.
58. Edwards, *Women in teacher training colleges*, pp. 53, 56 and 71.
59. Royal Holloway, University of London, Archives BC PH7/1–3, BC PH7/9.
60. Royal Holloway, University of London, Archives BC PH7/9.
61. Interview with Mrs J.B.
62. Royal Holloway, University of London, Archives RHC RF131/1, Pike, *Social Life Part II*, p. 212.
63. Royal Holloway, University of London, Pike, *Social Life Part II*.
64. Royal Holloway, University of London, Archives RHC RF 131/7, Pike, *Social Life Part IV*, pp. 490–1.
65. Berg, *A woman in history*, p. 145.
66. Berg, *A woman in history*, p. 154.
67. L. Martindale, *A Woman Surgeon* (Gollancz, 1951).
68. H. Martindale, *Women Servants of the State 1870–1938* (George Allen & Unwin, 1938).
69. National Portrait Gallery P363 (13); C. Townsend-Gault, 'Symbolic facades: official portraiture in British institutions since 1920', *Art History* 11, 4 (1988), pp. 511–26.

4. In Home and Garden

1. *Woman's Own*, October 1932, p. 15.
2. Lewis, *Women in England*, p. 152.
3. J. Burnett, *A social history of housing, 1815–1970* (Newton Abbot, David & Charles, 1978), p. 246.
4. McKibbin, *Classes and Cultures*, p. 73.
5. Jeffery, 'A Place in the Nation', p. 75.
6. A. Jackson, *Semi-Detached London: Suburban Development, Life and Transport, 1900–1939* (Allen & Unwin, 1973), p. 169.
7. Jackson, *Semi-Detached London*, p. 169.
8. D. Ryan, '"All the World and Her Husband": The *Daily Mail* Ideal Home Exhibition 1908–39', in M. Andrews and M. Talbot (eds), *All the World and Her Husband. Women in Twentieth-Century Consumer Culture* (Cassell, 2000), p. 15.
9. P. Horn, *Life Below Stairs in the 20th Century* (Stroud, Sutton Publishing, 2001), p. 35.
10. Smith, *New Survey, II*, I, p. 439; C.S. Peel, *Life's Enchanted Cup: An Autobiography* (1872–1933) (John Lane, 1933), p. 261.
11. *Punch*, 16 March 1921, p. 210.
12. Smith, *New Survey, II*, p. 442.
13. C. Horwood, '"Housewives' Choice". Women as Consumers Between the Wars', *History Today*, March 1997, p. 23.
14. S. Bowden and A. Offer, 'The Technological Revolution That Never Was: Gender, Class and the Diffusion of

Household Appliances in Interwar England', in V. de Grazia and E. Furlough (eds), *The Sex of Things: Gender and Consumption in Historical Perspective* (Berkeley, University of California Press, 1996), p. 245.

15. Bowden and Offer, 'Technological Revolution', p. 250.
16. M.-O. A., D.R. 1488 reply to April 1939 directive.
17. *Miss Modern*, December 1932, p. 29.
18. *Woman's Own*, October 1932, p. 15.
19. M.-O. A., D.R. 1488 reply to April 1939 directive.
20. M.-O. A., D.R. 1488 reply to July 1939 directive.
21. M.-O. A., D.R. 1559 reply to April 1939 directive.
22. Interview with Mrs D.R.
23. D. Woods, *Correct Dance-Room Behaviour: A Safe Guide for Avoiding Mistakes in the Dance Room* (Universal Publications, 1936), p. 70.
24. Woods, *Correct Dance-Room Behaviour*, p. 69.
25. Bowden and Offer, 'Technological Revolution', pp. 245–8.
26. L. Hirst, 'Dressing the part. Workwear for the home 1953–1965', *things* 9 (1998), p. 25.
27. M.-O. A., D.R. 1420 reply to July 1939 directive.
28. Jackson, *Semi-Detached London*, p. 169.
29. M.-O. A., D.R. 1488 reply to May 1939 directive.
30. M.-O. A., D.R. 1559 reply to May 1939 directive.
31. M.-O. A., D.R. 1362 reply to July 1939 directive.
32. Campbell, *Can I Help You, Madam?*, p. 103.

33. K. Silex, tr. H. Paterson, *John Bull at Home* (G.G. Harrap & Co., 1931), p. 150.
34. *Good Housekeeping*, February 1931, p. 58.
35. E. Elias, *Straw Hats and Serge Bloomers* (W.H. Allen, 1979), p. 140.
36. *Britannia and Eve*, July 1930, pp. 30–1.
37. M.-O. A., D.R. 1533 reply to May 1939 directive.
38. Polhemus and Procter, *Fashion & anti-fashion*, p. 69.
39. Interview with Mrs E.E.
40. M.-O. A., D.R. 1299 reply to May 1939 directive.
41. *Fashions for all*, January 1925, p. 10.
42. E.M. Forster, *Selected Letters of E.M. Forster 1879–1920*, Vol. 1, ed. M. Lago and P.N. Furbank (Collins, 1983), pp. 253–5.
43. M.-O. A., D.R. 1194 reply to June 1939 directive.
44. M.-O. A., D.R. 1384 reply to May 1939 directive.
45. M.-O. A., D.R. 1505 reply to April 1939 directive.
46. L. Bradstock and J. Condon, *The Modern Woman. Beauty, Physical Culture, Hygiene* (Associated Newspapers, 1936).
47. 1289 reply to July 1939 directive.
48. Interview with Mrs D.R.; C. Cannon (ed.), *Our Grandmothers, Our Mothers, Ourselves. A Century of Women's Lives* (Ogomos, 2000), p. 125.
49. Campbell, *Can I Help You, Madam?*, p. 103.
50. C. Zmroczek, 'The Weekly Wash', in S. Oldfield (ed.), *This Working Day World. Women's Lives and Culture(s) in Britain 1914–1945* (Taylor & Francis, 1994), p. 11.

51. N. Beauman, *A Very Great Profession. The Woman's Novel 1914–39* (Virago, 1983), p. 111.
52. Cutforth, *Later Than We Thought*, p. 31.
53. H. Forester, *Success Through Dress* (Duckworth, 1925), p. 166.
54. *Girls' Favourite*, 15 January 1927, p. 574.
55. M.-O. A., D.R. 1299 reply to May 1939 directive.
56. *Miss Modern*, October 1930, p. 30
57. *Miss Modern*, January 1932, p. 9.
58. *The Times*, 16 March 1932.
59. M.-O. A., D.R. 1285 reply to July 1939 directive.
60. M.-O. A., T.C. 38/1/1/K.
61. *Miss Modern*, September 1932, p. 50; November 1932, p. 50; January 1936, p. 48; February 1936, p. 57.
62. M.-O. A., D.R. 1542 reply to July 1939 directive.
63. *Statistical Review*, I, 1, October 1932, pp. 62–3; III, 1, October 1934, p. 90.
64. *Statistical Review*, I, 3, April 1933, p. 99.
65. *Statistical Review*, VI, 3, April 1938, p. 56.
66. *Statistical Review*, V, 3, April 1937, p. 54.
67. M.-O. A., D.R. 1459.1 reply to April 1939 directive; D.R.1470.1, reply to May 1939 directive.
68. M.-O. A., D.R. 1289 reply to July 1939 directive.
69. M.-O. A., D.R. 1068 reply to April 1939 directive.
70. *Statistical Review*, IV, 1, October 1935, p. 114; IV, 2, January 1936, p. 113; VI, 3, April 1938, p. 118; VII, 4, July 1939, p. 118.
71. *Good Housekeeping*, February 1931, p. 18.
72. *Good Housekeeping*, March 1930, p. 222.
73. *Good Housekeeping*, July 1935.
74. Graves and Hodge, *Long Weekend*, p. 39.
75. M.-O. A., D.R. 1474 reply to April 1939 directive.
76. *The Times*, 10 August 1932.
77. Cutforth, *Later*, p. 30.
78. *New Statesman and Nation*, 20 August 1938, p. 276.
79. Newby, *Something Wholesale*, p. 45.
80. John Osborne, *A better class of person. An autobiography 1929–1956* (Faber, 1981), p. 23.
81. M.-O. A., D.R. 1194 reply to May 1939 directive.
82. M.-O. A., D.R. 1264 reply to April 1939 directive.
83. M.-O. A., D.R. 1301 reply to May 1939 directive.
84. J. Waller (ed.), *A Man's Book* (Duckworth, 1977), p. 139.
85. M.-O. A., D.R. 1456 reply to April 1939 directive; D.R. 1301, 1318 and 1325 replies to May 1939 directive.
86. M.-O. A., D.R.s 1207, D.R.1141 replies to May 1939 directive.
87. M.-O. A., D.R. 1325 reply to May 1939 directive.
88. M.-O. A., D.R. 1040 reply to June 1939 directive.
89. M.-O. A., D.R. 1264 reply to May 1939 directive.
90. Byrde, *Male Image*, p. 154.
91. *The Sketch*, 29 June 1927, p. 660.
92. *Drapers' Record*, 5 April 1930, p. 16.
93. *Punch*, 18 June 1930, p. 685.
94. M.-O. A., D.R.s 1435; and 1465 replies to May 1939 directive.

95. M.-O. A., D.R. 1393 reply to May 1939 directive.
96. *Film Fashionland*, May 1934, pp. 16–17.

5. *From Seaside to Sports Club*

1. M. Dickens, *Mariana* (Michael Joseph, 1940, repr. Penguin, 1999), pp. 281–7.
2. Smith, *New Survey*, IX, p. 78.
3. J. Walton, *The British Seaside. Holidays and resorts in the twentieth century* (Manchester, Manchester University Press, 2000), p. 53.
4. J. Pimlott and R. Alfred, *The Englishman's Holiday: A Social History* (Faber & Faber, 1947), pp. 239–40.
5. Interviews with Mrs D.S. and Mrs T.C.
6. *The Lady*, 1 July 1937, p. 32.
7. Smith, *New Survey, IX*, p. 82.
8. V.S. Pritchett, 'Scarborough' in Y. Cloud (ed.), *Beside the Seaside* (Stanley Knott, 1934), p. 189.
9. Pritchett, 'Scarborough', p. 191.
10. M.-O. A., D.R. 1459 reply to April 1939 directive.
11. M.-O. A., D.R. 1474 reply to April 1939 directive.
12. Interview with Mrs D.R.
13. *Drapers' Record*, 13 August 1932, p. 12.
14. C. Horwood, '"Girls Who Arouse Dangerous Passions": women and bathing, 1900–39', *Women's History Review* 9, 4 (2000), p. 666.
15. Pimlott and Alfred, *Englishman's Holiday*, p. 219.
16. Horwood, 'Girls Who Arouse', p. 665.
17. M.-O. A., D.R. 1563 reply to July 1939 directive.
18. *Girls' Favourite*, 1 July 1922, p. 520.
19. *The Lady*, 22 July 1937, pp. 162–3.
20. Interview with Mrs E.E.
21. Interviews with Mrs E.E., Mrs D.R., Mrs G.R. and Mrs D.D.; K. Bill, 'Attitudes Towards Women's Trousers: Britain in the 1930s', *Journal of Design History* 6, 1 (1993), p. 47.
22. Greater Manchester County Record Office, Documentary Photography Archive 1872/38 and 40.
23. John Lewis Partnership Archive, 118/a Monthly Special Notice, June 1932.
24. Horwood, 'Girls Who Arouse', p. 663.
25. A. Holt, 'Hikers and Ramblers: Surviving a Thirties' Fashion', *International Journal of the History of Sport* (1987), pp. 56–67.
26. McKibbin, *Classes and Cultures*, p. 76.
27. C. Horwood, 'Dressing like a Champion: Women's Tennis Wear in Interwar England', in C. Breward, B. Conekin and C. Cox (eds), *The Englishness of English Dress* (Oxford, Berg, 2002), p. 46.
28. *Woman's Life*, 3 May 1924, p. 3.
29. Smith, *New Survey, I*, p. 281.
30. Jackson, *Semi-detached London*, p. 182.
31. McKibbin, *Classes*, p. 362.
32. Langhamer, *Women's leisure*, p. 80.
33. *Tennis Illustrated*, August 1927, p. 46.
34. D. Round, *Modern Lawn Tennis* (George Newnes, 1934), p. 13
35. Horwood, 'Dressing like a Champion', p. 46.
36. S. Lenglen, *Lawn Tennis for Girls* (George Newnes, 1919), pp. 28–9.
37. *Woman's Life*, 3 May 1924, pp. 20–1.
38. *Woman's Life*, 31 May 1924, p. 12.
39. *Woman's Life*, 31 May 1924, p. 5.
40. *Vogue*, May 1937, pp. 56–7 and 61.
41. *Wimbledon Championship Programme*, Kenneth Ritchie Wimbledon Library,

Wimbledon Lawn Tennis Museum (1937), p. 7.

42. *Punch*, 20 June 1932, p. 681.

43. F. Perry, *Fred Perry: an autobiography* (Hutchinson, 1984), p. 10.

44. C. Horwood, '"Anyone for Tennis?": Male Modesty on the Tennis Courts in Interwar Britain', *Costume* 38 (2004), pp. 103–4.

45. M.-O. A., D.R. 1212 reply to April 1939 directive.

46. D. Birley, *Playing the Game* (Manchester, Manchester University Press, 1995), p. 165.

47. G. Cousins, *Golf in Britain: a social history from the beginnings to the present day* (Routledge & Kegan Paul, 1975), p. 53.

48. B. Seymour, *All About Golf* (Ward Lock & Co., 1924), p. 24.

49. R. Cossey, *Golfing ladies. Five centuries of golf in Great Britain and Ireland* (Orbis, 1984), p. 114.

50. J. Farrell, *Socks and Stockings* (Batsford, 1992), p. 73.

51. Farrell, *Socks and Stockings*, p. 73.

52. Farrell, *Socks and Stockings*, p. 73.

53. *The Outfitter*, 11 July 1936, p. 14.

54. *Daily Mail*, 10 August 1920.

55. *Men's Wear*, 20 April 1929, p. 67.

56. Cossey, *Golfing Ladies*, p. 35.

57. *The Sketch*, 29 June 1927, p. ix.

58. *Vogue*, 30 May 1928, pp. 60–1.

59. K. McCrone, *Sport and the physical emancipation of women, 1870–1914* (Routledge, 1988), pp. 216–46.

60. *Punch*, 24 September 1930, p. 340.

61. M. Crane, *The Story of Ladies' Golf* (Stanley Paul, 1991), p. 146.

62. Cossey, *Golfing Ladies*, p. 114; *Punch*, 20 April 1921, p. 309.

63. Crane, *Ladies' Golf*, p. 146.

64. *Vogue*, 4 August 1937; Simpson's Guardbook K1 'B'.

65. Cossey, *Golfing Ladies*, p. 115.

66. *The Times*, 11 October 1934.

67. Graves and Hodge, *Long Weekend*, p. 276.

68. M.-O. A., D.R. 1264, 1393; and 1474 replies to May 1939 directive.

69. Greater Manchester County Record Office, 1141/2.

70. Obituary, *Daily Telegraph*, 25 January 2002.

71. Holt, 'Hikers and Ramblers', p. 59.

72. British Library 1883c13/2a.

73. R. Baden-Powell, *Lessons from the Varsity of Life* (A. Pearson, 1933), pp. 284–5.

74. Baden-Powell, *Lessons*, pp. 284–5.

75. M.-O. A., D.R. 1108 reply to May 1939 directive.

76. Baden-Powell, *Lessons*, pp. 284–5.

77. *Bernstein Questionnaire* (British Film Institute, 1937).

78. M.-O. A., D.R. 1264 reply to May 1939 directive.

79. M.-O. A., D.R. 1456 reply to April 1939 directive.

6. *Top Hats and Tulle*

1. Delafield, *Diary of a Provincial Lady*, p. 9.

2. *The Times*, 21 October 1957.

3. McKibbin, *Classes and Cultures*, pp. 390–1.

4. Rust, *Dance in society: an analysis of the relationship between the social dance and society in England from the Middle Ages to the present day* (Thames & Hudson, 1969), p. 93.

5. V. Buckley, *Good times: at home and abroad between the wars* (1979), p. 85; Rust, *Dance in society*, p. 92.

6. J. Stevenson, *British Society 1914–45* (Penguin, 1984, repr. 1990), p. 397.

7. V. Silvester, *Dancing is My Life* (Heinemann, 1958), p. 32.

8. Silvester, *Dancing*, p. 102.

9. Rust, *Dance in society*, p. 93.

10. Rust, *Dance in society*, p. 93.

11. *Middlesex County Times*, 30 July 1921.

12. Stevenson, *British Society*, p. 398.

13. B.S. Rowntree and G.R. Lavers, *English Life and Leisure* (Longman, Green & Co., 1951), p. 279.

14. M.-O. A., D.R. 1140 reply to January 1939 directive.

15. S. Messenger, 'The lifestyle of young middle-class women in Liverpool in the 1920s and 1930s', Ph.D., University of Liverpool (1999).

16. M.-O. A., D.R. 1159 reply to January 1939 directive.

17. Whipple, *High Wages*, p. 96.

18. M.-O. A., D.R. 1091 reply to January 1939 directive.

19. M.-O. A., D.R. 1207 reply to January 1939 directive.

20. M.-O. A., D.R. 1140 reply to January 1939 directive.

21. M.-O. A., D.R. 1122 reply to January 1939 directive.

22. M.-O. A., D.R. 1300 reply to July 1939 directive.

23. M.-O. A., T.C. 38/5/H.

24. A. de Courcy, *1939: The Last Season* (Thames & Hudson, 1989, repr. Phoenix, 2003), p. 198.

25. M.-O. A., D.R. 1040 reply to January 1939 directive.

26. M.-O. A., D.R. 1299 reply to July 1939 directive.

27. M.-O. A., D.R. 1135 reply to January 1939 directive.

28. A. MacCarthy, *The Dance Band Era: the dancing decades from ragtime to swing: 1910–1950* (Studio Vista, 1971), p. 76.

29. Rust, *Dance in society*, p. 129.

30. Magee, *Clouds of Glory*, p. 165.

31. E.F. Benson, *Queen Lucia* (Hutchinson, 1920, repr. Black Swan, 1970), p. 41.

32. *Punch*, 15 April 1936, p. 421.

33. *The Tatler*, 25 December 1929, p. 637.

34. *Man and His Clothes*, June 1927.

35. *The Times*, 30 May 1922.

36. *Man and His Clothes*, August 1927.

37. L. Lewis, *The Private Life of A Country House (1912–1939)* (Newton Abbot, David & Charles, 1980), p. 89.

38. Lewis, *Private Life*, p. 67.

39. M.-O. A., D.R. 1135 reply to January 1939 directive.

40. Woods, *Correct Dance-room Behaviour*, p. 76.

41. M.-O. A., D.R. 1086 reply to July 1939 directive.

42. O. Lancaster, *With an Eye to the Future* (Century, 1986), pp. 58–9.

43. *Man and His Clothes*, March 1927, p. 4.

44. *Men's Wear*, 30 July 1932, p. 12.

45. *Men's Wear*, 14 August 1920, p. 291.

46. *Man and His Clothes*, May 1927, p. 7.

47. *Man and His Clothes*, January 1933, p. 21.

48. Lewis, *Private Life*, p. 111.

49. *Punch*, 18 March 1925, p. 290.

50. M.-O. A., D.R. 1400, reply to January 1939 directive.

51. B. Burman and M. Leventon, 'The Men's Dress Reform Party 1929–37', *Costume* 21 (1987), p. 75.

52. *Men's Wear*, Special Shipping Number, June 1920, p. 59.

53. *Punch*, 26 June 1929, p. 720; 3 July 1929, p. 14; 10 July 1929, p. 54.

54. *Punch*, 15 March 1929, p. 546.

55. *The Times*, 28 May 1934.

56. *Man and His Clothes*, June 1933, p. 15.

57. Ritchie, *Touch of Class*, p. 74.

58. R. Rhodes James (ed.), *"Chips": The Diaries of Sir Henry Channon* (Weidenfeld & Nicholson, 1967, repr. Penguin, 1999), p. 60; *Man and His Clothes*, October 1927, p. 11.

59. Duke of Windsor, *A Family Album* (Cassell, 1960), p. 93.

60. *Man and His Clothes*, January 1933, p. 21.

61. *Man and His Clothes*, February 1937, p. 34.

62. *Punch*, 31 May 1933, p. 593.

63. T. Rattigan, *The Collected Plays of Terence Rattigan*, vol. 2 (Hamish Hamilton, 1953), pp. xi–xii.

64. *The Times*, 17 March 1932.

65. *The Times*, 15 March 1932.

66. *The Times*, 17 March 1932.

67. *The Times*, 23 March 1932.

68. *The Times*, 21 March 1932.

69. *The Times*, 22 March 1932.

70. *The Times*, 30 March 1932.

71. *The Times*, 30 March 1932.

72. *Punch*, 18 December 1929, p. 697.

73. *Men's Wear*, 25 December 1926, p. 412.

74. M.-O. A., D.R. 1040 reply to January 1939 directive.

75. *Bernstein Questionnaire* (British Film Institute, 1934), p. 5.

76. *World Film News* (1936), quoted in J. Richards, *The Age of the Dream Palace: Cinema and Society in Britain 1930–1939* (Routledge & Kegan Paul, 1984), p. 171.

77. Major R. Hoare, *This Our Country* (1934), quoted in Graves and Hodge, *Long Weekend*, p. 297.

78. A. Kuhn, 'Cinema, culture and femininity in the 1930s', in C. Gledhill and G. Swanson (eds), *Nationalising Femininity. Cultures, sexuality and British cinema in the Second World War* (Manchester, Manchester University Press, 1996), pp. 181–2.

79. Graves and Hodge, *Long Weekend*, p. 347; Richards, *Dream Palace*, p. 207.

80. *Bernstein Questionnaire* (1934), p. 1.

81. R. Lehmann, *Invitation to the Waltz* (Chatto & Windus, 1932, repr. Virago, 2001).

82. M.-O. A., D.R. 1963 reply to July 1939 directive.

83. M.-O. A., D.R. 1420 reply to July 1939 directive.

84. Richards, *Dream Palace*, pp. 178–9.

85. Wayne, *The Purple Dress*, p. 8.

86. Elias, *Straw Hats*, p. 76.

87. M.-O. A., D.R. 1408 reply to July 1939 directive.

88. *Daily Mail*, 13 May 1925.

89. *The Times*, 7 October 1927.

90. *Vogue*, 10 July 1929, p. 68.

91. Graves and Hodge, *Long Weekend*, p. 45.

92. *West Middlesex Gazette*, 10 July 1926.

93. *The Times*, 30 March 1932.

94. *Miss Modern*, October 1930, p. 54.

95. *Miss Modern*, November 1930, p. 88.

96. J. and M. Davidson, *Etiquette at a Dance: What to Do and What Not to Do* (W. Foulsham & Co., 1937), p. 29.

97. de Courcy, *1939: The Last Season*, p. 89.

98. M.-O. A., D.R.1077 reply to May 1939 directive.

99. Delafield, *Diary of a Provincial Lady*, p. 9.

100. Interview with Mrs T.R.

101. M.-O. A., D.R. 1086 reply to July 1939 directive.

102. M.-O. A., D.R. 1408 reply to July 1939 directive.

103. M.-O. A., D.R. 2318 reply to July 1939 directive.

104. *Punch*, 7 January 1920, p. 7.

105. John Lewis Partnership Archive, Monthly Special Notices, 118, September 1932.

106. M.-O. A., D.R. 1077 reply to January 1939 directive.

107. M.-O. A., D.R. 1051 reply to January 1939 directive.

108. Langhamer, *Women's leisure*, pp. 167–8.

109. M.-O. A., D.R. 1035 reply to January 1939 directive.

110. M.-O. A., D.R. 1462 reply to July 1939 directive.

111. M.-O. A., D.R. 1566 reply to January 1939 directive.

112. M.-O. A., D.R. 1534 reply to July 1939 directive.

113. M.-O. A., D.R. 2210 reply to January 1939 directive.

114. Lewis, *Private Life*; M.-O. A., D.R. 1060 reply to January 1939 directive.

115. M.-O. A., D.R. 2187 reply to January 1939 directive.

116. John Lewis Partnership Archive, Monthly Special Notices, 118a, September 1932.

117. S. Alexander, 'Becoming a Woman in London in the 1920s and 1930s', in D. Feldman and G. Stedman Jones (eds), *Metropolis, London. Histories and Representations* (Routledge, 1989), pp. 264–5.

118. McKibbin, *Classes and Cultures*, p. 397.

7. *Everything to Match*

1. *Miss Modern*, January 1936, p. 31.

2. Cutforth, *Later Than We Thought*, p. 28.

3. M.-O. A., D.R. 1456 reply to May 1939 directive.

4. P.G. Wodehouse, 'Jeeves and the Impending Doom', *Very Good, Jeeves!* (Herbert Jenkins, 1930, repr. 2001), p. 12.

5. *The Times*, 20 July 1928.

6. M.-O. A., D.R. 1384 reply to April 1939 directive.

7. Baldwin, *My Father*, p. 102.

8. Victoria & Albert Museum Archive, aad 2/11–1983.

9. J. Laver (ed.), *The Book of Public School Old Boys, University, Navy, Army Air Force & Club Ties* (Seeley Service, 1968), p. 34.

10. Laver, *Public School Old Boys*.

11. F. Chenoune, *A History of Men's Fashion* (Flammarion, 1993), p. 164.

12. Chenoune, *History of Men's Fashion*.

13. *Punch*, 18 June 1930, p. 681.

14. J. and D.L. Moore, *The Pleasure of Your Company* (Gerald Howe, 1933), p. 292.

15. P. Keers, *A Gentleman's Wardrobe. Class Clothes and the Modern Man* (Weidenfeld & Nicholson, 1987), p. 12.

16. A. Davidson, *Blazers, Badges and Boaters. A Pictorial History of School Uniform* (Horndean, Scope, 1990), p. 140.

17. A. Powell, *A Dance to the Music of Time I. A Question of Upbringing* (Heinemann, 1951, repr. Mandarin, 1991), pp. 88–91.

18. Cutforth, *Later Than We Thought*, p. 31.

19. *Men's Wear*, 25 December 1926, p. 411.

20. M.-O. A., D.R. 1457 reply to May 1939 directive.

21. M.-O. A., D.R. 210 reply to July 1939 directive.

22. *Miss Modern*, January 1936, p. 31.

23. Massey, 'Expenditure', p. 175.

24. M.-O. A., D.R. 1077 reply to April 1939 directive.

25. R.P. Weston and B. Lee, *Brahn Boots* (1910).

26. J. Jensen, H.M. Bateman. *The Man Who . . . and other drawings* (Methuen, 1975), p. 46.

27. *Punch*, 19 April 1922, p. 307.

28. *Punch*, 10 July 1929, p. 56.29.

29. M.-O. A., D.R. 1324 reply to May 1939 directive.

30. Graves and Hodge, *Long Weekend*, p. 278.

31. Interview with Mrs T.R.

32. Interview with Mrs T.C.

33. Interview with Mrs T.R.

34. J. Grove, 'Victorian Respectability and the Etiquette of Dress', *Strata of Society*, Costume Society Conference, Norwich (1973), p. 18.

35. N. Leyland and J. Troughton, *Glovemaking in West Oxfordshire* (Oxford, Oxford City and County Museum, 1974), p. 19.

36. Rose Harrison, *Rose. My Life in Service* (Cassell, 1979), p. 65.

37. *Girls' Favourite*, 1 July 1922, p. 516.

38. L. Bentley, *Educating Women. A Pictorial History of Bedford College University of London 1849–1985* (St Albans, Alma/RHUL, 1991), p. 53.

39. Forester, *Success Through Dress*, p. 156.

40. M.-O. A., T.C. 18/2/F.

41. Grove, 'Victorian Respectability', p. 18.

42. *Girls' Favourite*, 1 July 1922, p. 516.

43. Harrop, *Merchant Taylors'*, p. 102.

44. C.C. Collins, *Love of A Glove* (New York, Fairchild, 1947), p. 79.

45. M.-O. A., T.C. 18/1/C/40.

46. M.-O. A., T.C. 18/2/F.

47. V. Cumming, *Gloves* (Batsford, 1982), p. 82.

48. M.-O. A., T.C. 18/1/C/40.

49. M.-O. A., D.R. 1299 reply to May 1939 directive.

50. M.-O. A., T.C. 18/1/C/40.

51. E. Bland, 'With Hat and Gloves. A Career in Retailing', *Costume* 24 (1990), p. 116.

52. P. Corfield, 'Dress for Deference and Dissent: Hats and the Decline of Hat Honour', *Costume* 23 (1989), p. 64.

53. G.R.M. Devereux, *Etiquette for men. A book of modern manners and customs* (Arthur Pearson, 1902, repr. 1937), pp. 14–15.

54. *The Times*, 30 November 1934.

55. *The Times*, 12 December 1934.

56. *The Times*, 20 April 1929.

57. *Hatter's Gazette*, June 1934, p. 238; 15 April 1924, p. 188.

58. *Hatter's Gazette*, 1 February 1919, p. 59.
59. *Hatter's Gazette*, March 1934, p. 122.
60. J.G. Dony, *The History of the Straw Hat Industry* (Luton, Gibbs, Bamforth, 1947), p. 179.
61. *The Times*, 11 January 1934.
62. *Hatter's Gazette*, 5 September 1924, p. 429.
63. *Punch*, 11 March 1925, p. 264.
64. Hat Works, Stockport Museum of Hatting Archive, *The Wideawake*, March 1934, p. 2.
65. *Hatter's Gazette*, March 1934, p. 114.
66. *Hatter's Gazette*, December 1934, p. 540.
67. *Men's Wear*, 11 July 1936, p. 5; 29 August 1936, pp. 8–9.
68. *Punch*, 31 May 1922, p. 422.
69. Hat Works, *Manchester Evening Chronicle*, 20 July 1938, reprinted in *The Wideawake*, Autumn 1938, p. 3.
70. *Men's Wear Organiser*, February 1931, p. 92.
71. Luton Museum Services, LTNMG 1980/27/9; *Luton News*, 15 June 1935.
72. *Hatter's Gazette*, May 1939, pp. 176–7.
73. M.-O. A., D.Rs. 1141, 1151, 1285, 1324 and 1416 replies to April 1939 directive.
74. *Hatter's Gazette*, January 1939, p. 28; February 1939, p. 57.
75. *Hatter's Gazette*, July 1939, p. 63.
76. Luton Museum Services, LTNMG 1980/27/9; *Luton News*, 18 March 1926.
77. Forester, *Success Through Dress*, pp. 113–14.
78. Interview with Mrs T.R.
79. Bentley, *Educating Women*, p. 53.
80. Grove, 'Victorian Respectability', p. 18.
81. M.-O. A., D.R. 1044 reply to May 1939 directive.
82. M.-O. A., T.C. 18/5.
83. *Daily Mail*, 8 May 1939.
84. Luton Museum Services, Oral History Archive, Doris Green; see also Violet Vernon.
85. Bland, 'With Hat and Gloves', pp. 111–16.

8. *Radicals, Bohemians and Dandies*

1. E. Waugh, *Brideshead Revisited* (Chapman & Hall, 1945), p. 34.
2. Waugh, *Brideshead Revisited*.
3. S. Cole, *'Don we now our gay apparel': Gay Men's Dress in the Twentieth Century* (Oxford, Berg, 2000), p. 17.
4. S.M. Newton, *Health, art and reason: dress reformers of the 19th century* (John Murray, 1974).
5. Newton, *Health, art and reason*, p. 156.
6. Newton, *Health, art and reason*, p. 120.
7. D. Crane, 'Clothing Behavior as Non-Verbal Resistance: Marginal Women and Alternative Dress in the Nineteenth Century', *Fashion Theory* 3, 2 (1999), p. 248.
8. J.B. Paoletti, 'Ridicule and Role Models as Factors in American Men's Fashion Change, 1880–1910', *Costume* 19 (1985), pp. 121–34.
9. Newton, *Health, art and reason*, p. 139.
10. Newton, *Health, art and reason*, p. 157.
11. Newton, *Health, art and reason*, p. 155.
12. Crane, 'Clothing Behavior', p. 261.
13. K. Rolley, 'Fashion, Femininity and the Fight for the Vote', *Art History* 13, 1 (1990), p. 3.

14. Wilson, *Adorned in Dreams.*
15. M. Easton, 'Dorelia's Wardrobe: "There goes an Augustus John!"', *Costume* 8 (1974), pp. 30–4.
16. J. Laver, *Dandies* (Weidenfeld & Nicholson, 1968), p. 105.
17. B. Melman, *Women in the popular imagination in the Twenties. Flappers and nymphs* (Basingstoke, Macmillan, 1988), p. 145.
18. S. Zdatny, 'The Boyish Look and the Liberated Woman: The Politics and Aesthetics of Women's Hairstyles', *Fashion Theory* 1, 4 (1997), p. 38.
19. *Daily Mail*, 19 April 1927.
20. P. Nystrom, *Economics of Fashion* (New York, Ronald, 1928), pp. 498–9.
21. B. Cartland, *We Danced All Night* (Hutchinson, 1970), pp. 105–6.
22. Cartland, *We Danced All Night*, pp. 105–6.
23. D.L. Moore, *Pandora's Letter Box: being a discourse on fashionable life, etc.* (Gerald Howe, 1929), p. 94.
24. N. Nicolson, *Portrait of a Marriage* (Weidenfeld & Nicholson, 1973, repr. 1990), p. 110.
25. M. Costantino, *Men's fashion in the twentieth century. From frock coats to intelligent fibres* (New York, Costume & Fashion Press, 1997), pp. 36–7; H. Acton, *Memoirs of an Aesthete* (Methuen, 1948, repr. Hamilton, 1984), p. 119.
26. Acton, *Memoirs*, p. 119.
27. *Daily Mail*, 17 June 1925.
28. A. Adburgham, *A Punch History of Manners and Modes* (Hutchinson, 1961), p. 325.
29. *The Times*, 4 September 1935.
30. M.-O. A., D.R. 1403 reply to July 1939 directive.
31. J. Betjeman, *Betjeman's Oxford* (Oxford, Oxford University Press, 1990), p. 38.
32. Graves and Hodge, *Long Weekend*, p. 124.
33. H. Vickers, *Cecil Beaton. The authorised biography* (Weidenfeld & Nicholson, 1985), p. 86.
34. N. Mitford, *Love in a Cold Climate* (Hamish Hamilton, 1949), p. 184.
35. Acton, *Memoirs*, p. 2.
36. Cole, *'Don We Now'*, p. 19.
37. Cole, *'Don We Now'*.
38. M.-O. A., D.R. 1456 reply to May 1939 directive.
39. M.-O. A., D.R. 1465 reply to May 1939 directive.
40. C. Beaton, *The Wandering Years. Diaries 1922–1939* (Weidenfeld & Nicholson, 1961), p. 187.
41. M.-O. A., D.R. 1122 reply to April 1939 directive.
42. M.-O. A., D.R. 1359 reply to May 1939 directive.
43. Q. Crisp, *The Naked Civil Servant* (Cape, 1968), pp. 26–7.
44. N. Cohn, *Today there are no Gentlemen. The changes in Englishmen's clothes since the War* (Weidenfeld & Nicholson, 1971), p. 8.
45. E. Kelen, *Peace in their Time. Men who led us in and out of war, 1914–1945* (Victor Gollancz, 1964), p. 337.
46. D. Dutton, *Anthony Eden. A Life and Reputation* (Arnold, 1997), p. 463.
47. *Man and His Clothes*, January 1927, p. 7.
48. Elias, *Straw Hats*, p. 137.
49. Windsor, *Family Album*, p. 105.

50. Windsor, *Family Album*, p. 13.
51. Windsor, *Family Album*, p. 114.
52. Windsor, *Family Album*.
53. E. Wilson, *Bohemians. The Glamorous Outcasts* (I.B. Tauris, 2000), pp. 64–5.
54. M.-O. A., D.R. 1299 reply to May 1939 directive.
55. *Punch*, 31 May 1922, p. 423.
56. E. Mannin, *Young in the Twenties. A Chapter of Autobiography* (Hutchinson, 1971), p. 31.
57. *Punch*, 8 February 1922, p. 113.
58. *Punch*, 15 May 1929, p. 546.
59. *Punch*, 17 March 1937, p. 299.
60. A. Calder-Marshall, *The Magic of my Youth* (Hart-Davis, 1951), p. 24.
61. M.-O. A., D.R. 1040 reply to May 1939 directive.
62. M.-O. A., D.R. 1291 reply to May 1939 directive.
63. *Punch*, 6 January 1937.
64. M.-O. A., D.R. 1090 reply to April 1939 directive.
65. M.-O. A., D.R. 1291 reply to May 1939 directive.
66. 'The Intellectual Aristocracy', reprinted in N. Annan, *The Dons. Mentors, Eccentrics and Geniuses* (Harper Collins, 1999), pp. 304–41.
67. V. Nicholson, *Among the Bohemians. Experiments in Living 1900–1939* (Viking, 2002), p. 162.
68. F. Spalding, *Gwen Raverat. Friends, Family and Affections* (Harvill Press, 2001), p. 353.
69. E. Wilson, 'Bohemian Dress and the Heroism of Everyday Life', *Fashion Theory* 2, 3 (1998), pp. 169–70; E. Salter, *Edith Sitwell* (Oresko, 1979), p. 55.
70. Salter, *Sitwell*, pp. 38 and 59.
71. M.-O. A., D.R. 1470.1 reply to July 1939 directive.
72. Burman, 'Men's Dress Reform Party', p. 85.
73. Burman, 'Men's Dress Reform Party'; Horwood, 'Anyone for Tennis?'.
74. M.-O. A., D.R. 1361 reply to July 1939 directive.
75. Burman, 'Men's Dress Reform Party'; J. Bourke, 'The Great Male Renunciation: Men's Dress Reform in Inter-war Britain', *Journal of Design History* 9, 1 (1996), pp. 23–33.
76. *Men's Wear*, Special Shipping Number, June 1920, p. 59.
77. *Men's Wear*, 2 April 1927, p. 16.
78. E. Gill, *Clothes* (Cape, 1931), p. 49.
79. M.-O. A., D.R. 1210 reply to July 1939 directive.
80. R. Skidelsky, *Oswald Mosley* (Macmillan, 1975), pp. 292–3.
81. O. Mosley, *My Life* (Nelson, 1968), pp. 302–3.
82. S. Taylor, *The Great Outsiders. Northcliffe, Rothermere and the* Daily Mail (Weidenfeld & Nicholson, 1996), pp. 282–3.
83. Taylor, *Great Outsiders*.
84. Skidelsky, *Mosley*, p. 163.
85. E. Wilkinson, *Peeps at Politicians* (P. Allen, 1930), p. 38.
86. Newton, *Health, art and reason*, p. 157.
87. J. Parker, *Father of the House. Fifty years in politics* (Routledge & Kegan Paul, 1982), p. 31.
88. *Punch*, 25 September 1929, p. 341.
89. Moore, *Pandora's Letter Box*, p. 92.
90. Beaton, *Wandering Years*, p. 187.
91. M.-O. A., D.R. 1210 reply to April 1939 directive.

92. G. Orwell, *The Road to Wigan Pier* (Victor Gollancz, 1937, repr. Penguin, 1989), p. 162.
93. Orwell, *Road to Wigan Pier*, p. 126.

Conclusion

1. Macaulay, *Keeping Up Appearances*, p. 63.
2. Flugel, *Psychology of Clothes*, p. 113.
3. M.-O. A., D.R. 1264 reply to July 1939 directive.
4. M.-O. A., D.R. 2056 reply to July 1939 directive.
5. M.-O. A., D.R. 1044 reply to July 1939 directive.
6. M.-O. A., D.R. 2006 reply to July 1939 directive.
7. Alexander, 'Becoming a woman', fn.58, p. 271.
8. Alexander, 'Becoming a woman', p. 257.
9. M.-O. A., D.R. 1456 reply to May 1939 directive.
10. Beaton, *Wandering Years*, p. 61.
11. M.-O. A., D.R. 1533 reply to May 1939 directive.

Bibliography and Sources

Only printed sources given here. All manuscript and oral history material used is detailed in the endnotes. Place of publication is London unless otherwise listed.

ARCHIVES

British Film Institute
British Library
Greater Manchester County Record Office, Documentary Photography Archive
Hat Works, Stockport Museum of Hatting
History of Advertising Trust
John Lewis Partnership Archive
Luton Museum Services
Mass-Observation Archive, University of Sussex
Oxfordshire County Record Office
Royal Holloway, University of London, Bedford Centre for the History of Women (RHUL)
Simpson's Archive
Victoria & Albert Museum Archive
Kenneth Ritchie Wimbledon Library, Wimbledon Lawn Tennis Museum

NEWSPAPERS AND MAGAZINES

Bradford Times & Argus
Britannia and Eve
Daily Mail
Daily Telegraph
The Drapers' Record
Fashions for all
Film Fashionland

Girls' Favourite
Good Housekeeping
Hatter's Gazette
The Lady
Man and His Clothes
Manchester Evening Chronicle
Manchester Evening News
Men's Wear
Men's Wear Organiser
Middlesex County Times
Miss Modern
New Statesman and Nation
Outfitter
Picture Show
Punch
Sartorial Gazette
The Sketch
The Statistical Review of Press Advertising
Style Guide
Tatler
Tennis Illustrated
The Times
Vogue
West Middlesex Gazette
Woman and Home
Woman's Life
Woman's Magazine
Woman's Own

PRINTED BOOKS AND ARTICLES

Acton, H. *Memoirs of an Aesthete*, Methuen, 1948, repr. Hamilton, 1984

Adburgham, A. *A Punch History of Manners and Modes 1841–1940*, Hutchinson, 1961

——. *Shops and Shopping 1800–1914. Where, and in What Manner The Well-dressed Englishwoman Bought her Clothes*, George Allen & Unwin, 1964

Aldcroft, D.H. *The Inter-War Economy: Britain, 1919–1939*, Batsford, 1973

Alexander, S. 'Becoming a Woman in London in the 1920s and 1930s', in D. Feldman and G. Stedman Jones (eds), *Metropolis, London. Histories and Representations*, Routledge, 1989, pp. 245–75

——. 'Men's Fears and Women's Work: Responses to Unemployment in London Between the Wars', *Gender and History* 12, 2 (2000), 401–25

Annan, N. *The Dons. Mentors, Eccentrics and Geniuses*, HarperCollins, 1999

Baden-Powell, R. *Lessons from the Varsity of Life*, A. Pearson, 1933

Baldwin, A.W. *My Father: The True Story*, George Allen & Unwin, 1955

Beaton, C. *The Wandering Years. Diaries 1922–1939*, Weidenfeld & Nicholson, 1961

Beauman, N. *A Very Great Profession. The Woman's Novel 1914–39*, Virago, 1983

Beddoe, D. *Back to Home and Duty. Women Between the Wars 1918–1939*, Pandora, 1989

Benson, E.F. *Queen Lucia*, Hutchinson, 1920; repr. Black Swan, 1970

Benson, J. *The Rise of Consumer Society in Britain 1880–1980*, Longman, 1994

Bentley, L. *Educating Women. A Pictorial History of Bedford College University of London 1849–1985*, St Albans, Alma/RHUL, 1991

Berg, M. *A woman in history. Eileen Power, 1889–1940*, Cambridge, Cambridge University Press, 1996

Betjeman, J. *John Betjeman's Oxford*, Oxford, 1938, repr. Oxford University Press, 1990

Bill, K. 'Attitudes Towards Women's Trousers: Britain in the 1930s', *Journal of Design History* 6, 1 (1993), 45–54

———. 'Clothing Expenditure by a Woman in the Early 1920s', *Costume*, 21 (1993), pp. 57–60

Birley, D. *Playing the Game. Sport and British Society, 1910–45*, Manchester, Manchester University Press, 1995

Bland, E. 'With Hat and Gloves. A Career in Retailing', *Costume* 24 (1990), 111–16

Bland, W. 'Fashion for Pleasure', *Costume* 12 (1978), pp. 95–7

Bloome, D. et al. *Reading Mass-Observation Writing. Theoretical and Methodological Issues in Researching the Mass-Observation Archive*, Brighton, University of Sussex Library, 1993

Blunt, W. *Married to A Single Life. An Autobiography 1901–1938*, Salisbury, Michael Russell, 1983

Bourke, J. 'The Great Male Renunciation: Men's Dress Reform in Inter-war Britain', *Journal of Design History* 9, 1 (1996), 23–33

Bowden, S. and Offer, A. 'The Technological Revolution That Never Was: Gender, Class and the Diffusion of Household Appliances in Interwar England', in V. de Grazia and E. Furlough (eds), *The Sex of Things: Gender and Consumption in Historical Perspective*, Berkeley, University of California Press, 1996

Bowlby, R. 'The Cost of Living of Girls Professionally Employed in the County of London', *Economic Journal* 4 (1934), 328–33

Bradstock, L. and Condon, J. *The Modern Woman. Beauty, Physical Culture, Hygiene*, Associated Newspapers, 1936

Brazil, A. *Joan's Best Chum*, Blackie & Co., 1926

Breward, C. *The Culture of Fashion. A new history of fashionable dress*, Manchester, Manchester University Press, 1995

———. *The Hidden Consumer. Masculinities, fashion and city life 1860–1914*, Manchester, Manchester University Press, 1999

——. 'Men, fashion and luxury, 1870–1914', in A. de la Haye and E. Wilson (eds), *Defining Dress. Dress as object, meaning and identity*, Manchester, Manchester University Press, 1999, 48–61

Briggs, A. *Friends of the People: The Centenary History of Lewis's*, Batsford, 1956

Buckley, V. *Good times: at home and abroad between the wars*, Thames & Hudson, 1979

Burman, B. and Leventon, M. 'The Men's Dress Reform Party 1929–37', *Costume* 21 (1987), 75–87

Burnett, J. *A social history of housing, 1815–1970*, Newton Abbot, David & Charles, 1978

Byrde, P. *The Male Image. Men's Fashion in England 1300–1970*, Batsford, 1979

Campbell, E. *Can I Help You, Madam?*, Cobden-Sanderson, 1938

——. *Can I Help You, Sir?*, Peter Davies, 1939

Cannon, C. (ed.) *Our Grandmothers, Our Mothers, Ourselves. A Century of Women's Lives*, Ogomos, 2000

Caradog Jones, D. 'The Cost of Living of a Sample of Middle-class Families', *Journal of the Royal Statistical Society* IV (1928), 463–502

Carr-Saunders, A.M. and Caradog Jones, D. *A survey of the social structure of England and Wales, as illustrated by statistics*, Humphrey Milford, 1928

——. *A survey of the social structure of England and Wales, as illustrated by statistics*, Oxford, Clarendon Press, 1938

Cartland, B. *We Danced All Night*, Hutchinson, 1970

Chenoune, F. *A History of Men's Fashion*, Flammarion, 1993

Cobb, R. *Still Life. Sketches from a Tunbridge Wells childhood*, Chatto & Windus, 1983

Cohn, N. *Today there are no Gentlemen. The changes in Englishmen's clothes since the War*, Weidenfeld & Nicholson, 1971

Cole, S. *'Don We Now Our Gay Apparel'. Gay Men's Dress in the Twentieth Century*, Oxford, Berg, 2000

Collins, C.C. *Love of A Glove*, New York, Fairchild, 1947

Corfield, P. 'Dress for Deference and Dissent: Hats and the Decline of Hat Honour', *Costume* 23 (1989), 64–79

——. *Power and the Professions in Britain, 1700–1850*, Routledge, 1995

Corina, M. *Fine Silks and Oak Counters. Debenhams 1778–1978*, Hutchinson Benham, 1978

Cossey, R. *Golfing Ladies. Five centuries of golf in Great Britain and Ireland*, Orbis, 1984

Costantino, M. *Men's Fashion in the twentieth century. From frock coats to intelligent fibres*, New York, Costume & Fashion Press, 1997

Cousins, G. *Golf in Britain: a social history from the beginnings to the present day*, Routledge & Kegan Paul, 1975

Crane, D. 'Clothing Behavior as Non-Verbal Resistance: Marginal Women and Alternative Dress in the Nineteenth Century', *Fashion Theory* 3, 2 (1999), 241–68

Crane, M. *The Story of Ladies' Golf*, Stanley Paul, 1991

Crisp, Q. *The Naked Civil Servant*, Cape, 1968

Cumming, V. *Gloves*, Batsford, 1982

Cutforth, R. *Later Than We Thought. A Portrait of The Thirties*, Newton Abbot, David & Charles, 1976

Davidoff, L. and Westover, B. "'From Queen Victoria to the Jazz Age": Women's World in England, 1880–1939' in L. Davidoff and B. Westover (eds), *Our Work, Our Lives, Our Words*, Basingstoke, Macmillan Educational, 1986, 1–35

Davidson, A. *Blazers, Badges and Boaters. A Pictorial History of School Uniform*, Horndean, Scope, 1990

Davidson, J. and M. *Etiquette at a Dance: What to Do and What Not to Do*, W. Foulsham & Co., 1937

Davy, T. "'A Cissy Job for Men; a Nice Job for Girls": Women Shorthand Typists in London, 1900–1939', in Davidoff and Westover (eds), *Our Work*, 124–44

de Courcy, A. *1939: The Last Season*, Thames & Hudson, 1989, repr. Phoenix, 2003

de la Haye, A. 'The Dissemination of Design from Haute Couture to Fashionable Ready-to-wear during the 1920s', *Textile History* 24, 1 (1993), 39–48

Delafield, E.M. *The Diary of a Provincial Lady*, 1930, repr. Virago, 1985

Devereux, G.R.M. *Etiquette for Men. A book of modern manners and customs*, Arthur Pearson, 1902, repr. 1937

Dickens, M. *Mariana*, Michael Joseph, 1940, repr. Penguin, 1999

Donaldson, F. *Child of the Twenties*, Weidenfeld & Nicolson, 1959, repr. 1986

Dony, J.G. *The History of the Straw Hat Industry*, Luton, Gibbs, Bamforth, 1942

Dutton, D. *Anthony Eden. A Life and Reputation*, Arnold, 1997

Dyhouse, C. *Feminism and the family in England 1880–1939*, Oxford, Blackwell, 1989

Easton, M. 'Dorelia's Wardrobe: "There goes an Augustus John!"', *Costume* 8 (1974), 30–4.

Edwards, E. *Women in teacher training colleges, 1900–1960*, Routledge, 2000

Elias, E. *Straw Hats and Serge Bloomers*, W.H. Allen, 1979

Farrell, J. *Socks and Stockings*, Batsford, 1992

Flugel, J. *The Psychology of Clothes*, Hogarth Press, 1930

——. *Men and Their Motives*, Kegan Paul, Trench, Trubner, 1934

Forester, M. *Success Through Dress*, Duckworth, 1925

Forster, E.M. *Selected Letters of E.M. Forster 1879–1920, vol. 1*, (eds) M. Lago and P.N. Furbank, Collins, 1983

Fox, F. *The Langhorne Sisters*, Granta, 1999

Gathorne-Hardy, J. *The Public School Phenomenon*, Hodder & Stoughton, 1973

Gill, E. *Clothes*, Cape, 1930

Goffman, E. *The Presentation of Self in Everyday Life*, Penguin, 1959, repr. 1990

Goldman, L. *Brighton Beach to Bengal Bay*, Brighton, L. Goldman, 1999

——. *Oh What a Lovely Shore! Brighton in the Twenties through the Eyes of a Schoolboy*, Brighton, L. Goldman, 1999

Graves, R. and Hodge, A. *The Long Weekend. A Social History of Great Britain*, Faber & Faber, 1940, repr. Abacus, 1995

Grove, J. 'Victorian Respectability and the Etiquette of Dress', *Strata of Society* Costume Society Conference, Norwich (1973), 17–19

Haden, H.J. *The Rotary Club of Stourbridge 1922–1972. The Golden Jubilee History of Stourbridge Rotary Club*, Stourbridge, Stourbridge Rotary Club, 1973

Harrison, R. *Rose. My Life in Service*, Cassell, 1979

Harrop, S. *The Merchant Taylors' School for Girls, Crosby. One hundred years of achievement 1888–1988*, Liverpool, Liverpool University Press, 1988

Heimann, J.M. *The Most Offending Soul Alive. Tom Harrisson and his Remarkable Life*, Honolulu, University of Hawaii Press, 1999, repr. Aurum, 2002

Hewitt, C.R. *Towards my Neighbour: The Social Influence of the Rotary Club Movement in Great Britain & Ireland*, Rotary International Association of Great Britain and Ireland, 1950

Hirst, L. 'Dressing the part. Workwear for the home 1953–1965', *things* 9 (1998), 25–49

Holdsworth, A. *Out of the Doll's House: The Story of Women in the Twentieth Century*, BBC Books, 1988

Holt, A. 'Hikers and Ramblers: Surviving a Thirties' Fashion', *International Journal of the History of Sport* (1987), 56–67

Honeyman, K. 'Montague Burton Ltd: The creators of well-dressed men' in J. Chartres and K. Honeyman (eds), *Leeds city business 1893–1993*. (Leeds, University of Leeds, 1993), 186–216

Horn, P. *Life Below Stairs in the 20th Century*, Stroud, Sutton Publishing, 2001

Horwood, C. '"Housewives' Choice". Women as Consumers Between the Wars', *History Today* (March 1997), 23–8

——. '"Girls Who Arouse Dangerous Passions": Women and Bathing 1900–1939', *Women's History Review* 9, 4 (2000), 653–72

——. 'Dressing like a Champion: Women's Tennis Wear in Interwar England', in C. Breward, B. Conekin and C. Cox (eds), *The Englishness of English Dress*, Oxford, Berg, 2002, 45–78

——. '"Anyone for Tennis?": Male Modesty on the Tennis Courts in Interwar Britain', *Costume* 38 (2004), 100–5

Howard, E.J. *Slipstream. A Memoir*, Macmillan, 2002

Jackson, A. *Semi-Detached London: Suburban Development, Life and Transport, 1900–1939*, Allen & Unwin, 1973

——. *The Middle Class 1900–1945*, Nairn, David St John Thomas, 1991

Jeffery, T. 'A Place in the Nation: The Lower Middle Class in England', in R. Koshar (ed.), *Splintered classes. Politics and the lower middle classes in interwar Europe*, New York, Holmes & Meier, 1990

Jefferys, J.B. *Retail Trading in Britain 1850–1950*, Cambridge, Cambridge University Press, 1954

Jensen, J. (ed.) *H.M. Bateman. The Man Who . . . and other drawings*, Methuen, 1975

Judd, D. *Radical Joe. A Life of Joseph Chamberlain*, Cardiff, University of Wales Press, 1993

Keers, P. *A Gentleman's Wardrobe. Class, Clothes and the Modern Man*, Weidenfeld & Nicholson, 1987

Kelen, E. *Peace in their Time. Men who led us in and out of war, 1914–1945*, Victor Gollancz, 1964

Klingender, F.D. *The Condition of Clerical Labour in Britain*, Martin Laurence, 1935

Kuhn, A. 'Cinema, culture and femininity in the 1930s', in C. Gledhill and G. Swanson (eds), *Nationalizing Femininity. Cultures, Sexuality and the British Cinema in the Second World War*, Manchester University Press, 1996, 177–92

Lancaster, B. *The Department Store. A Social History*, Leicester University Press, 1995

Lancaster, O. *With an Eye to the Future*, Century, 1986

Langhamer, C. *Women's leisure in England 1920–1960*, Manchester, Manchester University Press, 2000

Laver, J. *Taste and Fashion*, Harrap, 1931, repr. 1945

—— (ed.). *The Book of Public School Old Boys, University, Navy, Army, Air Force & Club Ties*, Seeley Service, 1968

——. *Dandies*, Weidenfeld & Nicholson, 1968

Lehmann, R. *Invitation to the Waltz*, Chatto & Windus, 1932, repr. Virago, 2001

Lenglen, S. *Lawn Tennis for Girls*, George Newnes, 1919

Levy, H. *The Shops of Britain*, Kegan Paul, Trench, Trubner & Co., 1947

Lewes U3A Oral History Group. *Lewes Remembers Shops and Shopping*, Lewes, Lewes U3A Publications, 1999

Lewis, J. *Women in England, 1870–1950*, Hemel Hempstead, Harvester Wheatsheaf, 1984

Lewis, L. *The Private Life of A Country House (1912–1939)*, Newton Abbot, David & Charles, 1980

Lewis, R. and Maude, A. *The English Middle Classes*, Phoenix, 1949

Leyland, N. and Troughton, J. *Glovemaking in West Oxfordshire*, Oxford, Oxford City & County Museum, 1974

Lockwood, D. *The Blackcoated Worker. A Study in Class Consciousness*, George Allen & Unwin, 1958, repr. Oxford, Clarendon, 1989

Macaulay, R. *Keeping Up Appearances*, Collins, 1928, repr. Methuen, 1986

——. *Life Among the English*, Collins, 1942

MacCarthy, A. *The Dance Band Era: the dancing decades from ragtime to swing: 1910–1950*, Studio Vista, 1971

McCrone, K. *Sport and the physical emancipation of women, 1870–1914*, Routledge, 1988

McKibbin, R. *Classes and Cultures. England 1918–1951*, Oxford, Oxford University Press, 1998

Magee, B. *Clouds of Glory. A Hoxton Childhood*, Jonathan Cape, 2003

Mannin, E. *Young in the Twenties. A Chapter of Autobiography*, Hutchinson, 1971

Marley, J. and Campion, H. 'Changes in Salaries in Great Britain, 1924–1939', *Journal of the Royal Statistical Society, Part IV* (1940), 524–33

Marshall, A.C. *The Magic of My Youth*, Hart-Davis, 1951

Martindale, H. *Women Servants of the State 1870–1938*, George Allen & Unwin, 1938

Martindale, L. *A Woman Surgeon*, Gollancz, 1951

Marwick, A. *Class. Image and Reality in Britain, France and the USA since 1930*, Collins, 1980

Massey, P. 'The expenditure of 1,360 British middle-class households in 1938–39', *Journal of the Royal Statistical Society*, CV, part 3 (1942), 159–85

Mass-Observation. *Browns of Chester. Portrait of a Shop 1780–1946*, Lindsay Drummond, 1947

Melman, B. *Women and the Popular Imagination in the Twenties. Flappers and Nymphs*, Basingstoke, Macmillan, 1988

Mitford, M. *Love in a Cold Climate*, Hamish Hamilton, 1949

Moore, D.L. *Pandora's Letter Box: being a discourse on fashionable life, etc.*, Gerald Howe, 1929

—— and Moore, J. *The Pleasure of Your Company*, Gerald Howe, 1933

Mort, F. *Cultures of Consumption. Masculinities and Social Space in late twentieth-century Britain*, Routledge, 1996

Mosley, O. *My Life*, Nelson, 1968

Neal, L.E. *Retailing and the Public*, Allen & Unwin, 1933

Newby, E. *Something Wholesale. My Life and Times in the Rag Trade*, Secker & Warburg, 1962, repr. Picador, 1985

Newton, S.M. *Health, art and reason: dress reformers of the 19th century*, John Murray, 1974

Nicholas, S. 'The Construction of a National Identity: Stanley Baldwin, "Englishness" and the Mass Media in Inter-war Britain', in M. Francis and I. Zweiniger-Bargielowska (eds), *The Conservatives and British Society, 1880–1990*, Cardiff, University of Wales Press, 1996, 127–46

Nicholson, V. *Among the Bohemians. Experiments in Living 1900–1939*, Viking, 2002

Nicolson, N. *Portrait of a Marriage*, Weidenfeld & Nicholson, 1973, repr. 1990

Nystrom, P. *Economics of Fashion*, New York, Ronald, 1928

Orwell, G. *The Road to Wigan Pier*, Victor Gollancz, 1937, repr. Penguin, 1989

Osborne, J. *A better class of person. An autobiography 1929–1956*, Faber, 1981

Paoletti, J.B. 'Ridicule and Role Models as Factors in American Men's Fashion Change, 1880–1910', *Costume* 19 (1985), 121–34

Parker, J. *Father of the House. Fifty years in politics*, Routledge & Kegan Paul, 1982

Peel, C.S. *Life's Enchanted Cup: An Autobiography (1870–1933)*, John Lane, 1933

Peel, D.W. *A Garden In The Sky. The Story of Barkers of Kensington 1870–1957*, W.H. Allen, 1960

Perkin, P. *The Rise of Professional Society. England since 1880*, Routledge, 1989, repr. 2002

Perry, F. *Fred Perry: an autobiography*, Hutchinson, 1984

Pimlott, J. and Alfred, R. *The Englishman's Holiday: A Social History*, Faber & Faber, 1947

Polhemus, T. and Procter, L. *Fashion & anti-fashion: an anthropology of clothing and adornment*, Thames & Hudson, 1978

Powell, A. *A Dance to the Music of Time I. A Question of Upbringing*, Heinemann, 1951, repr. Mandarin, 1991

Priestley, J.B., *English Journey*, Heinemann, 1934, repr. Mandarin, 1996

Pritchett, V.S. 'Scarborough', in Y. Cloud (ed.), *Beside the Seaside*, Stanley Knott, 1934, 187–226

Pugh, M. *Women and the Women's Movement in Britain 1914–1939*, Basingstoke, Macmillan, 1992

Rattigan, R. *The Collected Plays of Terence Rattigan*, vol, 2, Hamish Hamilton, 1953

Rhodes James, R. (ed.) *'Chips': The Diaries of Sir Henry Channon*, Weidenfeld & Nicholson, 1967, repr. Penguin, 1999

Ribeiro, A. *Dress and Morality*, Batsford, 1986

Richards, J. *The Age of the Dream Palace: Cinema and Society in Britain 1930–1939*, Routledge & Kegan Paul, 1984

Ritchie, B. *A Touch of Class. The Story of Austin Reed*, James & James, 1990

Rolley, K. 'Fashion, Femininity and the Fight for the Vote', *Art History* 13, 1 (1990), 47–71

Round, D. *Modern Lawn Tennis*, George Newnes, 1934

Rowntree, B.S. and Lavers, G.R. *English Life and Leisure*, Longman, Green & Co., 1951

Rust, F. *Dance in society: an analysis of the relationship between the social dance and society in England from the Middle Ages to the present day*, Routledge & Kegan Paul, 1969

Ryan, D. "All the World and Her Husband": The *Daily Mail* Ideal Home Exhibition 1908–39', in M. Andrews and M. Talbot (eds), *All the World and Her Husband. Women in Twentieth–Century Consumer Culture*, Cassell, 2000

Ryan, M. *Office Training for Girls*, Pitman, 1933

Salter, E. *Edith Sitwell*, Oresko, 1979

Samuel, R. 'The middle class between the wars: part one', *New Socialist* (Jan/Feb 1983), 30–6

——. 'The middle class between the wars: part three', *New Socialist* (May/June 1983), 28–31

Sanderson, K. "'A Pension to Look Forward to . . . ?": Women Civil Service Clerks in London, 1925–1939', in Davidoff and Westover (eds), *Our Work*, 145–60

Seymour, B. *All About Golf*, Ward Lock & Co., 1924

Shaw, G.B. *Man and Superman*, Constable, 1903

Shaw, L.J. *The Rotary Club of Poole, Dorset 1923–1973*, Poole, Rotary Club of Poole, 1973

Sigsworth, E. *Montague Burton. The tailor of taste*, Manchester, Manchester University Press, 1990

Silex, K, tr. H. Paterson. *John Bull at Home*, G.G. Harrap & Co., 1931

Silvester, V. *Dancing is My Life*, Heinemann, 1958

Skidelsky, R. *Oswald Mosley*, Macmillan, 1975

Smith, H.L. *The New Survey of London Life and Labour, II, London Industries I*, London School of Economics and Political Science, 1931

——. *The New Survey of London Life and Labour, III, Survey of Social Conditions (I) The Eastern Area*, London School of Economics and Political Science, 1932

——. *The New Survey of London Life and Labour, V, London Industries II*, London School of Economics and Political Science, 1933

Spalding, F. *Gwen Raverat. Friends, Family and Affections*, Harvill Press, 2001

Stevenson, J. *British Society 1914–45*, Penguin, 1984, repr. 1990

Sykes, C. *Nancy: the life of Lady Astor*, Panther, 1972

Taylor, S.J. *The Great Outsiders. Northcliffe, Rothermere and the* Daily Mail, Weidenfeld & Nicholson, 1996

Townsend-Gault, C. 'Symbolic facades: official portraiture in British institutions since 1920', *Art History* 11, 4 (1988), 511–26

Tute, W. *The Grey Top Hat. The Story of Moss Bros. of Covent Garden*, Cassell, 1961

Ugolini, L. 'Clothes and the Modern Man in 1930s Oxford', *Fashion Theory* 4, 4 (2000), 427–46

Vickers, H. *Cecil Beaton. The authorised biography*, Weidenfeld & Nicholson, 1985

Vickery, A. 'Golden Age to Separate Spheres: A Review of the Categories and Chronology of English Women's History,' *Historical Journal* 36, 2 (1993), 383–414

Wainwright, D. *The British Tradition. Simpson – a World of Style*, Quiller Press, 1996

Waller, J. (ed.) *A Man's Book*, Duckworth, 1977

Walton, J. *The British Seaside. Holidays and resorts in the twentieth century*, Manchester, Manchester University Press, 2000

Waugh, E. *Brideshead Revisited*, Chapman & Hall, 1945

Wayne, J. *The Purple Dress: growing up in the thirties*, Gollancz, 1979

Whipple, D. *High Wages*, John Murray, 1930, repr. New York, Harmondsworth, 1946

White, C. *Women's Magazines 1693–1968*, Michael Joseph, 1978

Whiteing, E. *'Anyone for tennis?' Growing up in Wallington between the wars*, Sutton, Sutton Libraries, 1979

Wilkinson, E. *Peeps at Politicians*, P. Allen, 1930

Williams, A.S. *Ladies of Influence. Women of the Elite in Interwar Britain*, Allen Lane, 2000

Wilson, E. *Adorned in Dreams. Fashion and Modernity*, Berkeley, University of California Press, 1985

——. 'Bohemian Dress and the Heroism of Everyday Life', *Fashion Theory* 2, 3 (1998), 225–44

——. *Bohemians. The Glamorous Outcasts*, I.B. Tauris, 2000

Windsor, Duke of. *A Family Album*, Cassell, 1960

Wise, A. 'Dressmaking in Worthing', *Costume* 32 (1998), 82–6

Wodehouse, P.G. 'Jeeves and the Impending Doom', in *Very Good, Jeeves!*, Herbert Jenkins, 1930, repr. 2001

Woods, D. *Correct Dance-Room Behaviour: A Safe Guide for Avoiding Mistakes in the Dance Room*, Universal Publications, 1936

Zdatny, S. 'The Boyish Look and the Liberated Woman: The Politics and Aesthetics of Women's Hairstyles', *Fashion Theory* 1, 4 (1997), 367–98

Zmroczek, C. 'The Weekly Wash', in S. Oldfield (ed.), *This Working Day World. Women's Lives and Culture(s) in Britain 1914–1945*, Taylor & Francis, 1994

Index

Page numbers in italic refer to illustrations.